Psychological
Trauma

Psychological Trauma

Bessel A. van der Kolk, M.D.

*Massachusetts Mental Health Center,
Harvard Medical School,
Boston, Massachusetts*

1400 K Street, N.W.
Washington, DC 20005

Note: The authors have worked to ensure that all information in this book concerning drug dosages, schedules, and routes of administration is accurate as of the time of publication and consistent with standards set by the U.S. Food and Drug Administration and the general medical community. As medical research and practice advance, however, therapeutic standards may change. For this reason and because human and mechanical errors sometimes occur, we recommend that readers follow the advice of a physician who is directly involved in their care or the care of a member of their family.

Books published by American Psychiatric Press, Inc., represent the views and opinions of the individual authors and do not necessarily reflect the policies and opinions of the Press or the American Psychiatric Association.

91 92 93 6

Library of Congress Cataloging in Publication Data

van der Kolk, Bessel A., 1943–
  Psychological trauma.

  Includes bibliographies and index.
  1. Post-traumatic stress disorder. 2. Post-traumatic stress disorder in children. 3. Parent and child. I. Title.
[DNLM: 1. Life Change Events. 2. Stress, Psychological. 3. Violence. WM 172 V234p]
RC552.P67V36   1986   616.85'2   86-14149
ISBN 0-88048-233-8

To Hanna, Nicholas, and Nina,
for their delightful lessons about attachment,
the separation cry, and the ways in which
children learn to make sense of the world;

and to Betta,
for providing the safe base.

When on all sides assailed by prospects of disaster . . . the soul of man . . . never confronts the totality of its wretchedness. The bitter drug is divided into separate draughts for him; today he takes on part of his woe; tomorrow he takes more; and so on, till the last drop is drunk.

Herman Melville, *Pierre*

Contents

Additional Contributors

Caroline C. Fish-Murray, Ed.D.
Coordinator, Child Services, Trauma Clinic,
Massachusetts Mental Health Center,
Harvard Medical School

Raymond B. Flannery, Jr., Ph.D.
Chief Psychologist,
Somerville Mental Health Center,
Cambridge Hospital,
Harvard Medical School

Mark S. Greenberg, Ph.D.
Chief Psychologist,
Deaconess Hospital,
Harvard Medical School

Judith L. Herman, M.D.
Women's Mental Health Collective; and
Medical Director, Trauma Clinic,
Cambridge Hospital,
Harvard Medical School

William Kadish, M.D.
Chief Resident in Psychiatry,
Massachusetts Mental Health Center,
Harvard Medical School

Elizabeth V. Koby, M.D.
Research Fellow in Child Psychiatry,
National Institutes of Mental Health,
Washington, DC

Steven Krugman, Ph.D.
Co-Director, Trauma Clinic,
Massachusetts Mental Health Center,
Harvard Medical School

Preface

The frame of mind with which a clinician or researcher approaches a patient or subject largely determines the nature and outcome of both therapy and research. Since the beginnings of modern psychiatry, clinicians have had quite sharply divergent views about the nature and origin of psychopathology. The field has often been polarized between clinicians with a biologic–genetic orientation and those who see most mental illness as the result of intrapsychic conflicts. This polarization may well result from our relative ignorance of the basic nature of psychological processes; it is likely that factionalism in psychiatry will decrease as we gain a better understanding of the interrelationships between psychology and biology.

Until recently neither the psychodynamic nor the biological orientations have paid much attention to the impact of overwhelming life experiences on both the soma and the psyche. In view of the horrendous life stories told by so many of our patients, the relative neglect by psychiatry of the issue of psychological trauma is almost as intriguing as the impact of trauma itself. Except for some work by Ferenczi, research on the war neuroses during and after World War II, and studies of concentration camp survivors, little work was done between 1898 and 1976 to explore the psychological and biological effects of traumatic life events. After a virtual hiatus of almost 70 years, interest has dramatically resurged in the past decade with the work of Horowitz and studies on the impact of the Vietnam War, rape, incest, child abuse, and other environmental trauma. Kardiner, who first described the trauma response as we currently understand it, called the human reaction to trauma a "physioneurosis." Posttraumatic stress disorder, perhaps more than any other mental disorder, demonstrates the close interdependence of psychological and physiological reactions. Current research on the trauma response, aided by animal models of early social deprivation and inescapable stress, is beginning to shed light on the biological concomitants of psychological symptoms.

Mainstream psychiatry has usually studied individuals as self-contained entities, relatively divorced from the social contexts within which they mature and thrive. Despite the abundance of family studies and the prominence of social psychiatry in the 1960s, clinicians have not consistently recognized the virtual inseparability between individuals and their social frameworks. A human being is a biological organism embedded in a social environment from the moment of birth. Disruption of the social matrix, particularly in childhood, has serious long-term effects on both psychological and biological functioning.

This book considers the impact of experiences that overwhelm both psychological and biological coping mechanisms. Lindemann's definition of psychological trauma as "the sudden, uncontrollable disruption of affiliative bonds" is interpreted broadly and the effects of trauma on emotional and cognitive processes, underlying biological changes, and resulting psychopathology are reviewed. A large number of research findings from a variety of theoretical perspectives are presented and their treatment implications examined. Childhood trauma is particularly significant because uncontrollable terrifying experiences may have their most profound effects when the central nervous system and cognitive functions have not yet fully matured, leading to a global impairment that may be manifested in adulthood in psychopathological conditions. Although long-term prospective studies of traumatized children are not yet available, retrospective studies are reviewed to examine the impact of early psychological trauma on the development of mental illness.

Building on the work of Bowlby, Harlow and his successors, and other psychoanalytic, cognitive, biological, and behavioral psychologists, a general theory of the human trauma response as a biopsychosocial entity is presented. As Kurt Lewin once remarked, nothing is so practical as a good theory. I hope that this attempt to develop a theoretical framework for the study of trauma will lead to practical results by suggesting new ways to prevent and treat the human trauma response.

Acknowledgments

This work is the result of an intensely rewarding collaboration among the members of the Harvard Trauma Study Group. Some of the members of the Study Group contributed to this volume; others fertilized our thinking with their contributions during our many discussions at the home of Henry and Nina Murray. Sarah Haley, Elaine Carmen, Pat Rieker, Dan Brown, Rich Mollica, Mary Harvey, Dante Cicchetti, and Betty Canick made particularly valuable contributions. We came from a variety of backgrounds, and we had done clinical work and research in such diverse areas as incest, rape, family violence, child abuse, refugees, and war veterans. Although we started with different vocabularies to describe our observations, there was a clear consensus that we were all dealing with very similar clinical issues.

Aldo Tartaglini and Mark Braverman did a tremendous amount of research gathering material for this book. The editorial work of Jim Bakalar of the Harvard Mental Health Newsletter made much of the writing comprehensible. David Bear, Jim Beck, Jules Bemporad, Yael Danielli, Allan Hobson, Ed Khantzian, Chester Pearlman, Roger Pitman, and Carl Salzman made generous comments and suggestions.

Finally, I want to thank my teachers who taught the importance of thinking in various "frames of mind": Bruno Bettelheim, who urged us that "the patient is always right"; Elvin Semrad and Leston Havens, who taught me to pay attention to the language of the body; and Ernest Hartmann and Dick Shader, two psychoanalysts who were my mentors in biological research.

CHAPTER 1

The Psychological Consequences of Overwhelming Life Experiences

Bessel A. van der Kolk, M.D.

The psychological damage resulting from uncontrollable, terrifying life events was a central focus of psychiatric interest around the turn of this century. Many early psychiatrists understood psychological trauma to be the ultimate source of much psychopathology. Freud at first regarded many psychiatric problems as manifestations of early childhood traumas; for example, he interpreted the cognitive, emotional, and behavioral symptoms of hysterical patients as symbolic repetitions of early traumatic events (1). After Freud came to believe that the development of neuroses was more intimately related to childhood fantasies and misinterpretations of childhood events, external psychological trauma lost its central importance in psychoanalytic thinking. Although Freud continued to show interest in the consequences of psychological trauma (see Chapter 8), dynamic psychiatry in general has paid little attention to the consequences of actual overwhelming experiences until a recent resurgence of interest.

In the past two decades psychiatry has gradually shifted from

The author wishes to acknowledge the assistance in the preparation of this chapter by Mark Braverman and Aldo Tartaglini.

1

a dynamic, intrapsychic model to a biomedical model, emphasizing genetic and biological determinants of major mental illness. But neither the biomedical nor the psychoanalytic points of view have adequately addressed the impact of traumatic life events on people's identities and psychopathology. Much of the present renewed interest can be attributed to a heightened concern about the impact of child abuse, the attention paid by the women's movement to the consequences of rape and incest, the unexpectedly high incidence of delayed stress reactions in Vietnam veterans, and the recognition of psychiatric consequences of political persecution.

Until recently, the consequences of specific traumas—such as wars, concentration camp experiences, rape, civilian disasters, and child abuse—were generally described as separate entities. However, closer examination makes it clear that the human response to overwhelming and uncontrollable life events is remarkably consistent. Although the nature of the trauma, the age of the victim, predisposing personality, and community response all have an important effect on ultimate posttraumatic adaptation, the core features of the posttraumatic syndrome are fairly constant across these variables. The American Psychiatric Association implicitly recognized this in the *Diagnostic and Statistical Manual of Mental Disorders*, Third Edition (DSM-III) (2) when it introduced a separate category for the human response to overwhelming life events under the heading of "Post-Traumatic Stress Disorder" (PTSD).

The Clinical Symptomatology of Post-Traumatic Stress Disorder

Kardiner (3) first described the full syndrome, using descriptions that essentially coincide with the contemporary formal DSM-III diagnostic criteria for PTSD. Kardiner noted that many sufferers of PTSD continue to live in the emotional environment of the traumatic event, with "enduring vigilance for and sensitivity to environmental threat." He described the five principal features of the human response to trauma as 1) a persistence of startle response and irritability, 2) proclivity to explosive outbursts of aggression, 3) fixation on the trauma, 4) constriction of the general level of personality functioning, and 5) atypical dream life. In mild cases the trauma is eventually successfully resolved with an integration of the traumatic events into the totality of a person's life experiences (4). But in many other cases, some or all of the symptoms may persist, or recur during periods of later stress (see Chapters 8 and 9).

The Trauma Response as a Biphasic Response

Hyperarousal and Intrusion Versus Numbing and Constriction

Starting with Lindemann (5), and refined by Horowitz (4), the response to psychological trauma has been described as a phasic reliving and denial, with alternating intrusive and numbing responses. The intrusive responses are hyperreactivity, explosive aggressive outbursts, startle responses, intrusive recollections in the form of nightmares and flashbacks, and reenactment of situations reminiscent of the trauma. Traumatized people have a poor tolerance for psychological and physiological arousal. Their usual response to stress consists of either motoric discharge, including acts of aggression against the self or others, or social and emotional withdrawal (6). Intrusive reexperiencing also may take the form of seemingly voluntary reenactment; for example, some Vietnam veterans enlist as mercenaries (7), victims of sexual assault may become prostitutes (8), and physically abused children may expose themselves to constant danger (9). Freud was struck by this voluntary reexposure to trauma, and he saw it as an attempt to gain mastery (10). Rangell (11) and Horowitz (4) have called this "traumatophilia." These issues will be discussed in detail in Chapter 3.

The numbing response consists of emotional constriction, social isolation, retreat from family obligations, anhedonia, and a sense of estrangement. It can be understood as a way of warding off recurrent intrusive recollections of the trauma. Traumatized individuals may gain some sense of subjective control by shunning all situations or emotions related to the trauma. Often they avoid intimate relationships, apparently out of fear of a renewed violation of the attachment bond. Avoiding emotional involvement further diminishes the significance of life after the trauma, and thus perpetuates the central role of the trauma (6).

Rorschach tests on Vietnam veterans with PTSD (13) support the concept of two primary dimensions of the trauma response: their responses were either severely constricted or represented the traumatic events. After seeing traumatic percepts, their thought processes became disorganized and colored by emotions appropriate only to the original trauma. In other words, they responded either hardly at all, or with an intensity appropriate to the traumatic experience—an all-or-nothing response. These Rorschachs, as well as projective tests on abused children (see Chapter 4) indicate that people with PTSD lose the capacity to symbolize, fantasize, and sublimate as a way of anticipating and modifying emotional responses. Hence, they are deprived of precisely the psychological mechanisms that allow others to cope with the small injuries of daily life. This lack of affect tolerance interferes with the ability to grieve and work through ordinary conflicts and thus limits their capacity to accumulate restitutive and gratifying experiences.

This alternation of numbing and reexperiencing has been noticed not only following combat trauma (14–16), but also after rape (17), kidnapping (18), spouse abuse (19), natural disasters (20), accidents (5, 21), concentration camp experiences (12), incest (22, 23), burns (24), and child abuse (9).

Etiological Models of PTSD

PTSD so clearly has both psychological and physiological components that Kardiner (3) coined the term "physioneurosis" when describing the trauma response. Freud and Pavlov proposed primarily psychological models, whereas other observers, starting with Selye (25), viewed PTSD primarily as a physiological disturbance. (The physiological sequelae of trauma will be discussed in detail in Chapter 3.) Pavlov (26) coined the term "defensive reaction" to denote the cluster of innate reflexive responses to environmental threat. He found that after repeated aversive stimulation, the cues associated with the trauma (conditional stimuli, CS) become capable of eliciting the defensive reaction by themselves (conditional response, CR). For a Vietnam veteran, the sound of a passing helicopter can still evoke the experience of combat as many as 15 years later. This analysis of PTSD as a conditioned emotional response has in recent years been further elaborated and tested by Kolb (27) and others.

Both Janet and Freud noted the impoverished mental life of trauma victims and ascribed it to the energy used in warding off the impact of the traumatic experience. Janet (28) wrote: "Stress is often experienced in later points in time much the same way as the actual earlier traumatic insult. The trauma remains isolated, more or less completely separated from all other ideas; it can envelop and suppress all else." A decade later Freud (10) made a similar observation: "An external trauma is bound to provoke a disturbance on a large scale in the functioning of the organism's energy and to set in motion every possible defensive measure. An 'anticathexis' on a large scale is set up, for whose benefit all other psychical systems are impoverished, so that the remaining psychical functions are extensively paralysed or reduced." Freud believed that trauma caused increased libidinal excitation, leading to a break in the "stimulus barrier." He described a compulsion to repeat the trauma, which he saw as an attempt of the organism to drain this excess energy. He thought that by redoing and repeating the trauma (in dreams and in waking life), the victims attempted to change a passive stance to one of active coping. By recognizing that the enduring psychological reality of the trauma can be observed both in intrusive symptoms and in generally impoverished functioning, Freud anticipated the observations and theoretical formulations of many later researchers. Subsequent writers on the subject, such as Kardiner (3), Lindemann (5), Krystal (6), and Horowitz (4), noting that the trauma dominates the mental life of the victim long after the original experience, have advanced varying theories to explain the forms taken by the post-traumatic symptoms. In subsequent chapters further elaborations based on recent findings in psychobiology (Chapters 2 and 3) and in cognitive psychology (Chapters 4 and 9) are proposed.

Fixation on the Trauma

When the trauma fails to be integrated into the totality of a person's life experiences, the victim remains fixated on the trauma. Despite avoidance of emotional involvement, traumatic memories cannot be avoided: even when pushed out of waking consciousness, they come back in the form of reenactments, nightmares, or feelings related to the trauma. The nightmares often are exact replicas of the traumatic event (29) (Chapter 3). Recurrences may continue throughout life during periods of stress.

Focusing on how victims of trauma manage emotional expression and interpersonal communication, Krystal (30) presented a picture of profound personality change. As part of the "disaster syndrome" he listed: 1) loss of capacity to use community supports, 2) chronic recurrent depression with feelings of despair, 3) psychosomatic symptoms, 4) emotional "anesthesia" or blocked ability to react affectively, and 5) "alexithymia" or inability to recognize and make use of emotional reactions. The result is a robot-like existence, devoid of fantasy and empathy for others, often accompanied by chronic physical illness, alcoholism, or drug dependence. Krystal found that it was not the intensity of the experience but the meaning for the individual that "posed the challenge and generated the affective response" that caused the ultimate posttraumatic adaptation. Krystal's reviews of World War I and World War II trauma victims and his study and treatment of holocaust survivors led to the theory that PTSD is the response of the whole personality to overwhelming stress, superimposed on the "psychic reality" of the individual. The "stimulus barrier," in his view, was not a passive barrier against excitation, but "the totality of the apparatus involved in perception, registration and evaluation" of the trauma. Horowitz (4) further expanded this notion of the meaning of the trauma, showing how preexisting psychological defense mechanisms affect the way the trauma is perceived and impede or facilitate resolution of the trauma response.

Integration or Dissociation

The overwhelming nature of the trauma makes psychological integration difficult. Both dissociative and conversion reactions have been related to overwhelming experiences. Researchers have found that stress was a precipitant in up to 93 percent of patients with conversion symptoms (31). The DSM-III criteria for conversion symptoms acknowledge the etiological importance of stress.

The connection between psychological trauma and various forms of dissociation was recognized in the earliest days of modern psychiatry. The concept of dissociation was first formulated by Briquet (32), who explained hysterical symptoms as the result of a traumatic event that affected the brain's ability to process emotions. In 1869, Reynolds (33) proposed a similar model in which dissociation of pain originated from changes in the patient's body image. In his studies on hypnosis, Charcot (31) adapted these theories; he continued to believe that symptoms of dissociation were caused by brain changes after a traumatic event. Contemporary research in neurobiology supports the view that dissociation in multiple personality disorder (MPD) is the result of severe childhood trauma and is accompanied by physiological alterations in the central nervous system (34, 35).

Janet (36) first pointed out that dissociated states often followed childhood sexual or physical abuse. Multiple personality is probably the most extreme example of how severe traumatization can lead to dissociation and subsequent reexperiencing or reenactment of the trauma. There is overwhelming evidence that MPD results from child abuse (37). For example, Bliss (38) hypnotized nine patients with MPD and found, with the help of family and other informants, that the various personalities were related to actual traumatic events such as sexual and physical brutalization. Dissociative processes are mobilized as defenses against severe stress: multiple personalities alternate in the face of further stress and conflicts. MPD illustrates how dissociation, and its resulting loss of memory for the trauma, allows the original distress to be walled off, while leaving the patient with a tendency to react to subsequent stress as if it were a recurrence of the trauma. The patient experiences the emotional intensity of original trauma without conscious awareness of the historical reference.

Freud (10) related the defense mechanism of dissociation to the issue of fixation on the trauma. He proposed that the repetition compulsion originated in repression of the trauma, which he described as a dissociative phenomenon:

> We found that the perceptual content of pathogenic existing experiences and the ideational content of pathogenic structures of thought were forgotten and debarred from being reproduced in memory, and we therefore concluded that the keeping away from consciousness was the main characteristic of hysterical repression . . . the patient can not remember the whole of what is repressed in him and what he cannot remember is precisely the essential part of it . . . he is obliged to REPEAT the repressed material as a contemporary experience, instead of remembering it as something belonging to the past.

Lindemann (5) wrote that "walling off" of awareness or memory of the traumatic event is a valuable defense as long as the threat persists. However, he and most later clinicians believe that the trauma must eventually be brought into awareness and put into perspective, lest the repressed material return in the form of intrusive thoughts, reenactments, or disruptions in emotional functioning (4) (Chapters 8 and 9).

Loss of Capacity to Modulate Anxiety and Aggression

Because they respond with hyperarousal to emotional or sensory stimuli, many traumatized individuals have difficulty controlling their anxious and aggressive feelings. Thus, warding off anxiety and aggression becomes a focal issue for many trauma victims. Both Kardiner (3) and Lindemann (5) saw irritability and the loss of capacity to modulate anger as central to the trauma response. The persistent difficulty with modulating the intensity of affect seems to be the reason why so many traumatized individuals medicate themselves with alcohol and drugs (39). A Vietnam veteran stated:

> After a certain moment you just keep running the hundred yard dash: you are always ready for it to come back. I have to isolate myself to keep myself from exploding. It all comes back, all the time. The nightmares come two, three times a week for awhile. Then they let up for a bit. You can never get angry, because there is no way of controlling it. You can never feel just a little bit: it is all or nothing. I am constantly and totally preoccupied with not getting out of control.

In recent years the subject of aggression following trauma has received scant attention in the literature. Studies by Fox (40) and van der Kolk (41) found that the loss of a buddy in combat often caused narcissistic rage that led to atrocities (42) (Chapter 7). Similarly, Krystal (6) has described "hate addiction" in many concentration camp survivors. An inpatient study by Carmen et al. (43) revealed marked differences in the expression of aggression between male and female victims of child abuse and incest: 33 percent of the males dealt with anger by becoming physically aggressive, compared with 16 percent of the females; 66 percent of the females directed anger inward with self-destructive behavior, compared with 20 percent of the males.

Helplessness and Loss of Control

People in whom the effects of the trauma become ingrained often develop a chronic sense of helplessness and victimization. The experience is so unexpected and overwhelming that the very foundations of a person's coping mechanisms are challenged. If the victims already have tenuous personal control, or if the stress persists, they may lose the feeling that they can actively influence their destinies. In this state of "learned helplessness" their minds and bodies are on constant alert for return of the trauma (6) (Chapters 3 and 10). Since intrusive reexperiencing is not under control of the person, the original experience of helplessness is reenforced by dissociated reliving of elements of the traumatic event. Sounds, smells, or situations easily stimulate the recurrence of a traumatic memory or the overwhelming feelings associated with earlier traumatic events. Thus even minor sensory or emotional arousal reminds them of the helplessness associated with the original trauma. Studies of rape victims (44) suggest that loss of sense of trust and control in relationships may persist long after the initial symptoms of PTSD subside. The personality changes that often follow trauma can be seen as a rearrangement of ego structures to deal with both chronic hyperarousal and the dread that the loss of control will return.

This sense of helplessness often makes it hard to modulate the degree of intimate involvement with others. Many people who were traumatized as children suffer from a "disorder of hope": new acquaintances are either idealized or hated (Chapters 5 and 7). Both extremes lead to new disappointments that further confirm a sense of helplessness and victimization. After rape and incest, many women have difficulty in defining the boundaries of their involvement with men: they often get indiscriminantly involved or shun all contact. Their decreased capacity to protect themselves against further danger supports the tendency of others to blame them for their misfortunes (45, 46) and confirms their own sense of their essential "badness."

Vulnerability

It is not clear why some people sustain major psychological assaults without lasting effects while others become "fixated" on the trauma. Because there often is a long latency in the appearance of symptoms, it is difficult to determine whether the trauma response has been successfully resolved. Long-term successful repression of memories and behavioral (mal)adaptations further complicate accurate assessment of the resolution of the trauma. One illustration, presented in Chapter 8, describes a survivor of the Coconut Grove Fire of 1942 who did not develop symptoms of reenactment of the trauma until 1981 and did not start retrieving memories of the fire until 1984. Manifestations of posttraumatic responses to combat may not appear until long after the traumatic events. Archibald and Tuddenham (47) found that new symptoms continued to appear as late as 15 years after the trauma. Veterans and concentration camp survivors who have no apparent symptoms for many years may develop florid PTSD in response to a stressful event in later life, such as the birth of a child, the loss of a spouse, retirement, or physical illness. These expectable life stresses may elicit unbidden images, feelings, or reenactments of earlier traumas so emotionally intense that they can severely disrupt psychological functioning and make it impossible to deal with the immediate crisis.

Factors Affecting the Duration and Severity of the Trauma Response

Six factors apparently affect the long-term adjustment to traumatization: 1) severity of the stressor, 2) genetic predisposition, 3) developmental phase, 4) a person's social support system, 5) prior traumatization, and 6) preexisting personality.

1. Severity of the Stressor

The severity of the stressor is certainly a major factor; for example, few survived a Nazi extermination camp without at least some psychological impairment. Eitinger (48) found that 99 percent of 226 concentration camp survivors in Norway had some psychiatric disturbances: 87 percent had cognitive disturbances, 85 percent had persistent nervousness and irritability, 60 percent had sleep disturbances, and 52 percent had nightmares. Lifton (49) found similar effects in survivors of the atom bomb in Hiroshima and Nagasaki. Comparable findings exist in the literature on rape (44) and on Vietnam veterans (50, 51).

2. Genetic Predisposition

Studies on attachment and separation in nonhuman primates at the Wisconsin Primate Laboratory (52) (Chapter 2) demonstrated that they can be bred in stress-resistant and stress-vulnerable strains, which have a markedly different vulnerability in long-term response to environmental manipulations such as maternal separation. In Maier and Seligman's (53) studies on learned helplessness in dogs, one-third of the animals did not develop the helplessness syndrome in response to repeated traumatization. In children, Kagan et al. (54) found that:

> A small proportion . . . , estimated at 10%, has a low threshold of reactivity in those parts of the Central Nervous System that are responsive to unfamiliarity and challenge, while another 10% has a high threshold in these circuits. . . . Children differ in the ease of excitability of those parts of the CNS that generate states of psychological uncertainty and physiological arousal.

It is likely that genetic vulnerabilities contribute in a major way to the likelihood of developing chronic stress responses.

3. Developmental Phase

It has long been known that "every man has his breaking point" (15). This clearly is, in part, determined by the developmental phase at which the trauma occurs; for example, an adult with a firm sense of identity and good social support (55) is infinitely better protected against psychological trauma than a child. Psychological development in secure surroundings allows a person to build up a repertoire of coping behaviors and references to conquered stressful situations that serve as guides to subsequent coping (see Chapter 4). Children are thought to be extraordinarily sensitive to the long-term effects of uncontrollably traumatic events (9, 18, 55–57). Evidence from Garmezy and Rutter's (58) and Fish-Murray's (Chapter 4) studies indicates that this sensitivity is in part related to the level of cognitive development. As we will see in Chapter 7, adolescents who fought in Vietnam were much more prone than older soldiers to become intensely attached to their combat units, reacting to the loss of a buddy by committing atrocities and later developing PTSD (51, 59, 60).

4. A Person's Social Support System

Disruption or loss of social support is intimately associated with inability to overcome the effects of psychological trauma (see Chapters 6 and 7). Lack of support during traumatic experiences may leave enduring marks on subsequent adjustment and functioning (61, 62). Conversely, many people remain fairly intact after psychological trauma as long as their environment restores a sense of trust and safety. The effects of lost social support have been observed in burned children (63) and in civilian disasters that disrupted social communities such as Buffalo Creek (64) and Three Mile Island (65). This effect is even more poignant in children who are physically or sexually abused by the very people on whom they depend for safety and nurturance (9) (Chapters 4 and 6). Their lost sense of basic safety often leads to a life-long inability to trust and a chronic rage that may be turned against others or against the self. In both children and adults, lack of social support following trauma heightens the sense of lost security (66).

5. Prior Traumatization

People with a prior history of traumatization are especially likely to develop long-term symptomatology in response to later trauma. Lidz (67) and Fairbairn (68) correlated disrupted early family relationships with the development of chronic PTSD in response to the death of a comrade. However, another study (41) found that some Vietnam veterans with a stressful childhood history were less likely to develop PTSD than a control group. These subjects stated that they had learned not to trust anyone in childhood and therefore did not form close attachments to their comrades (see Chapter 7). Perhaps they had been inoculated against stress by avoiding the attachments that might render them vulnerable to object loss. How the latent effects of early childhood deprivation can be reactivated by stress in later life is discussed in Chapter 2.

6. Preexisting Personality

There is a strong relationship between preexisting personality factors and chronic PTSD symptomatology (4, 17). Brill (69) found that soldiers with preexisting neurosis had a seven to eight times greater chance of psychiatric reactions in combat. Some clinicians (e.g., 70) believe that failure to recover from chronic stress reactions is primarily due to personality predisposition. Personality results not only from genetic predisposition, but also from adaptation to previous stressful life events. In a study by Burgess and Holstrom (71) on the long-term effects of rape, the 29 percent who had not recovered after 5 years were women with a poorer premorbid adjustment than the 39 percent who had recovered after 6 months. The women with preexisting personality problems had become fixated in a chronic state of helplessness with chronic anxiety and phobic behavior after the rape.

Resolution

Horowitz (4) defined successful resolution as the capacity to recall the trauma at will, while being equally capable of turning one's mind to other matters. He remarked: "There is general agreement on the causal relationship of stressful events and acute reactions. There is less agreement on the causal relation between stressful events and chronic reactions." He accounted for this disagreement among clinicians by the frequency with which trauma victims refuse long-term follow-up. In a follow-up study of 26 kidnapped children in California, Terr (18) found that all subjects suffered from intrusive posttraumatic symptomatology 4 years later. In a retrospective study of World War II combat veterans, Hocking (72) found that of 303 individuals involved in military combat, more than half suffered from depression, insomnia, nightmares, anxiety, tension, irritability, startle reactions, impairment of memory, and obsessive thoughts related to wartime experiences. In addition, many were denying trauma by transforming emotional problems into psychosomatic symptoms.

Aside from Terr's (18) work, few studies have prospectively charted the persistent effects of trauma on psychological functioning. An exception is the study of the long-term effects of rape, beginning with the work of Burgess and Holstrom (17) on symptoms of PTSD in rape victims. However, most of these studies have methodological limitations; most of them have addressed such variables as anxiety and depression (73–76) but not the core symptoms of PTSD.

Over the last 6 years, the longitudinal studies on the clinical aftermath of rape by Kilpatrick and his colleagues (44, 73, 74) have painted an increasingly clear picture of a syndrome with the hallmarks of PTSD. In a study comparing 46 rape victims with 35 nonvictim controls, they concluded that after a year most symptoms, such as depression, were no different in victims and controls. However, they noted persistent

> generalized signs such as nervousness, tension and trembling . . .
> [and] panic attacks, feelings of terror, feelings of apprehension and
> dread, and some of the somatic correlates of anxiety and . . . a
> persistent fear response to a specific place, object, or situation which
> is characterized as being irrational and disproportionate to stim-
> ulus, and which leads to avoidance or escape behavior.

These data suggest that symptoms related to autonomic hyperarousal and intrusive reexperiencing persist independently of other clinical symptoms. Although the persistent symptoms, called "a core of distress" by the authors, resemble the PTSD symptoms of chronic hyperarousal and intrusive reexperiencing, Kilpatrick and his colleagues classed these symptoms within the confines of the standard diagnostic framework as anxiety and phobic anxiety. This led them to the erroneous conclusions that, since the preponderance of intrusive symptoms had subsided, "the victims seem to have regained their psychological equilibrium." A descriptive system based on a biphasic model of PTSD suggests another interpretation.

Thus the diagnosis of PTSD presents unique problems. Recent research by van der Kolk (41) suggests that many trauma victims with a semblance of normal functioning are in fact suffering from profound constriction in their involvement with others and reduced capacity to modulate feelings. After the initial intrusive, "positive" symptoms subside, they may leave profound psychological changes in their wake. During times of heightened arousal, either behavioral disturbances or intolerable intrusive memories allow for a ready diagnosis of PTSD. When controls dominate and intrusive events are warded off, only emotional constriction, chronic passivity, and a vague sense of victimization may remain—symptoms of PTSD that are easily missed. Laufer et al. (51) have criticized the DSM-III diagnostic criteria because both intrusive reexperiencing and denial are required for a positive diagnosis. They call for a clearer bidimensional approach in defining PTSD, in which either dimension may dominate, at the exclusion of the other, at different stages.

The intensity of the initial response may be related to long-term symptoms. In a recent monograph, Kilpatrick et al. (44) concluded: "There is clear evidence that most rape victims meet the . . . diagnostic criteria for PTSD, that of reexperiencing the traumatic event." They cite studies (e.g., 77) indicating that the initial response to the traumatic event is the best predictor of long-term outcome. It seems reasonable to assume that the initial trauma alters the biological substrate mediating emotional response (see Chapter 3). Symptoms that originate from this biological shift are probably the most resistant to resolution, even though understanding the meaning of the event in the context of personal history may allow a high degree of cognitive control over later intrusive reexperiencing (see Chapters 8 and 9).

Trauma in Children

The emotional development of children is intimately connected with the safety and nurturance provided by their environment. Children universally attach themselves intensely to their caregivers. This is a survival mechanism necessary to provide the needs that a child is unable to satisfy alone. Certainty of the presence of a "safe base" allows for normal emotional and cognitive development through assimilation and accommodation of new experiences (78–80).

In the absence of such a safe base, as in cases of child abuse and neglect, a child goes through a variety of psychological maneuvers to preserve maximum protection. Abused and neglected children often become fearfully and hungrily attached to their caregivers, with timid obedience, and an apparent preoccupation with the anticipation and prevention of abandonment (80) (see Chapters 2, 4–6). As Bowlby (81) put it: "Should his caregivers, in addition, actively reject him, he is likely to develop a pattern of behavior in which avoidance of them competes with his desire for proximity and care and in which angry behavior is apt to become prominent."

Many children who have been exposed to disruptions of their attachment to their primary caregivers through separation or through abuse or neglect develop extreme reactivity to internal and external stimulation: they overreact to frustrations and have trouble tolerating anxiety. When not faced with actual threatening situations, these children often appear depressed, anxiously withdrawn, dependent, clinging, and passive (81–83). They make few, or fearful, attempts at socialization and are uncomfortable in play with other children (84–86).

Traumatized children often have a heightened sense of vulnerability. They suffer from cognitive and perceptual changes, a reliance on rhythmical activities, and time distortions. They are prone to attach magical explanations to events beyond their control (9, 18) (Chapter 4). Unfortunately, there is still too little research on how the severity of trauma and the developmental level of the child affect the outcome. There is a slowly emerging body of knowledge about why some children are much more resistant to the long-term effects of psychological trauma than others (58) (Chapter 4). Developing special areas of competence and finding a secure school environment, a nurturing attachment figure, and, ultimately, a supportive spouse all make significant contributions to good posttraumatic adaptation (58).

The Chowchilla Studies

Most studies of psychic trauma concern death, physical catastrophe, or sexual assault. In contrast, the school bus kidnapping of 26 children in Chowchilla, California, in 1976 left all of them physically unharmed. Lenore Terr (18, 56) studied the effects of psychic traumatization in these children, who did not suffer a violation of basic trust in their primary caregivers. On follow-up 4 years later, she found that every one of them had some degree of posttraumatic stress, such as posttraumatic dreams, posttraumatic play, reenactment of the kidnapping, time distortions, cognitive and perceptual changes, and a heightened sense of vulnerability. Attempts to gain cognitive control led to a belief in omens, a sense of clairvoyance, and a foreshortened sense of the future. She noted some degree of collapse of earlier developmental accomplishments in all victims.

Although the severity of the posttraumatic symptoms was to some extent correlated with preexisting family pathology, lack of community bonding, and individual vulnerability, the symptoms were strikingly similar in all the children. This was particularly remarkable since the group included children between the ages of 5 and 14 who were at different phases of development. Terr (18, 56) concluded that all these children had lost some autonomy and were preoccupied with self-preservation: "None of the children was toughened by the experience: they simply had narrowed their spheres of concern to their own rooms at night and had lost hope to be able to affect their own future." Like Anna Freud (87), Terr noted that repeated reenactments and other attempts to deal with the aftermath of the trauma caused permanent personality change.

Child Physical Abuse

Children are particularly vulnerable to the long-term effects of psychological trauma and these effects are most psychologically disruptive when the perpetrator of the trauma is at the same time the adult on whom a child relies for love and protection. Between 1.5 and 2 million American children are thought to be at risk of physical injury from their parents each year (55). Green (9, 82) outlined the psychological defenses that children use to deal with parental abuse: hypervigilance, projection, splitting, and denial. Like Terr (18, 56), he described a driven, compulsive repetition and reenactment that permeates the dreams, play, fantasies, and object relationships of these children. Bowlby (81) and Green (82) have observed that children often blame themselves or an outside agency rather than their caregivers in order to maintain a modicum of trust in the people on whom they are physically and emotionally dependent. Like adults who identify with their terrorist kidnappers (88), abused children usually make a rapid accommodation to their environment by protecting and identifying with their abusers (89).

Aggression Following Abuse:
The Victim to Victimizer Process

Traumatized children have trouble modulating aggression. They tend to act destructively against others or themselves, sometimes to the point of self-mutilation (90). Many traumatized children have temper tantrums and fight with siblings and schoolmates (82, 90–92). Green (82) found that 41 percent of a sample of abused children, compared with 7 percent of control subjects, exhibited self-destructive behavior, such as biting, burning, head banging, and suicide attempts. Several observers have noted that some abused children provoke abuse by parents and other care-takers. This tendency to provoke abuse may serve a need to obtain otherwise unavailable physical contact and attention (92). This way of obtaining physical contact may establish a lifelong sado-masochistic character style (93).

The frequency of aggressive interactions in abused children suggests to Green (9) a link between the compulsion to repeat trauma and identification with the aggressor, which replaces fear and helplessness with feelings of omnipotence. Carmen et al. (43) suggested that boys are most likely to identify with the aggressor and perpetuate the abuse on their spouse and children. Abused girls may be more likely to identify with the victim. They often become the wives and lovers of violent and abusive men, and they tend to abuse their own children either actively or passively (9) (Chapter 6). Parents who batter each other are likely to abuse their children as well, and many parents who batter their children have been victims of parental abuse themselves (86, 92) (Chapter 6).

Incest

Childhood incest can be followed by a chronic PTSD (94). Incest victims often suffer phasic alterations between numbing and de-nial, with repetitive intrusions that may be dissociated as either affective (bodily) states or as vivid recollections (22, 23). The un-derlying problem often is obscured by chronic depression, self-destructive behavior, and drug and alcohol abuse (23). Estimates of the incidence of sexual abuse in the general population range from 4 to 14 percent (57), whereas the incidence among psychia-tric patients is thought to be higher. The abuse may go on for a long time. In the Harborview studies, 40 percent of the incest victims were abused for a year or longer (95).

There is a well-documented relationship between childhood incest and subsequent antisocial behavior: 15 percent of girls in a school for delinquent girls reported having had sex with fathers or step-fathers (8). Rosenfeld (96) cited an early finding that 51 of 103 women arrested by the Chicago vice squad said that their first sexual experience had been with their father. In his paper on "Confusion of Tongues Between Adults and the Child: The Language of Tenderness and Passion," Ferenczi (97) pointed out that incest left a lifelong residue of fear about the violation of trust in intimate relationships. Freud may have been right to believe that some women's overactive imaginations produced distorted memories of childhood sexual violations. However, contemporary clinicians who work with actual victims of incest are more impressed by their attempts to ward off memories of the trauma and their intense desire to protect and make excuses for the abusers. Shengold (98) stated: "Most patients who have an actual history of incest intensely wish that their memories were merely fantasies."

Learning Disabilities Following Childhood Abuse

Abuse affects children on many levels of mental and emotional development (84, 85) (Chapter 4). Consistent lack of parental protection against overwhelming external or internal stimulation is thought to interfere with learning to modulate affective responses to stimuli. Field (99) (Chapter 2) proposed that the mother serves as a mediator of soothing and arousal in the child. Failure to develop "the essential synchronicity between mother and child" causes physiological disorganization, which leads to extremes of under- and overarousal. This physiological instability can interfere with the capacity to assimilate and accommodate new information. Abused children often have learning disabilities and perform poorly on intelligence tests (9). Fish-Murray et al. (Chapter 4) have shown that abused children often respond to interpersonal anxiety with an affective intensity that suggests a reliving of their traumatic experiences. This may result in severe cognitive disorganization. Their data indicate that overwhelming feelings interfere with the capacity to organize information logically: when presented with stimuli even remotely reminiscent of the trauma, these children often suffered a psychotic disorganization that contained many elements of actual traumatic incidents. They tended to have an all-or-nothing response to emotional stimulation, and were unable to accommodate the demands of their current environment.

Many abused children with learning disabilities are now treated in remedial reading classes, often unsuccessfully, because no attention is paid to the traumatic elements that interfere with perception and cognition.

Abuse and Neurological Abnormalities

Many abused children show evidence of neurological damage, even when there is no evidence of head injury. Green et al. (100) found many soft neurological signs and nonspecific electroencephalogram (EEG) abnormalities. Green (9) thinks that this central nervous system damage is usually not due to head trauma, but "can be seen as an additional source of trauma which potentiates the pathological impact of the abusive environment." Evidence that childhood emotional trauma itself interferes with maturation of the central nervous system and causes lasting neurological changes is examined in Chapter 2.

Several studies suggest a link between hysterical seizures and childhood incest (101). Others show an unusually high incidence of abnormal EEGs in these patients (102). In patients with MPD, different personalities are accompanied by different physiological states, with differences in EEG and galvanic skin response (103). A relationship between MPD and temporal lobe epilepsy (104, 105) has also been noted. Elucidation of the temporal relationship between traumatization and neurological damage remains a challenge for further research (see Chapter 2).

The Victim to Patient Process: Trauma and Psychiatric Illness

The secondary reactions to psychological trauma—such as emotional constriction, sensation seeking and reenactment, and drug and alcohol abuse—all create new and usually overwhelming problems. These maladaptations often make it very difficult at first to establish the proper diagnosis of PTSD. Since people with preexisting character problems are more vulnerable to PTSD, one can understand that these patients develop complex diagnostic pictures (Chapters 8 and 9).

Psychiatrists and other mental health professionals are not routinely taught to inquire into a history of sexual or physical abuse or other traumatic precedents in their patients. When a history of such a psychological trauma is obtained, it usually is recorded as a fact with little relevance to current psychiatric problems. However, in recent studies where these questions were specifically addressed, some surprising findings emerged, shedding light on the extent of prior traumatization in psychiatric patients. In one study by Carmen et al. (43), 43 percent of a sample of adult psychiatric inpatients had a history of severe physical or sexual abuse.

It revealed a marked sex difference in both the incidence and consequences of abuse and incest. Female patients were much more likely to have been abused than males: the incidence was 53 percent of female inpatients, compared with 26 percent of the males. Abused males were much more likely to turn their aggression outwards, whereas the women tended to be more self-destructive. Beck and van der Kolk (106) surveyed 26 chronically hospitalized female patients in a state hospital. Their chart reviews uncovered 12 cases in which incest was reported and 10 cases in which there was no reported incest. The four remaining patients had inadequate records, which prevented classification in one group or the other. The incest victims were found to seek significantly more staff contact than did those without a history of incest. They had received a variety of psychiatric diagnoses over time, with schizophrenia being most prevalent. However, the incest victims had a higher incidence of affective symptoms and substance abuse. Many did not fit clearly into any diagnostic category. All patients had failed to respond to neuroleptics enough to be discharged, even to a nursing home.

Previous studies (13) (Chapters 4 and 5) have shown that in PTSD affective stimulation may cause a disorganization of thought processes. It is possible that the psychotic decompensations in these women were caused by a response to affective stimulation that was appropriate to earlier childhood trauma. In their psychotic states they may have been partially reliving earlier traumatic events. The authors (106) believe that there is a need to examine the content of psychotic thoughts in incest victims to determine to what degree their "delusions" may be related to actual events. The authors concluded that:

> Chronically hospitalized patients with a history of childhood trauma, recurrent psychotic episodes, with fluctuating levels of involvement with their environment, and severely restricted capacity for self care, have typically not been diagnostically separated from the group of schizophrenias. In our chronically institutionalized sample, the possibility of such a separate sub-group can only be raised, not confirmed.

In two outpatient surveys, almost half of the female psychiatric patients had a history of physical or sexual abuse (107, 108). In one private psychiatric practice (96), 6 of 18 female patients were found to have a history of incest, but only 1 patient had volunteered this information spontaneously. Hilberman and Munson (109) described a syndrome in battered women that they viewed as similar to the rape trauma syndrome (17) and that largely coincides with the DSM-III description of PTSD. The features of this syndrome include agitation and anxiety bordering on panic, intense fear when confronted with events even remotely connected with violence, a chronic sense of apprehension, and heightened vigilance leading to inability to relax and insomnia. These women were characterized by passivity and paralysis. Numbness coexisted with a pervasive sense of helplessness and despair. They all had sleep disturbances and nightmares with undisguised themes of violence. "Like rape victims, battered women rarely experienced anger directly." They (109) concluded that this syndrome reflected not only fear for another assault, but also a constant struggle to control aggressive impulses. They noted that these women usually turned their aggression against themselves in the form of suicidal behavior, depression, grotesque self-imagery, alcoholism, and self-mutilation. In studies in outpatient clinics, traumatized women presented with somatic complaints and depression. In a survey of 100 wife-battering cases (108), 71 women had symptoms that were treated with antidepressants or major tranquilizers, 42 women had attempted suicide, and 21 carried a primary diagnosis of depression.

Conclusions

While there is no predictable psychopathological diagnosis following childhood physical or sexual abuse, these traumas have been implicated in the genesis of several psychopathological conditions, including borderline personality disorder (110, 111) (Chapter 5), MPD (34, 35, 112), panic disorders (113), and chronic pain syndromes (114). Herman (111), Greaves (115), and Rosenfeld (96) have shown the validity of Freud's early impression that trauma was often followed by the hysterical symptoms of dissociation and conversion. In a retrospective study, Herman found that the majority of abused women in an outpatient psychiatric population carried the diagnosis of either hysterical or borderline personality. Five of six of Rosenfeld's patients had a diagnosis of hysterical personality. Herman found that males with a history of physical or sexual abuse often were diagnosed as antisocial personalities. Many traumatized males probably end up in the criminal justice system and may never come to the attention of psychiatrists.

Much work remains to be done to clarify the link between childhood emotional trauma and later psychiatric illness. In the next three chapters the many neurological, cognitive, psychological, and biochemical functions that can be affected by disruptions of affiliative bonds and other traumas throughout life are discussed. People who become fixated at a level of helplessness and loss of control are likely to end up in the mental health system, where they will receive a variety of psychiatric diagnoses, depending on the particular presentation during any particular admission. Ignoring the cause of the patient's distress is likely to result in increasingly hostile demands on the part of the patient, and equally firm rejections on the part of the caregivers. The particular form that this hostile dependent relationship takes may give a clue to the nature of the traumatic constellation that gave rise to the psychiatric symptoms.

Preliminary data from several studies indicate that some of the hallmarks of childhood traumatic antecedents of mental illness include a multiplicity of clinical presentations, a variety of diagnoses given, and a number of different medications prescribed. More knowledge about the human response to trauma would allow a better understanding of these fluctuating clinical presentations and suggest psychological treatments to alleviate hyperarousal, dissociation, helplessness, and inability to modulate aggression and intimacy.

References

1. Freud S: The neuro-psychoses of defense (1984), in Complete Psychological Works. Standard Ed. Vol 2. Translated and edited by Strachey J. London, Hogarth Press, 1954

2. American Psychiatric Association: Diagnostic and Statistical Manual of Mental Disorders, 3rd ed. Washington, DC, American Psychiatric Association, 1980

3. Kardiner A: The Traumatic Neuroses of War. New York, P Hoeber, 1941

4. Horowitz MJ: Stress Response Syndromes. New York, Jason Aronson, 1976

5. Lindemann E: Symptomatology and management of acute grief. Am J Psychiatry 101:141–148, 1944

6. Krystal H: Trauma and affects. Psychoanal Study Child 33:81–116, 1978

7. Shatan CF: Bogus manhood and bogus honor: surrender and transfiguration in the US Marine Corps, in Psychoanalytic Perspectives on Aggression and Violence. Edited by

Milman D, Goldman, G. Springfield, Ill, Charles C Thomas, 1975

8. Sharfman MA, Clark RW: Delinquent adolescent girls: residential treatment in a municipal hospital setting. Arch Gen Psychiatry 17:441–447, 1967

9. Green AH: Dimensions of psychological trauma in abused children. J Am Assoc Child Psychiatry 22:231–237, 1983

10. Freud S: Beyond the pleasure principle (1920), in Complete Psychological Works. Standard Ed. Vol 18. Translated and edited by Strachey J. London, Hogarth Press, 1959

11. Rangell L: Discussion of the Buffalo Creek Disaster: the course of psychic trauma. Am J Psychiatry 133:313–316, 1976

12. Krystal H: Massive Psychic Trauma. New York, International Universities Press, 1968

13. van der Kolk BA, Ducey CP: Clinical implications of the Rorschach in posttraumatic stress, in Post-Traumatic Stress Disorder: Psychological and Biological Sequelae. Edited by van der Kolk BA. Washington, DC, American Psychiatric Press, 1984

14. Southard EE: Shellshock and Neuropsychiatry. Boston, WM Leonard, 1919

15. Grinker RR, Spiegel JJ: Men under Stress. New York, McGraw-Hill, 1945

16 Figley C: Stress Disorders among Vietnam Veterans: Theory, Research and Treatment Implications. New York, Brunner/Mazel, 1978

17. Burgess AW, Holstrom L: Rape trauma syndrome. Am J Psychiatry 131:981–986, 1974

18. Terr L: Chowchilla revisited: the effects of psychic trauma four years after a school bus kidnapping. Am J Psychiatry 140:1543–1550, 1983

19. Hilberman, E: Overview: the wife-beater's wife "reconsidered." Am J Psychiatry 137:974–975, 1980

20. Titchener JL, Kapp F: Family and character change in Buffalo Creek. Am J Psychiatry 133:295–299, 1976

21. Wilkinson CB: Aftermath of disaster, collapse of Hyatt Regency Hotel Skywalks. Am J Psychiatry 140:1134–1139, 1983

22. Herman JL: Father-Daughter Incest. Cambridge, Harvard University Press, 1981

23. Gelinas DJ: The persistent negative effects of incest. Psychiatry 46:312–332, 1983

24. Andreasen N, Norris AS: Long term adjustment and adaptation mechanisms in severely burnt adults. J Nerv Ment Dis 154:352–360, 1972

25. Selye H: The Stress of Life. New York, McGraw-Hill, 1956

26. Pavlov IP: Conditioned Reflexes: An Investigation of the Physiological Activity of the Cerebral Cortex (1927). Edited and translated by Anrep GV. New York, Dover, 1960

27. Kolb L: The posttraumatic stress disorders of combat: a subgroup with a conditional emotional response. Milit Med 149:237–243, 1984

28. Janet P: The Mental State of Hystericals. Paris, Alcan, 1911

29. van der Kolk BA, Blitz R, Burr W, et al: Nightmares and trauma. Am J Psychiatry 141:187–190, 1984

30. Krystal H: Psychoanalytic views on human emotional damages, in Post-Traumatic Stress Disorder: Psychological and Biological Sequelae. Edited by van der Kolk BA. Washington, DC, American Psychiatric Press, 1984

31. Whitlock F: The aetiology of hysteria. Acta Psychiatry Scand 43:144–162, 1967

32. Briquet P: Traite clinique et therapeutique de l'hysterie. Paris, Balliere, 1859

33. Reynolds JR: Remarks on paralysis, and other disorders of motion and sensation, dependent on idea. Br Med J 2: 483–485, 1869

34. Braun BG: Towards a theory of multiple personality and other dissociative phenomena. Psychiatry Clin North Am 7:171–193, 1984

35. Putnam FW: The psychophysiological investigation of multiple personality disorder. Psychiatr Clin North Am 7:31–41, 1984

36. Janet P: L'automatisme psychologique. Paris, Balliere, 1889

37. Kluft RP (Ed): Childhood Antecedents of Multiple Personality. Washington, DC, American Psychiatric Press, 1985

38. Bliss EL: Multiple personalities: a report of 14 cases with implications for schizophrenia and hysteria. Arch Gen Psychiatry 37:1388–1397, 1980

39. Lacoursiere R, Godfrey K, Rubey L: Traumatic neurosis in the etiology of alcoholism. Am J Psychiatry 137: 966–968, 1980

40. Fox RP: Narcissistic rage and the problem of combat aggression. Arch Gen Psychiatry 31:807–811, 1974

41. van der Kolk BA: Adolescent vulnerability to post-traumatic stress. Psychiatry 20:365–370, 1985

42. Haley S: When the patient reports atrocities. Arch Gen Psychiatry 30:191–196, 1974

43. Carmen EH, Reiker PP, Mills T: Victims of violence and psychiatric illness. Am J Psychiatry 141: 378–379, 1984

44. Kilpatrick DG, Veronen LJ, Best CL: Factors predicting psychological distress in rape victims, in Trauma and Its Wake. Edited by Figley C. New York, Brunner/Mazel, 1985, pp 113–141

45. Burgess AW, Holstrom E: Adaptive strategies in recovery from rape. Am J Psychiatry 136:1278–1282, 1979

46. Schucker E: Psychodynamics and treatment of the sexual assault victim. J Am Acad Psychoanal 7:553–573, 1979

47. Archibald H, Tuddenham R: Persistent stress reactions after combat. Arch Gen Psychiatry 12:475–481, 1965

48. Eitinger L: The concentration camp syndrome and its late sequelae, in Victims, Survivors and Perpetrators. Edited by Dimsdale JE. New York, Hemisphere, 1980

49. Lifton RJ: The Broken Connection. New York, Simon and Schuster, 1979

50. Lindy JD, Grace MC, Green BL: Building a conceptual bridge between civilian trauma and war trauma, in Post-Traumatic Stress Disorder: Psychological and Biological Sequelae. Ed-

ited by van der Kolk BA. Washington, DC, American Psychiatric Press, 1984

51. Laufer RS, Frey-Wouters E, Gallops MS: Traumatic stressors in the Vietnam war and post-traumatic stress disorder, in Trauma and Its Wake. Edited by Figley C. New York, Brunner/Mazel, 1985

52. Sackett GP: Genotype determines social isolation rearing effects on monkeys. Dev Psychol 17:313–318, 1981

53. Maier SF, Seligman MEP: Learned helplessness: theory and evidence. J Exp Psychol [Gen] 105:3–46, 1976

54. Kagan J, Reznick S, Snidman N: The biology and psychology of behavioral inhibition in young children. Child Dev (in press)

55. Hendin H, Pollinger Haas A: Combat adaptations of Vietnam veterans without post traumatic stress disorder. Am J Psychiatry 141:956–960, 1984

56. Terr L: Children of Chowchilla: a study of psychic trauma. Psychoanal Study Child 34:547–623, 1979

57. Finkelhor D: Child Sexual Abuse: New Theory and Research. New York, Free Press, 1984

58. Garmezy N, Rutter M (Eds): Stress, Coping, and Development in Children. New York, McGraw-Hill, 1983

59. Laufer RS, Brett E, Gallops MS: Post-traumatic stress disorder reconsidered: PTSD among Vietnam veterans, in Post-Traumatic Stress Disorder: Psychological and Biological Sequelae. Edited by van der Kolk BA. Washington, DC, American Psychiatric Press, 1984

60. Hendin H, Pollinger Haas A, Singer P, et al: The influence of precombat personality on posttraumatic stress disorders. Compr Psychiatry 24:530–534, 1983

61. Pynoos RS, Eth S: Developmental perspective on psychic trauma in childhood, in Trauma and Its Wake. Edited by Figley CR. New York, Brunner/Mazel, 1985

62. Janoff-Bulman R: The aftermath of victimization: rebuilding shattered assumptions, in Trauma and Its Wake. Edited by Figley CR. New York, Brunner/Mazel, 1985

63. Stoddard F: Stress disorders in burned children and adolescents. Paper presented at the Annual Meeting of the American Psychiatric Association, 1985

64. Erikson KT: Everything in Its Path: Destruction of Community in the Buffalo Creek Flood. New York, Simon and Schuster, 1976

65. Bromet E, Schulberg HC, Dunn L: Reactions of psychiatric patients to the Three Mile Island nuclear accident. Arch Gen Psychiatry 39:725–730, 1982

66. Kobasa SC, Pucetti MC: Personality and social resources in stress resistance. J Pers Soc Psychol 45:839–850, 1982

67. Lidz T: Nightmares and the combat neuroses. Psychiatry 9:37–49, 1946

68. Fairbairn WRD: The War Neuroses: Their Nature and Significance. Psychoanalytic Studies of the Personality. Boston, Routledge & Kegan Paul, 1952

69. Brill NQ: Gross stress reactions: II traumatic war neuroses, in Comprehensive Textbook of Psychiatry. Edited by Freedman AM, Kaplan HL. Baltimore, Williams & Wilkins Co, 1967

70. Moses R: Adult psychic trauma: the question of early predisposition and some detailed mechanisms. Int J Psychoanal 54:353–363, 1978

71. Burgess AW, Holstrom E: Adaptive strategies in recovery from rape. Am J Psychiatry 136:1278–1282, 1979

72. Hocking F: Psychiatric aspects of extreme environmental stress. Diseases of the Nervous System 31:542–545, 1970

73. Kilpatrick DG, Veronen LJ, Resick PA: The aftermath of rape: recent empirical findings. Am J Orthopsychiatry 49:658–669, 1979

74. Kilpatrick DG, Resick PA, Veronen LJ: Effects of the rape experience: a longitudinal study. Journal of Social Issues 37:105–122, 1981

75. Atkeson BM, Calhoun KS, Resick PA, et al: Victims of rape: repeated assessment of depressive symptoms. J Consult Clin Psychol 50:96–102, 1982

76. Veronen LJ, Best CI: Assessment and treatment of rape-

induced fear and anxiety. The Clinical Psychologist 36:99–101, 1983

77. McCahill TW, Meyer LC, Fishman AM: The aftermath of rape. Lexington, Mass, DC Heath & Co, 1979

78. Bowlby J: Attachment and Loss. Vol 1: Attachment. New York, Basic Books, 1969.

79. Bowlby J. Attachment and Loss. Vol 2: Separation. New York, Basic Books, 1973

80. Bowlby J: Separation: Anxiety and Anger. New York, Basic Books, 1973

81. Bowlby J: Violence in the family as a disorder of the attachment and caregiving systems. Am J Psychoanal 44:9–27, 1984

82. Green A: Child Maltreatment. New York, Aronson, 1980

83. Greensbauer TJ, Sands K: Distorted affective communications in abused/neglected infants and their potential impact on caretakers. J Am Acad Child Psychiatry 18:236–250, 1979

84. Cichetti D: The emergence of developmental psychopathology. Child Dev 55:1–7, 1984

85. Cichetti D, Rizley A: Developmental perspectives on the etiology, intergenerational transmission, and sequelae of child maltreatment. New Directions for Child Development 11:31–55, 1981

86. Malone CA: Safety first: comments on the influence of external danger in the lives of children of disorganized families. Am J Orthopsychiatry 36:6–12, 1966

87. Freud A: A psychoanalytic view of developmental psychopathology. Journal of the Philadelphia Association of Psychoanalysis 1:7–17, 1974

88. Ochberg FM: Victims of terrorism. J Clin Psychiatry 41:73–76, 1980

89. Cichetti D, Rosen KS: Theoretical and empirical considerations in the investigation of the relationship between affect and cognition in an atypical population of infants, in Emo-

tions, Cognition and Behavior. Edited by Izard C, Kagan J, Zajanc R. New York, Cambridge University Press, 1984

90. Ross RR: Violence in, violence out: child abuse and self-mutilation in adolescent offenders. Juvenile and Family Court Journal 31:33–44, 1980

91. Lewis DO, Shanok SS, Pincus JH, et al: Violent juvenile delinquents: psychiatric, neurological, psychological and abuse factors. J Child Psychiatry 18:307–319, 1979

92. Lewis D, Balla D: Delinquency and Psychopathology. New York, Grune & Stratton, 1976

93. Jaffe P, Wolfe D, Wilson SK, et al: Family violence and child adjustment: a comparative analysis of girls' and boys' behavioral symptoms. Am J Psychiatry 143:74–77, 1986

94. Donaldson MA, Gardner R: Diagnosis and treatment of traumatic stress among women after childhood incest, in Trauma and Its Wake. Edited by Figley C. New York, Brunner/Mazel, 1985, pp 356–377

95. Harborview Sexual Assault Center: Response to Violence and Sexual Abuse in the Family. Washington, DC, Center for Women's Policy Studies, 1980

96. Rosenfeld A: Incidence of a history of incest in 18 female psychiatric patients. Am J Psychiatry 136:791–795, 1979

97. Ferenczi S: Confusion of tongues between adults and the child: the language of tenderness and passion, in Problems and Methods of Psychoanalysis. Edited by Ferenczi S. London, Hogarth Press, 1955

98. Shengold L: The parent as sphinx. J Am Psychoanal Assoc 11:725–751, 1963

99. Field T: Attachment as psychobiological attunement, in The Psychobiology of Attachment and Separation. Edited by Reite M, Field T. Orlando, Florida, Academic Press, 1985, pp 415–454

100. Green A, Voeller K, Gaines R, et al: Neurological impairment in maltreated children. Child Abuse Negl 5:129–134, 1981

101. Davies RK: Incest: some neuropsychiatric findings. Int J Psychiatry Med 9:117–120, 1979

102. Gross M: Incestuous rape: a cause for hysterical seizures in four adolescent girls. Am J Orthopsychiatry 49:704–708, 1979

103. Brende JO: The psychophysiologic manifestations of dissociation. Psychiatr Clin North Am 7:41–49, 1984

104. Schenk L, Baer D: Multiple personality and related dissociative phenomena in patients with temporal lobe epilepsy. Am J Psychiatry 138:1311–1316, 1981

105. Mesulam MM: Dissociative states with abnormal temporal lobe EEG: multiple personality and the illusion of possession. Arch Neurol 38: 176–181, 1981

106. Beck J, van der Kolk B: Women with a history of incest in the mental hospital. Manuscript submitted for publication

107. Post RD, Willett AA, Franks RD, et al: A preliminary report on the prevalence of domestic violence among psychiatric inpatients. Am J Psychiatry 137:974–975, 1980

108. Gayford JJ: Wife battering: a preliminary survey of 100 cases. Br Med J 1:194–198, 1980

109. Hilberman E, Munson M: Sixty battered women. Victimology 2:460–471, 1978

110. Bemporad JR, Smith HF, Hanson G, et al: Borderline syndromes in childhood: criteria for diagnosis. Am J Psychiatry 139:596–602, 1982

111. Herman J: Histories of violence in an outpatient clinic. Am J Orthopsychiatry 57:137–141, 1986

112. Horevitz RP, Braun BG: Are multiple personalities borderlines? Psychiatr Clin North Am 7:69–87, 1984

113. Favarelli C, Webb T, Ambonetti A, et al: Prevalence of traumatic early life events in 31 patients with panic attacks. Am J Psychiatry 142: 1493–1495, 1985

114. Muse M: Stress related, posttraumatic chronic pain: criteria for diagnosis, and preliminary report on prevalence. Pain 23:295–300, 1985

115. Greaves GB: Multiple personality 165 years after Mary Reynolds. J Nerv Ment Dis 168:577–596, 1980

CHAPTER 2

The Separation Cry and the Trauma Response: Developmental Issues in the Psychobiology of Attachment and Separation

Bessel A. van der Kolk, M.D.

The essence of psychological trauma is the loss of faith that there is order and continuity in life. Trauma occurs when one loses the sense of having a safe place to retreat within or outside oneself to deal with frightening emotions or experiences. This results in a state of helplessness, a feeling that one's actions have no bearing on the outcome of one's life. Since human life seems to be incompatible with a sense of meaninglessness and lack of control, people will attempt to avoid this experience at just about any price, from abject dependency to psychosis. Much of human endeavor, in religion, art, and science, is centrally concerned with exactly these grand questions of meaning and control over one's destiny.

Emotional attachment is essential for survival in children as well as for a sense of existential meaning in adults. A person is a biological organism that develops from the moment of birth in a social context, which begins with the mother–infant bond and continually incorporates wider interpersonal and cultural influences. For a long time, psychologists and psychiatrists have been

---

The author wishes to acknowledge the assistance of Aldo Tartaglini in gathering the material for this chapter.

debating the nature of the mother—infant bond and other social affiliations, and investigating the effects of their disruption. Studies by Spitz (1), Mahler (2), Bowlby (3, 4), and others have brought modern psychiatry to reconsider the ways in which failure of attachment and traumatic separation affect the developing psyche. Bowlby (3) emphasized that attachment behavior is first of all a vital biological function, indispensable for both reproduction and survival. He sees the human need for deep and long-lasting attachments as the result of a long-term evolutionary development. By attaching themselves to caregivers, children put themselves in constant touch with a powerful protector. The assurance of a "safe base" to which children can return after exploring their surroundings promotes self-reliance and autonomy, while instilling a sense of sympathy and helpfulness to others in distress. Attachment and caring also give powerful emotional satisfactions to caregivers, providing further insurance for the child's survival.

The earliest and possibly most damaging psychological trauma is the loss of a secure base. When caregivers who are supposed to be sources of protection and nurturance become simultaneously the main sources of danger, a child must maneuver psychologically to reestablish some sense of safety, often becoming fearfully and hungrily attached, unwillingly or anxiously obedient, and apprehensive lest the caregiver be unavailable when needed (see Chapters 1, 3–6). Bowlby (5) called this "a pattern of behavior in which avoidance of them competes with his desire for proximity and care and in which angry behavior is apt to become prominent."

In an essay on the long-term consequences of child abuse and neglect, Bowlby (6) suggested that expression of anger between members of a family can serve to maintain attachment bonds. Family violence is often a distorted or exaggerated version of behavior that is potentially functional. Pain, fear, fatigue, and inaccessibility of the primary caregiver elicit increased efforts to attach to parents. In both children and adults, severe stress, such as illness and other situations involving loss of control, dramatically increase the need for attachment and protection. In fact, the most powerful influence in overcoming the impact of psychological trauma seems to be the availability of a caregiver who can be blindly trusted when one's own resources are inadequate.

In recent years much has been learned about the neurobiology of attachment and the long-term effects of maternal and peer separation in a variety of animal species. At the same time, a rapidly expanding body of human research is showing that disturbances of childhood attachment bonds may have lifelong psychobiological consequences. There may be particularly vulnerable stages of development related to maturational processes in the central nervous system (CNS).

Children whose attachment to their primary caregivers has been disrupted by separation, abuse, or neglect develop several symptoms. They become extremely reactive to internal and external stimulation; that is, they overreact to many situations and tolerate anxiety poorly. Boys often display a constant high level of motor activity. At rest, these children seem depressed, anxiously withdrawn, clinging, and passive (7, 8). They do not participate in social play, and they make few, or fearful, attempts at socialization (9). They display frozen watchfulness toward the abusing parents, or show an unusual sensitivity to their parents' needs (10). They have trouble modulating aggression against others and may be self-destructive, even to the point of self-mutilation. In later life they are prone to depression and find it difficult to form stable relationships or work commitments. Depending on the severity of the trauma and the developmental level at which separation occurs, such children also suffer from a heightened sense of vulnerability, cognitive and perceptual changes, a reliance on rhythmical activities, time distortions, and a tendency to attach magical explanations to events beyond their control (11) (Chapter 4).

Studies on Imprinting

Over the past few decades, many theories have been proposed to explain the strong infant–mother attachment bonds that have been observed in both mammals and birds (12). Recent primate research (13) confirms the view of Bowlby (3) and Ainsworth (14) that an attachment figure provides the infant with the security necessary to explore the limits of its surroundings, thus permitting exploration and affiliation even at some distance from the attachment figure. Nonhuman primates express attachment mainly through physical contact such as clinging; in contrast, human beings predominantly use signaling to maintain adult–infant proximity (15). The infantile separation cry induces adults to provide safety, nurturance, and social (i.e., pleasurable) stimulation.

The offspring of mammals have developed highly complex ways of attracting their mother's attention. In all mammalian species abandoned pups emit a distress cry, which stimulates complex complementary behaviors in mothers (and other caregivers) that allow infants to develop safely. In most species, the separation response appears to be nonspecific: care giving by any female animal of the same species will abolish separation distress. Only in primates is the response specific to the mother, at least after a certain stage of development (16).

MacLean (15) considers human verbal communication to be an evolutionary development from this infantile attachment cry. He sees the capacity to maintain attachment bonds over space and time by means of verbal communication as one of the principal reasons for the human ascendancy in the animal kingdom. But this capacity also has a dark side: "When mammalians opted for a family way of life, they set the stage for the most distressful forms of suffering, [what] makes being a mammal so painful, . . . is having to endure separation and isolation from loved ones, and, in the end, the utter desolation of death."

At least in nonhuman primates, attachment behavior seems to be rather nonspecific during the first 6 to 9 months of life; after that one adult can no longer substitute for any other without eliciting responses of protest or despair (17, 18). The protest phase consists of a generalized disoriented increase in activity accompanied by loud and repeated signs of arousal and distress; the signs of despair are decreased motor activity, vocalizations, eating, and drinking, accompanied by general withdrawal (19, 20). The protest signals are aimed at bringing the primary attachment figure back, and they cease on the adult's return. Failure to return results in a despair response. Research on monkeys by McKinney and Kraemer and colleagues (21–27), Suomi and colleagues (13, 19, 20, 28–31), and Reite and colleagues (16, 32) and other studies of nonhuman primates have extended many of Bowlby's and Ainsworth's observations on the response of human infants to separation.

An infant seeks increased attachment in the face of any external danger, including threats emanating from the attachment object itself. Thus attachment remains strong, even when the imprinted object no longer provides effective protection and nurturance. Increased imprinting to abusing objects has been demonstrated in birds (33), dogs (34), monkeys (35, 36), and human beings (7). Sackett et al. (37) found that monkeys raised by abusive mothers cling to them more than average: "The immediate consequence of maternal rejection is the accentuation of proximity seeking on the part of the infant." After similar experiments, Harlow and Harlow (35) concluded: "Instead of producing experimental neurosis we had achieved a technique for enhancing maternal attachment."

Studies of different species using different methodologies all agree that traumatic separation of an infant from its mother, or a child from its peers, is a far-reaching biopsychosocial event (21). Harlow and his successors have conclusively demonstrated that secure attachment is a prerequisite for normal social development in nonhuman primates. Prospective studies on the long-term effects of loss of attachment bonds in humans are currently incomplete, but research by Spitz (1), Mahler (2), and Cicchetti (9) indicate that failure to develop such bonds is devastating. Small children, unable to anticipate the future, experience separation anxiety as soon as they lose sight of the mother. After the development of object constancy, overwhelming traumatic experiences cause a loss of trust that the separation call will be answered. In both children and adults, this may lead to temporary or lasting disruptions in the capacity to modulate emotions and engage in social affiliation. The clinical symptoms of this lost trust can be as severe as the symptoms of those in whom basic trust never developed.

Attachment and Separation in Nonhuman Primates: Lessons from Harlow's Heirs

The Effects of Social Deprivation

Starting with Harlow's work, a long series of experiments have documented the response of nonhuman primates to separation from mothers and peers, demonstrating the remarkable similarities to the reactions of human beings. The great advantage of working with monkeys is their short life-span, which allows for easier observation of the long-term consequences of environmental manipulation. Researchers have only recently begun to explore the implications of this work for the understanding of both the normal and abnormal development of human beings.

In both male and female monkeys, social isolation for various periods during the first year of life produces grossly abnormal social and sexual behavior. Isolated monkeys do not produce offspring, and artificially inseminated females will mutilate or kill their babies. Young monkeys who are separated from their mothers become socially withdrawn and unpredictably aggressive. They also develop self-destructive and self-stimulating behaviors such as huddling, self-clasping, self-sucking, and biting (35, 37–39). They do not learn to discriminate such social stimuli as facial expressions (40) because they lack the early experience of the essential synchrony between mother and child and its associated expressions. Remnants of this deficit persist throughout their lives, even after later exposure to social situations. Isolation does not seem to affect the long-term capacity to regulate basic physiological functions, such as feeding and sleep (21).

The Relevance of Critical Periods

Surprisingly, monkeys separated from their mothers during the first few months of life and otherwise socially isolated develop normally, provided they are soon reunited with their mothers or with peers (41). Even if socially isolated during critical periods of development, the effects can be partially reversed if they are reunited fairly quickly with their mothers or with peers. While these behavioral changes are nearly universal, males are more seriously affected by isolation than are females (19). There is also evidence that individual genetic vulnerability influences the severity of the damage (42).

The age at which monkeys are separated from either their mothers or their peers is crucial in accounting for both the immediate intensity of the protest/despair response and its long-term effects. With variations depending on the species, separations at the end of the first year of life (corresponding roughly to the third year in human infants) have devastating short-term as well as permanent consequences. Sackett (39) found that rhesus monkeys isolated at 12 months show a much greater loss of social competence than those isolated at 6 to 9 months. Suomi (13) found that monkeys isolated at 90 days after birth were much more affected than those isolated at either 30 or 120 days. He also found that when infants are separated from their mothers but allowed to remain with peers, they showed much less protest and despair than those who were housed alone: monkeys apparently substitute strong peer attachments for maternal care.

Repeated peer separation evokes responses similar to those of repeated maternal separations. According to Kraemer and McKinney (25), peer-reared monkeys showed a stronger response to peer separation than did mother-reared animals. Suomi et al. (20) selected monkeys who had been housed with peers since 15 days after birth to 20 separations of 4 days each, starting at 90 to 300 days of age. The protest/despair response was consistent and persisted undiminished through all 20 separations. In contrast, Seaman (43) subjected peer-raised monkeys to three 19-day separations, finding that protest, but not despair, abated by the third separation. He thus established that number of separations is not crucial to the despair response; while protest abates over time, despair persists.

Reversibility of Early Deprivation and the Persistence of Latent Effects

The effects of early social deprivation in monkeys used to be considered largely irreversible (44). However, Suomi and Harlow (28) demonstrated that raising separated monkeys with younger monkeys can provide a nurturing environment that eliminates most of the bizarre behavior caused by isolation. They coined the term "monkey therapists" for these younger peers. After an initial period in which they were extraordinarily aggressive, the separated monkeys slowly developed appropriate behavior during prolonged periods of group housing. By 3 to 4 years, the previously isolated monkeys were nearly indistinguishable from monkeys who were normally reared (29).

However, this adaptation can be lost under social stress, when complex social discriminations are required (43, 46, 47). Heightened emotional or physical arousal causes previously separated animals to show inappropriate social behavior; they become either withdrawn or aggressive and they display an increase in stereotyped activity. Even monkeys that recover in other respects may have persistent deficits in sexual behavior and may continue to misperceive social cues; for example, they may fail to withdraw after a threat by a dominant animal (45, 48, 49).

Latent Effects of Separation Uncovered by Amphetamines and Alcohol

McKinney et al. (23, 24) demonstrated the differential effects of amphetamine on previously separated monkeys and those who were always properly socialized. They examined the behavioral and neurobiological effects of *d*-amphetamine on 3-year-old preadolescent rhesus monkeys who had been separated from their peers during the second month after birth and isolated during the first year of life, but had for several years been successfully reunited with stable affiliative and peer relationships. They became acutely violent when given low doses of amphetamines and killed several of their peers. This behavior was not seen in monkeys who were not socially deprived.

Social separation also alters the response of rhesus monkeys to alcohol (24). Intermittently separated and socially isolated monkeys consumed more alcohol both during separation and after reunion. The increased response to alcohol was dose dependent: at low doses (1 g/kg) the usual separation response was attenuated, whereas at high doses (3 g/kg) the despair response was exacerbated. Thus alcohol in low doses had antidepressant effects and in higher doses produced behavioral signs of depression. When a mixed group of monkeys was given free access to alcohol, consumption was significantly higher in monkeys who had been exposed to early social isolation. This result, like the reaction to amphetamines, substantiates the notion of neurobiological links among social attachment mechanisms, social stressors, and vulnerability to substance abuse and addiction.

Social Isolation in Older Primates

Studies on separation in older animals indicate that the depressive response seen in younger monkeys does not necessarily abate as the animal matures. Suomi et al. (31) demonstrated that the protest/despair response persists into adulthood. When 5-year-old adult monkeys who were separated from their nuclear families were placed in cages with other animals, they displayed transient behavioral disturbances but rapidly established normal social relationships after an initial spurt of aggression. However, adult monkeys separated from their nuclear families and put in a cage by themselves showed the typical protest/despair response. The despair response seems to result specifically from losing attachment objects; animals did not develop such a pronounced despair response when separated from peers if they had lived a large part of their lives in single cages and had not sustained an abrupt loss of their nuclear families.

The Offspring of "Motherless Monkeys"

Suomi and Ripp (19) studied the effects of social deprivation on the second generation. When a female monkey was separated early in life from her mother, she herself had severely impaired mothering capacities. "Motherless monkeys" were prone to parental abuse, including mutilation and killing of offspring. The younger the mother, the greater was the likelihood of abuse. The inadequacy of the care provided to the offspring was directly correlated with the degree of early social deprivation experienced by their mothers. In contrast, the vast majority of mother-raised females became competent mothers themselves. Peer socialization again compensated for parental deprivation: females separated from their mothers who had spent their juvenile and adolescent years in stable conspecific arrangements were at very low risk for becoming abusive mothers. Peer-reared females were three times more likely to provide adequate maternal care to firstborn offspring than were surrogate- and wire-cage-reared females. There was a striking sexual difference in vulnerability to abuse: motherless monkeys were three times more likely to provide adequate care to female offspring than to male offspring. Finally, even motherless monkeys appeared to learn mothering from their offspring: most monkeys who were abusive with firstborns proved quite competent with later offspring if they had not been immediately separated from the firstborn children. The issue of child abuse by deprived human mothers is discussed in Chapter 6.

Implications for Human Psychopathology

This research has profound implications for understanding the effects of child neglect and abuse in human beings. The protest/despair response to separation is seen in all primates, human and nonhuman. Sudden loss of a love object leads to acute depressions in all primates. Anaclitic depressions can be improved, but not totally resolved, by peer group interactions. Vulnerability to both depression and abuse of offspring is intimately related to early experiences. Later experiences only partially offset the effects of early social deprivation. An adequate support network may attenuate the devastating effects of early deprivation, but altered cognitive functioning, incapacity to deal with autonomic arousal, and the loss of ability to fantasize and sublimate may continue to render a person vulnerable to loss of self-esteem, substance abuse, and problems in coping with aggression. Thus early deprivation enhances vulnerability to later traumatic life events. However, the superior human learning capacity can provide vulnerable people with tools unavailable to lower primates to overcome some of the handicaps created by early abuse and neglect.

Affiliative Behavior and the Brain

The Separation Cry

Primate research demonstrates that social attachment is not only a psychological event; it is related to the development of core neurobiological functions in the primate brain. MacLean (15) pointed out that certain evolutionary changes in the brain are associated with family-related behavior. In lower animals such as amphibians and fish, the reproductive process ends with the laying of eggs, and offspring easily fall prey to their own parents' predatory behavior. In mammals, some way to communicate danger and relatedness was necessary for further development and nurturance outside the womb.

Research in the past few decades has established that the limbic system controls the emotions that stimulate the behavior necessary for self-preservation and survival of the species. It governs such complex behaviors as feeding, fighting, fleeing, and reproduction. As studies of people with temporal lobe epilepsy indicate, the limbic system is also responsible for free-floating feelings of what is real, true, and meaningful (50).

Cortical activity is not necessarily involved in attachment behaviors, at least in lower mammals. Murphy et al. (51) found that when the neocortex of hamsters was ablated shortly after birth, leaving them with only an R-complex and limbic system, their self-preservative and affiliative behaviors remained normal. They grow normally, go through normal daily routines, mate, produce offspring, and engage in species-specific maternal behavior. Generally, they are behaviorally indistinguishable from intact hamsters. However, destruction of the cingulate cortex abolishes all social behavior, including care of the young. In hamster pups, destruction of the cingulate cortex also abolishes play. MacLean (15) believes that play serves the evolutionary function of providing a way to learn to experiment with peer attachments and social collaboration.

In most mammalian species, dependency on adult caregivers has become so strong that separation from the mother alone, even without external danger, causes distress in infants. Pups of many species show a behavioral and physiological response to removal from the mother, including a drop in temperature, cardiac and respiratory depression, and behavioral arousal (32). A series of studies by Coe et al. (70, 71) showed that even brief (½-hour) separations in squirrel monkeys caused highly elevated plasma cortisol levels. After repeated separations, these physiological changes persisted over time, even though the animals were behaviorally indistinguishable from controls.

The Endogenous Opioid System and the Separation Call

Studies on a variety of species have demonstrated that the distress call is mediated by endogenous opioids. For example, Newman et al. (52) found that a dose of morphine insufficient to interfere with general behavior abolishes the separation call; the opiate antagonist naloxone then reinstates it (53, 54). The maternal response to the distress call also appears to be mediated by opioids: it is abolished by low-dose morphine (53). In fact, no other behavior is as powerfully and consistently modified by low doses of opiate receptor agonists (53, 55). Conversely, opiate receptor blockade enhances the need for social attachment; for example, in a group of male monkeys, the opiate antagonist naltrexone increases the amount of mutual grooming (56, 57).

Many other psychoactive agents have been studied for their effects on distress vocalizations. Reserpine, meprobamate, diazepam, sodium pentobarbital, amphetamines, and alcohol do not abolish the separation cry (54). The only two psychotropic agents besides opiates that had some effect on separation distress are imipramine (30) and clonidine. Clonidine, an alpha-2 noradrenergic receptor agonist, was most consistently found to have the same effects as the opiates (60). This effect of clonidine was thought not to be mediated by its effect on the noradrenergic system. It is interesting that clonidine alleviates the symptoms of opiate withdrawal in humans (58, 59) (Chapter 3). Thus the evidence suggests that the opioid system specifically controls separation distress.

There is also evidence that social isolation directly affects the number or sensitivity of brain opiate receptors, at least during critical stages of development. In one study, social isolation in young mice was found to cause decreased brain opiate receptor density (61). A few days of social isolation causes hyperalgesia and reduced morphine sensitivity in young rats (62).

The areas of the brain with the highest binding for μ-like opiate receptors are precisely those that have been found to be involved in the maintenance of social bonding (63). Also, the brain circuits that mediate separation distress are apparently related to those that mediate pain: stimulation of the areas around the anterior commissure, dorsomedial thalamus, dorsolateral quadrants of the neocortex, amygdala, and hypothalamus—all areas known to be involved in pain perception—elicit distress vocalizations in animals (53). These are also precisely the areas which Kling and Steklis (64) implicated as mediating affiliative behavior in nonhuman primates. Thus there now is some evidence that pain perception, separation distress, and affiliative behavior are all mediated, at least in part, by the brain opiate system, and that all three are related to discrete and interconnected neuroanatomical areas.

While it is attractive to apply our knowledge about the role of endogenous opioids in animal separation distress to human beings who have been exposed to unresponsive or abusive parents, the data on mature animals and human beings do not support a simple correlation. Low-dose naloxone seems to have no psychotropic properties in human adults who are not opiate addicts (65). Even if early social deprivation affects opiate receptor activity in humans, only a minute fraction of neglected and abused infants become opiate addicts, and there is no evidence that all opiate addicts were abused and neglected as children. Childhood deprivation seems to predispose a person to a large variety of addictive behaviors, including alcohol and nicotine addiction. The relationship between these behaviors and the endogenous opiate system is still largely unknown. However, opiates do have the capacity to relieve feelings of separation and alienation in human adults (66). It is conceivable that unalleviated separation distress during infancy makes a person more likely to seek the comfort of actions that stimulate the opioid system to cope with adult separation distress.

The Mother as Mediator of Soothing and Arousal

Field (67) has suggested that normal play and exploratory activity in children require the presence of a familiar attachment figure who modulates their physiological arousal by providing a balance between soothing and stimulation. Field, Reite et al. (68), and others (69–71) have shown that, in the absence of the mother, an infant may experience extremes of under- and overarousal that are physiologically aversive and disorganizing. Masson (72) suggests that the capacity to reduce arousal is the major maternal quality that reinforces the early infant's attraction or attachment. A study of young chimpanzees (72) found that they played most often when the mother was nearby. After separation, they tended to abandon play and clung to their mothers; the longer they had been separated, the more they clung. The administration of amphetamines, which increase physiological arousal, decreased play and increased clinging. Thus play increased and clinging decreased physiological arousal. Although no direct measurements of endogenous opioid levels during play and clinging have as yet been published, current knowledge about the role of endogenous opioids in alleviating the separation response suggests that young organisms may alternately stimulate the opioid and the noradrenergic systems, the former by physical contact with the mother and the latter by play and exploration, thus maintaining an optimal level of physiological arousal. Unresponsive or abusive mothers may cause hyperarousal that may have long-term effects on the child's ability to modulate strong emotions. As Field (67) noted: "On a continuum from low to high physiological arousal there is an optimal level for every organism. The shape of an individual's optimal stimulation curve may depend on the level of stimulation received during early experience."

Neurotransmitter Changes Related to Attachment and Separation

A detailed discussion of the neurochemistry of affiliative behavior is beyond the scope of this chapter. Critical reviews of recent developments can be found in articles by McKinney (22), Coe et al. (73), Timiras (74), and Ciaranello (75). The psychobiology and psychopharmacology of the trauma response itself will be discussed in detail in Chapter 3. This section will present a very selective review of recent data indicating relationships between affiliative behavior and catecholamine, serotonin, and cortisol activity. It should be emphasized that any given behavior is undoubtedly influenced by a variety of interacting neurochemical systems. Thus any attempt to establish connections between a particular neurotransmitter and a specific type of behavior is bound to be an oversimplification.

In infants who are separated from their mothers, changes have been observed in hypothalamic serotonin (5-HT) (73–75), adrenal gland catecholamine synthesizing enzymes (70, 71), plasma cortisol (73, 75, 76), heart rate, body temperature, and sleep (32). These changes are not transient or mild, and their persistence suggests that long-term neurobiological alterations underlie the psychological effects of early separation.

Catecholamines.   Some of the earliest evidence that the noradrenergic system plays a role in attachment responses came from studies showing that drugs that increase noradrenergic activity in the brain could reverse or ameliorate the effects of separation and social isolation. Imipramine decreased the separation response of monkeys during and immediately after peer separation (30). This effect was transitory; when the drug was discontinued, the separation response returned (30). This capacity of antidepressants to reverse the behavioral effects of early separation confirmed for some investigators the notion that early maternal deprivation in monkeys is a good model of depression (77).

Norepinephrine seems to have a biphasic effect on social bonding: both increased and decreased brain norepinephrine cause a decrease in affiliative behavior. High levels of brain norepinephrine produced by amphetamines cause social withdrawal in both human beings and animals (78). Agents that reduce norepinephrine and dopamine activity in the brain can produce depression in all primates. These include dopamine-blocking agents, such as reserpine and the neuroleptics; agents that inhibit noradrenergic activity, such as propranolol; and drugs that interfere with the synthesis of norepinephrine, such as alpha-meta-paratyrosine (AMPT). Drugs that decrease the availability of the catecholamines norepinephrine and dopamine also aggravate the behavioral expression of separation stress in separated monkeys. By administering drugs that depleted catecholamines in free-ranging monkeys, Redmond et al. (79) produced behavioral changes similar to those caused by social isolation. Monkeys treated with catecholamine-depleting agents also engaged in less grooming and showed less social initiative. Several of them failed to return to their social group.

The work of Kraemer et al. (27) suggests lasting alterations in noradrenergic receptor sensitivity following early social deprivation. Previously separated monkeys responded to low doses of amphetamines with significantly higher levels of cerebrospinal fluid (CSF) norepinephrine than did controls. Kraemer et al. concluded that deprivation of early social experience produces changes in CNS neurochemical systems that are later translated into altered behavior in challenge situations or altered responses to drugs that act through noradrenergic pathways. Similarly, McKinney et al. (24) found that the increased alcohol consumption in monkeys who have been exposed to early social isolation was related to lowered CSF norepinephrine levels.

The reciprocal relationship between the brain opioid system and the noradrenergic system is well established. In general, opiate receptor activity inhibits noradrenergic activity and vice versa. For example, the symptoms of opiate withdrawal are mediated in part by increased noradrenergic activity. The locus ceruleus, hippocampus, amygdala, and anterior hypothalamus—the areas of the brain most concerned with emotions and stress responses—all share a very high density of both norepinephrine and opioid receptors (80, 81). Prolonged treatment with antidepressant agents induces a down regulation of sensitivity to norepinephrine postsynaptically (83). Perhaps it is by reducing this supersensitivity of noradrenergic receptors that antidepressant drugs blunt the severity of the separation response (21).

Cortisol.   Stress causes the release of adrenocorticotropic hormone (ACTH) from the anterior pituitary, which in turn stimulates the release of cortisol from the adrenal glands. Chronically stressed animals have a chronically high level of ACTH, and a concomitant decrease in cortisol responsiveness (72). In one study, avoidant infants showed low cortisol responsiveness, whereas secure infants were highly responsive to ACTH stimulation (84). Increased ACTH raises tryptophan hydroxylase levels; this results in increased serotonin metabolism and thus possibly lower serotonin levels (85). In adult monkeys, high social status has been correlated with low basal plasma cortisol levels and a rapid rise and fall in plasma cortisol in response to stress (85). High stress responsiveness and high social status are also correlated with low resting levels of ACTH (86). This stress responsiveness may be passed on to the next generation. One study found a correlation between the cortisol response to separation in monkey infants and the position of their mothers in the dominance hierarchy (87). The capacity to deal with stress is apparently passed on both genetically and through upbringing.

Serotonin.   Serotonin (5-hydroxytryptamine) plays a role in affect modulation, the capacity to tolerate pain, and the ability to feel pleasure. Its principal metabolic product, 5-hydroxy indole amino acid (5-HIAA), seems to be higher in grouped than in solitary animals (88). Decreased 5-HIAA has been correlated with increased despair (89) and with suicide in humans (90). Serotonin is highly concentrated in cortical and subcortical areas related to social-affiliative behavior (53).

The effects of serotonin on social behavior have been thoroughly studied in nonhuman primates. In vervet monkeys (91), serotonergic drugs stimulate such affiliative behaviors as grooming and approaching and reduce behavior indicating fear and anxiety. High levels of plasma tryptophan (the precursor of serotonin) and whole blood serotonin are correlated with social behavior, and inversely correlated with social avoidance (92). Redmond et al. (79) found that monkeys treated with PCPA, a serotonin inhibitor, initiated fewer social contacts.

A series of studies by McGuire et al. (91) showed that dominant male monkeys have higher serotonin levels than subordinate males.

Blood serotonin levels were state dependent: they were greatly affected by spontaneous and induced changes in social status and by temporary isolation. Conversely, administration of L-tryptophan increased grooming and approach behavior and decreased locomotion and solitary and vigilant behaviors in all monkeys. Dominant males had larger increases in approach, grooming, eating, and resting than nondominant monkeys, and their platelet concentrations of L-tryptophan were raised three times more than those of nondominant monkeys. When the administration of the L-tryptophan was discontinued, all monkeys returned to their baseline levels of behavior.

Implications for Separation Anxiety and Depression in Humans

Klein (92), noting that both panic attacks and depression in humans responded to treatment with tricyclic antidepressants and monoamine oxidase inhibitors, postulated that both conditions are rooted in a neurobiological sensitivity to abandonment precipitated by early life experiences. He proposed that the adult pathological forms of both the protest and despair responses to abandonment are associated with a lowered threshold for release of these distressing affective regulatory states: "If the threshold is lowered in that portion of the regulatory mechanism that controls protest, then spontaneous panic attacks occur, whereas if the lowered threshold occurs in the segment that regulates despair, then a phasic depressive episode occurs."

Depression and severe anxiety are both part of the adult response to psychological trauma and stress. Anxiety causes clinging and a search for human comfort. Depression is often accompanied by detachment from social affiliation and a loss of pleasure in human company. Both anxiety and depression can be relieved by antidepressant medications, which have both noradrenergic and serotonergic activity. However, the differential serotonergic and noradrenergic activities of various antidepressants have not yet been definitively correlated with their various clinical effects (93). It is likely that certain childhood experiences make people vulnerable to disorders of these neurotransmitter systems, which may later be activated under stress, particularly after the loss of affiliative bonds. The nature and severity of childhood stress may determine which neurotransmitter system is most vulnerable to later disruption.

Altered Immune Response Following Social Isolation

Early separation does not only affect psychological processes and the CNS. In recent years a link between social isolation and cellular immune competence has been established as well. Premature weaning of young rats causes suppression of lymphocyte proliferation at 40 days of age and is also associated with an increase in opportunistic infections and premature death at 100 days (94). Monkeys with early separation experience were found to have reduced proliferative responses to B and T cell mitogens (95). Social dominance also has a marked effect on immune response in animals: stress produced an increased antibody response in dominant mice and a decreased response in submissive animals (96). Both the opioid and the cortisol systems have been implicated in mediating this altered immune response that occurs after social isolation. Opioids facilitate natural killer cell activity (53, 97), and animals with high endogenous opioid levels are thought to have increased resistance to cancer (98). Increased ACTH and serum cortisol both have been correlated with decreased immune competence (99). In human beings, psychological trauma has repeatedly been implicated in decreased disease resistance and increased mortality (100), but systematic prospective studies to substantiate these clinical impressions have not yet been published.

Neuroanatomical Correlates of Affiliative Behavior

The relationship between affiliative behaviors and specific areas in the CNS is still speculative. However, brain lesion studies in nonhuman primates provide some indications that bonding, nurturance, and social cohesion are severely affected by ablations of particular areas of the brain. Kling and Steklis (63) found that lesions of the amygdala, the cingulate cortex, the anterior temporal pole, and the prefrontal cortex all cause dramatic deficits in social behavior, such as maternal protection of the young. In contrast, lesions of the dorsolateral cortex increase grooming and play in some species (101). The role of the cingulate cortex in bonding and affiliation is well established (64, 102). Interestingly, cingulotomy decreases the perception of opioid withdrawal, and hence social withdrawal (56). Ablations of the cingulate cortex consistently produce maternal deficits in nest building, nursing, and retrieval of the young. In one study of monkeys, this maternal neglect resulted in a mere 12 percent survival of the offspring (64). Cingulectomized animals treated others as if they were inanimate (e.g., walking over them and sitting on them). This did not lead to fights because they avoided even aggressive contact with others (101). In human beings, cingulotomy has been used to treat obsessive-compulsive disorder and other emotional disturbances related to conflicts over social relationships.

Kling and Steklis's (103) electrical recording studies of the amygdala suggest that it responds to an external stimulus with an intensity proportional to its "emotional" significance. They believe that the intensity of the discharge may determine the extent of the projection field from the amygdala to the hypothalamus, brainstem, and, possibly, cortical structures. Temporal lobe lesions reduce the capacity to make differential responses to specific stimuli and thus impair affiliative behavior by a decrease in facilitatory inputs and a diminution in amygdaloid activity.

Lesioning of the amygdala in captive primates results in the Kluever–Bucy syndrome, which consists of hyperactivity, hypersexuality, unresponsiveness to danger, and decreased aggression. Until about a decade ago this syndrome had been studied mainly in socially isolated monkeys. With the advent of primate colonies that preserved a more natural setting, it was found that feral amygdalectomized monkeys lost all social bonding (104). Instead of hypersexuality, they developed a loss of sexual behavior. This apparently resulted from a loss of social standing because the lesioned males resumed sexual activity on removal of normal males from the colony (64). Amygdalectomized animals often became so seclusive that investigators had difficulty finding them under the dense foliage of the colonies. They lost all association with the troop, became frequent victims of attack, and often died of wounds or malnourishment (104). Lesions of the frontal lobe, especially after the age of 1 year, caused similar changes in social behavior (104). It is well known that lesions of the prefrontal cortex through prefrontal lobotomy or through diseases such as Alzheimer's cause indifference and impaired social awareness in humans.

Deficits in the social bonding of prepubertal monkeys following lesions of the cingulate cortex, amygdala,and the prefrontal area are similar to those seen in older monkeys. However, in the first year of life, there appears to be considerable plasticity of the nervous system. For example, Kling and Green (105) performed bilateral ablations of the amygdala on two neonate rhesus macaques and returned them to their mothers 6 to 12 hours later. They grew up no different from normal controls. They began to wean, separate from the mother, and respond to strangers by returning to the mother in the manner of normal infants. At 20 months they did not display any of the behaviors characteristic of amygdala-lesioned subjects, such as hyperorality, decreased fear of normally threatening objects, hypersexuality, or emotional blunting. In a study of amygdalectomized free-ranging vervet monkeys (106), only the youngest, a 2-year-old female, gave distress calls. Although she, like the others, eventually lost contact with the group, she spent more time near the group than did any of the amygdalectomized adults.

The Social Environment as Mediator of Brain Development

Thus it appears that, during the first 2 years of life, social affiliative bonds remain relatively intact after prefrontal and temporal cortical ablation in nonhuman primates, provided there is adequate mothering. However, monkeys with either prefrontal or amygdaloid lesions are even more responsive to the effects of maternal deprivation than are intact monkeys (105). Contemporary psychiatrists have done much research to elucidate the relationship between subtle, implicitly genetic, brain abnormalities and human psychopathology. Studies on nonhuman primates indicate that the brains of neonates are plastic enough to permit compensation for a number of gross brain abnormalities in early life if parental care is adequate. On the other hand, mothers of damaged and unresponsive offspring tend to avoid close physical contact with their infants and show little emotional expressiveness (107). Therefore, brain abnormalities themselves can lead to inadequate mothering, which exacerbates their effects.

However, primate studies suggest that early social deprivation may itself cause lasting changes in neuronal functioning. Hubel (108) proposed that "early starvation of social interaction, such as contact with mother, may lead to mental disturbances that have their counterpart in actual structural abnormalities of the brain." In monkeys, there are intriguing similarities between the behavioral effects of maternal neglect and those of ablations of the amygdala and cingulate cortex. Amygdalectomized mothers usually neglect or abuse their offspring until the offspring die (64). We have already discussed neglect or abuse of children by primate mothers reared in isolation from their own mothers or peers—Suomi and Ripp's (19) motherless monkeys. There are other behavioral similarities between lesioned and isolated monkeys as well. For example, both develop an attentional deficit, with distractability and difficulty in performing complex tasks (104).

There are no morphological studies indicating that the behavioral effects of amygdalectomy and early social deprivation are, in fact, based on the same structural abnormalities. However, it is striking that the effects of social deprivation are most pronounced during critical periods in a monkey's life. As we have noted, in Suomi's (13) studies, the effects of maternal deprivation were more pronounced at 90 days than at either 60 or 120 days. This critical period may coincide with the myelinization of the parts of the nervous system related to bonding and affiliative behavior.

Thus it is conceivable that early social deprivation causes lasting damage to brain structures concerned with affiliation and bonding, analogous to the irreversible damage that results in the visual system from sensory deprivation during critical periods (109). Kraemer (21) comments:

> The hypothetical social attachment system must . . . be responsive to specific stimuli from a variety of input modalities, and this information must be integrated in an almost unimaginably complex manner to provide a cohesive perception of social environment. Deprivation of complex social stimuli during development of this system could result in neurological effects similar to those observed in the visual system following sensory deprivation. . . . Thus the abnormal behavior of previously isolated subjects might be in part due to the fact that, when social stimulation is experienced after a period of deprivation, the effect is to activate inputs to neural systems with supersensitive receptors . . . the effect of denervation, or lesions of the CNS neurotransmitter systems, is that the receptors that would normally receive input from the system become hypersensitive.

Other evidence for lasting alterations in receptor sensitivity following the overwhelming sensory input that accompanies psychological trauma is examined in Chapter 3. However, altered receptor sensitivity is not the only way to account for altered brain function following sensory over- or understimulation during critical periods of development. The data (61, 62) on the alterations in the number and receptivity of opiate receptors in animal brains following social deprivation suggest that there may be actual morphological changes in the brain following social deprivation, or other disruptions of affiliative bonds. There also is evidence that the number and nature of brain receptors for particular neurotransmitters can continue to change throughout a person's lifetime, as illustrated by dopamine receptor alterations leading to the clinical symptoms of tardive dyskinesia (110). Thus it is conceivable that receptor changes induced by early deprivation or trauma in the CNS can to some degree be modified by later life experiences.

Conclusion

Environment, Genetics, and Human Development

Contemporary psychiatrists have justifiably paid much attention to both the neurological and genetic concomitants of mental disorders. They have found intriguing leads toward understanding the biology of schizophrenia, affective disorders, phobias, and attention deficit disorder. But often, researchers have implicitly assumed that abnormal biological conditions must be genetically transmitted, and are encoded in DNA. Recent primate studies indicate that the social environment can have profound effects on neurobiological development. The precise relationship between early experiences and subsequent psychopathology remains as elusive as the relationship between DNA and mental illness. However, given the importance of secure social attachment during infancy for normal development in humans, it is surprising how little attention has been paid to the long-term effects of early disruptions of these attachment bonds.

Disruptions of attachment during infancy can lead to lasting neurobiological changes. Lack of parental response to separation typically results in a biphasic protest/despair response that may be correlated with hyperactivity or underactivity of neurotransmitter systems. In humans, damage related to protest may lead to panic attacks in adulthood, while excessive exposure to despair in infancy may give rise to cyclical depressions in adults. A lack of synchrony between mother and child may result in impaired modulation of physiological arousal: disruptions of the attachment bond may cause extremes of under- and overarousal, which can result in lasting psychobiological changes. Norepinephrine, dopamine, serotonin, and the endogenous opioid and endocrine systems are all involved in the protest/despair response; this suggests the potential for great complexity and variety in resulting clinical syndromes. The developmental stage at which the disruption occurs as well as its severity and duration probably all effect the degree and reversibility of the resulting psychobiological damage.

In Chapter 1, it was noted that neurological abnormalities are often observed in victims of child abuse and neglect (111–115). These symptoms of (soft) neurological damage are usually assumed to be contributors to the abuse, rather than rooted in the abuse itself. Similar nonspecific CNS abnormalities have been observed in adults subjected to extreme stress (116, 117). Further research is needed to provide a better understanding of the relationship between overwhelming stress and neurological damages, and to suggest ways to reverse or modify the impact of this damage.

References

1. Spitz R: Hospitalism: An inquiry into the genesis of psychiatric conditions in early childhood. Psychoanal Study Child, 1:53–74, 1945

2. Mahler MS: A study of the separation-individuation process and its possible application to borderline phenomena in the psychoanalytic situation. Psychoanal Study Child 26:403–426, 1971

3. Bowlby J: Attachment and Loss, Vol 1; Attachment. New York, Basic Books, 1969

4. Bowlby J: Attachment and Loss, Vol 2: Separation. New York, Basic Books, 1973

5. Bowlby J: Separation: Anxiety and Anger. New York, Basic Books, 1973

6. Bowlby J: Violence in the family as a disorder of the attachment and caregiving systems. Am J Psychoanal 44:9–27, 1984

7. Green A: Child Maltreatment. New York, Aronson, 1980

8. Greensbauer TJ, Sands K: Distorted affective communications in abused/neglected infants and their potential impact on caretakers. J Am Acad Child Psychiatry 18:236–250, 1979

9. Cicchetti D: The emergence of developmental psychopathology. Child Dev 55:1–7, 1984

10. Malone CA: Safety first: comments on the influence of ex-

ternal danger in the lives of children of disorganized families. Am J Orthopsychiatry 36:6–12, 1966

11. Eth S, Pynoos RS (eds): Post-Traumatic Stress Disorders in Children. Washington, DC, American Psychiatric Press, 1985

12. Rajecki DW, Lamb ME, Obmascher P: Toward a general theory of infantile attachment: a comparative review of aspects of the social bond. The Behavioral and Brain Sciences 3:417–464, 1978

13. Suomi SJ: The development of affect in rhesus monkeys, in The Psychobiology of Affective Development. Edited by Fox N, Davidson R. Hillsdale, NJ, Lawrence Erlbaum Associates, 1984, pp 119–159

14. Ainsworth MDS: Infancy in Uganda: Infant Care and the Growth of Attachment. Baltimore, Johns Hopkins University Press, 1967

15. MacLean PD: Brain evolution relating to family, play, and the separation call. Arch Gen Psychiatry 42:505–417, 1985

16. Reite M, Seiler C, Short R: Loss of your mother is more than loss of a mother. Am J Psychiatry 135:370–371, 1978

17. Bowlby J: The nature of the child's tie to his mother. Int J Psychoanal 39:350–373, 1958

18. Ainsworth MDS: The development of the infant-mother attachment, in: Review of Child Development Research, Vol. 3. Edited by Caldwell BM, Ricutti HN. Chicago, University of Chicago Press, 1973, pp 1–94

19. Suomi SJ, Ripp C: A history of motherless mother monkey mothering at the University of Wisconsin Primate Laboratory, in Child Abuse: The Non-Human Primate Data. Edited by Reite M, Caine N. New York, Alan R Liss, 1983, pp 49–78

20. Suomi SJ, Harlow HF, Domek CJ: Effects of repetitive infant-infant separation of young monkeys. J Abnorm Psychol 76:161–172, 1970

21. Kraemer GW: Effects of differences in early social experiences on primate neurobiological-behavioral development, in: The Psychobiology of Attachment and Separation. Edited

by Reite M, Fields T. Orlando, FL, Academic Press, 1985, p 141

22. McKinney WT: Separation and depression: biological markers, in The Psychobiology of Attachment and Separation. Edited by Reite M, Fields T. Orlando, FL, Academic Press, 1985, pp 201–222

23. McKinney WT, Kraemer G, Ebert MH: Explosive violence in primates. Paper presented at the American Psychiatric Association Meeting, Dallas, 1985

24. McKinney WT, Kraemer G, Ebert MH: Separation and alcohol consumption in monkeys. Paper presented at the American Psychiatric Association Meeting, Dallas, 1985

25. Kraemer GW, Ebert MH, Lake CR, et al: Hypersensitivity to d-amphetamine several years after early social deprivation in rhesus monkeys. Psychopharmacology 82:266–271, 1984

26. Kraemer GW, McKinney WT: Interactions of pharmacological agents which alter biogenic amine metabolism and depression: an analysis of contributing factors within a primate model of depression. J Affective Disord 1:33–54, 1979

27. Kraemer GW, Ebert MH, Lake CR, et al: Cerebrospinal fluid measures of neurotransmitter changes associated with pharmacological alteration of the despair response to social separation in rhesus monkeys. Psychiatry Res 11:303–315, 1984

28. Suomi SJ, Harlow HF: Social rehabilitation of isolate-reared monkeys. Dev Psychol 6:487–496, 1972

29. Suomi SJ, Harlow HF, Novak MA: Reversal of social deficits produced by isolation rearing in monkeys. Journal of Human Evolution 3:527–534, 1974

30. Suomi SJ, Seaman SF, Lewis JK, et al: Effects of imipramine treatment of separation induced social disorders in rhesus monkeys. Arch Gen Psychiatry 35:321–325, 1978

31. Suomi SJ, Eisele CD, Grady S, et al: Depressive behavior in adult monkeys following separation from family environment. J Abnorm Psychol 84:576–578, 1975

32. Reite M, Short R, Seiler C, et al: Attachment, loss and depression. J Child Psychol Psychiatry 22:141–169, 1981

33. Ratner AM: Modifications of duckling filial behavior by aversive stimulation. J Exp Psychol [Anim Behav] 2:266–284, 1976

34. Stanley WC, Elliot O: Differential human handling as reinforcing events and as treatments influencing later social behavior in Baseji puppies. Psychol Reports 10:775–788, 1962

35. Harlow HF, Harlow MK: Psychopathology in monkeys, Experimental Psychopathology. Edited by Kimmel HD. New York, Academic Press, 1971

36. Seay B, Alexander BK, Harlow HF: Maternal behavior of socially deprived rhesus monkeys. J Abnormal and Social Psychology 69:345–354, 1964

37. Sackett GP, Griffin GA, Pratt C, et al: Mother-infant and adult female choice behavior in rhesus monkeys after various rearing experiences. J Comp Physiol Psychol 63:376–381, 1967

38. Sackett GP: Effects of rearing conditions on the behavior of the rhesus monkey. Child Dev 36:855–868, 1965

39. Sackett GP: Isolation rearing in monkeys: Diffuse and specific effects on late behavior, in Colloquia Internationaux du CNRS, No. 198, Models Animaux du Comportement Humain. Paris, Editions du Centre National de la Recherche Scientifique, 1972, pp 61–110

40. Mirsky IA: Communication of affects in monkeys, in Environmental Influences. Edited by Glass DC. New York, Rockefeller University Press, 1968, pp 129–137

41. Griffin GA, Harlow HF: Effects of three months of total soccial deprivation on social adjustment and learning in the rhesus monkey. Child Dev 37:535–547, 1966

42. Sackett GP, Ruppenthal GC, Fahrenbruch CE, et al: Social isolation rearing effects in monkeys vary with genotype. Dev Psychol 17:313–318, 1981

43. Seaman SF: The effects of Tofranil, SC-27123, or placebo on the peer-peer separation syndrome. Quoted in Kraemer (21).

44. Novak MA, Harlow HF: Social recovery of monkeys isolated

for the first year of life: I. Rehabilitation and therapy. Dev Psychol 11:453–465, 1975

45. Novak MA, Harlow HF: Social recovery of monkeys isolated for the first year of life: II. Long term assessment. Dev Psychol 15:50–61, 1979

46. Sackett GP, Bowman RE, Meyer JS, et al; Adrenocortical and behavioral reactions by differentially raised rhesus monkeys. Physiol Psychol 1:209–212, 1973

47. Anderson CO, Mason WA: Early experience and complexity of social organization in groups of young rhesus monkeys. Journal of Comparative and Physiological Psychology 87:681–690, 1974

48. Anderson CO, Mason WA: Competitive social strategies in groups of deprived and experienced rhesus monkeys, Dev Psychobiol 11:289–299, 1978

49. Mason WA: Early social deprivation in the non-human primates; implications for human behavior, in Environmental Influences. Edited by Glass DC. New York, Rockefeller University Press, 1968, pp 70–100

50. MacLean PD: On the evolution of three mentalities in man. Environmental Systems 5:213–224, 1975

51. Murphy MR, McLean PD, Hamilton SC: Species-typical behavior of hamsters deprived from birth of the neocortex. Science 213:459–461, 1981

52. Newman JD, Murphy MR, Harbough CR: Naloxone-reversible suppression of isolation call production after morphine injections in squirrel monkeys. Social Neuroscience Abstracts 8:940, 1982

53. Panksepp J, Sivey SM, Normansell LA: Brain opioids and social emotions, in The Psychobiology of Attachment and Separation. Edited by Reite M, Fields T. Orlando, FL, Academic Press, 1985

54. Scott JP: Effects of psychotropic drugs on separation and distress in dogs: Proceedings IX Congress Neurospychopharmcology (Paris). Excerpta Medica Internationale Series 359:735–745, 1974

55. Meller RE, Keverne EB, Herbert J: Behavioural and endo-

crine effects of naltrexone in male talapoin monkeys. Pharmacol Biochem Behav 13:663–672, 1980

56. Fabre-Nys C, Meller RE, Keverne EG: Opiate antagonists stimulate affiliative behavior in monkeys. Pharmacol Biochem Behav 6:653–659, 1982

57. Sahley TL, Panksepp J, Zolovick AJ: Cholinergic modulation of separation distress in the domestic chick. Eur J Pharmacol 72:261–264, 1981

58. Gold M, Pottash AC, Sweeney D, et al: Antimanic, anti-depressant and antipanic effects of opiates: clinical neuroanatomical and biochemical evidence. Ann NY Acad Sci 398:140–150, 1982

59. Gold MS, Redmond DE, Kleber HD: Clonidine in opiate withdrawal. Lancet 1:929–930, 1978

60. Panksepp MJ, Meeker R, Bean NJ: The neurochemical control of crying. Pharmacol Biochem Behav 12:437–443, 1980

61. Bonnett KS, Miller JM, Simon EJ: The effects of chronic opiate treatment and social isolation on opiate receptors in the rodent brain, in Opiate and Endogenous Opioid Peptides. Edited by Kosterlitz HW. Amsterdam, Elsevier, 1976, pp 335–343

62. Panksepp J: Brief social isolation, pain responsivity and morphine analgesia in young rats. Psychopharmacology 72:111–112, 1980

63. Lewis WE, Miskin M, Bragin E, et al: Opiate receptor gradients in the monkey cerebral cortex: correspondence with sensory processing hierarchies. Science 211:1166–1169, 1981

64. Kling A, Steklis HD: A neural substrate for affiliative behavior in non-human primates. Brain Behav Evol 13:216–238, 1976

65. Judd LL, Janowsky DS, Segal DS, et al: Naloxone-induced behavioral and physiological effects in normal and manic subjects. Arch Gen Psychiatry 37:583–586, 1980

66. Khantzian E: The self-medication hypothesis of addictive disorders: focus on heroin and cocaine dependence. Am J Psychiatry 142:1259–1264, 1985

67. Field T: Attachment as psychobiological attunement: being on the same wavelength, in The Psychobiology of Attachment and Separation. Edited by Reite M, Fields T. Orlando, FL, Academic Press, 1985, pp 431–432

68. Reite M, Short R, Seiler C: Physiological correlates of separation in surrogate-reared infants: a study in altered attachment bonds. Dev Psychobiol 11:427–435, 1978

69. Smotherman WP, Wiener S, Mendoza SP, et al: Maternal pituitary-adrenal responsiveness as a function of differential treatment of rat pups. Dev Psychobiol 10:113–122, 1977

70. Coe CL, Mendoza SP, Smotherman WP, et al: Mother-infant attachment in the squirrel monkey: adrenal responses to separation. Behav Biol 22:256–263, 1978

71. Coe CL, Glass JC, Wiener SG, et al: Behavioral, but not physiological adaptation to repeated separation in mother and infant primates. Psychoneuroendocrinology 8:401–409, 1983

72. Mason WA: Motivational aspects of social responsiveness in young chimpanzees, in Early Behavior: Comparative and Developmental Aspects. Edited by Stevenson H. New York, John Wiley and Sons, 1967

73. Coe CL, Wiener S, Rosenberg LT, et al: Endocrine and immune responses to separation and maternal loss in nonhuman primates, in The Psychobiology of Attachment and Separation. Edited by Reite M, Fields T. Orlando, FL, Academic Press, 1985, pp 163–197

74. Timiras PS: The timing of hormone signals in the orchestration of brain development, in The Development of Attachment and Affiliative Systems. Edited by Emde RN, Harmon RJ. New York, Plenum Press, 1982

75. Ciaranello RD: Neurochemical aspects of stress, in Stress, Coping and Development. Edited by Garmezy N, Rutter M. New York, McGraw-Hill, 1983

76. Konner M: Biological aspects of the mother-infant bond, in The Development of Attachment and Affiliative Systems. Edited by Emde RN, Harmon RJ. New York, Plenum Press, 1982

77. Harlow HF, Mears C: The Human Model: Primate Perspectives. New York, John Wiley and Sons, 1979

78. Haber S, Barchas PR, Barchas JD: A primate analogue of amphetamine induced behavior in humans. Biol Psychiatry 16:181–195, 1981

79. Redmond DE, Maas JW, Kling A, et al: Social behavior of monkeys selectively depleted of monoamines. Science 174:428–431, 1971

80. Arbilla S, Langer SZ: Morphine and beta endorphin inhibit release of noradrenaline from cerebral cortex but not of dopamine from rat striatum. Nature 271:559, 1978

81. Korf J, Bunney BS, Aghajanian CK: Noradrenergic inhibition of spontaneous activity. Eur J Pharmacol 25:165–169, 1974

82. Susler F, Vetulani J, Mobley PL: Mode of action of antidepressant drugs. Biochem Pharmacol 27:257–261, 1982

83. Sulser F: Antidepressant drug research: its impact on neurobiology and psychobiology, in Typical and Atypical Antidepressants. Vol 31. Edited by Costa E, Racagni G. New York, Raven Press, 1982, pp 1–20

84. Tennes K: The role of hormones in mother-infant transactions, in The Development of Attachment and Affiliative Systems. Edited by Emde RN, Harmon RJ. New York, Plenum Press, 1982, pp 75–80.

85. Capitanio JP, Weissberg M, Reite MR: The biology of maternal behavior, in The Psychobiology of Attachment and Separation. Edited by Reite M, Fields T. Orlando, FL, Academic Press, 1985, pp 163–197

86. Joffe LS, Vaughn BE, Barglow P, et al; Biobehavioral antecedents in the development of infant-mother attachment, in The Psychobiology of Attachment and Separation. Edited by Reite M, Fields T. Orlando, FL, Academic Press, 1985, pp 163–197

87. Raleigh MJ, Yuweiler A, Brammer GL, et al: Peripheral correlates of serotonergically influenced behaviors in vervet monkeys. Psychopharmacology 72:241–246, 1981

88. Raleigh MJ, McGuire MT, Brammer GL, et al: Social and

environmental influences on blood serotonin concentrations in monkeys. Arch Gen Psychiatry 41:505–510, 1984

89. Brown GL, Ebert MH, Goyer P, et al: Aggression, suicide and serotonin. Am J Psychiatry 134:741–745, 1982

90. Asberg M, Thorer SP, Trushman L: Serotonin depression: a biochemical subgroup within affective disorders. Science 191:478–480, 1975

91. McGuire MT, Raleigh MJ, Brammer GL: Adaptation, selection and benefit-cost balances: implications of behavioral-physiological studies of behavioral studies of social dominance in male vervet monkeys. Ethology and Social Biology 5:269–277, 1984

92. Klein DF: Anxiety reconceptualized. Compr Psychiatry 6:411–427, 1980

93. Schildkraut JJ: Current status of the catecholamine hypothesis of affective disorders, in Psychopharmacology: A Generation of Progress. Edited by Lipton MA, DiMascio A, Kellam S. New York, Raven Press, 1978

94. Hofer MA: Studies on how early maternal deprivation produces behavioral change in young rats. Psychosom Med 37:245–264, 1975

95. Laudenslager M, Capitano JP, Reite M: Possible effects of early separation on subsequent immune function in adult macaque monkeys. Am J Psychiatry 142:862–864, 1985

96. Fauman MA: Isolation, aggression and antibody response in mice. Paper presented at the American Psychiatric Association Meeting, Dallas, 1985

97. Gonzales CA, Gunnar MR, Levine S: Behavioral and hormonal responses to social disruption and infant stimuli in the female rhesus monkey. Psychoneuroendocrinology 6:53–64, 1981

98. Matthews PM, Froehlich CJ, Sibbit WL, et al: Enhancement of natural cytotoxicity with beta endorphin. J Immunol 130:1658–1662, 1983

99. Thompson CI, Kreider JW, Black PL, et al: Genetically obese mice: resistance to metastases of B16 melanoma and en-

hanced T-lymphocytic mitogenic responses. Science 220: 1183–1185, 1983

100. Krystal H: Psychoanalytic views on human emotional damages, in Post Traumatic Stress Disorder; Psychological and Biological Sequelae. Edited by van der Kolk B. Washington, DC, American Psychiatric Press, 1984, pp 1–28

101. Tucker JT, Kling A: Differential effects of early and late lesions of the frontal granular cortex in the monkey. Brain Res 5:377–389, 1967

102. Ward AA: The cingulate gyrus, area 24. J Neurophysiol 11: 13–23, 1948

103. Kling A, Steklis HD, Deutsch S: Radiotelemetered activity from the amygdala during social interactions in the monkey. Exp Neurol 66:88–96, 1979

104. Steklis H, Kling A: Neurobiology of affiliation in primates, in The Psychobiology of Attachment and Separation. Edited by Reite M, Fields T. Orlando, FL, Academic Press, 1985

105. Kling A, Green PC: Effects of amygdalectomy in maternally reared and maternally deprived neonatal and juvenile Macaques. Nature 213:742–751, 1967

106. Kling A, Lancaster J, Benitone J: Amygdalectomy in the free ranging vervet. J Psychiatr Res 7:191–199, 1970

107. Ainsworth MD, Blehar ML, Waters E, et al: Patterns of Attachment. Hillsdale, NJ, Lawrence Erlbaum Associates, 1978

108. Hubel DH: Effects of deprivation on the visual cortex of cat and monkey. Harvey Lectures 72:1–51, 1978

109. Prescott JW: Early somatosensory deprivation as an ontogenetic process in the abnormal development of the brain and behavior, in Medical Primatology. Edited by Goldsmith EI, Moore-Janowski J. Basel, S. Karger, 1971

110. Klawans HL: The pharmacology of tardive dyskinesia. Am J Psychiatry 130:82–86, 1978

111. Lewis DO, Shanok SS, Pincus JH, et al: Violent juvenile delinquents: psychiatric, neurological, psychological and abuse factors. J Child Psychiatry 18:307–319, 1979

112. Green A, Voeller K, Gaines R, et al: Neurological impairment in maltreated children. Child Abuse Negl 5:129–134, 1981

113. Davies RK: Incest: some neuropsychiatric findings. Int J Psychiatry Med 9:117–120, 1979

114. Bemporad JR, Smith HF, Hanson G, et al: Borderline syndromes in childhood: criteria for diagnosis. Am J Psychiatry 139:596–602, 1982

115. Gross M: Incestuous rape: a cause for hysterical seizures in four adolescent girls. Am J Orthopsychiatry 49:704–708, 1979

116. Hocking F: Psychiatric aspects of extreme environmental stress. Diseases of the Nervous System 31:542–545, 1970

117. Cohen BM, Cooper MZ: A Follow-Up Study of World War II Prisoners of War. Washington, DC, US Government Printing Office, 1954

CHAPTER 3

The Psychobiology of the Trauma Response: Hyperarousal, Constriction, and Addiction to Traumatic Reexposure

Bessel A. van der Kolk, M.D.
Mark S. Greenberg, Ph.D.

The human response to overwhelming trauma has been thought to have a biological basis since the consequences of psychological trauma were first described a century ago. Since the early accounts of "railroad spine" (1) and the investigations of "shell shock" (2) in World War I, the lasting effects of traumatization have been ascribed to physiological or neuroanatomical alterations. Even Freud (3) considered a biological explanation for traumatic neuroses when he postulated:

> We may tentatively venture to regard the traumatic neurosis as a consequence of an extensive breach being made in the protective shield against stimuli . . . the old naive theory of shock . . . regards the essence of the shock as being direct damage to the molecular structure or even to the histological structure of the elements of the nervous system, whereas what we seek to understand are the effects produced on the organ of the mind by the breach in the shield against stimuli and by the problems that follow in its train.

Freud hypothesized that when this "stimulus barrier" is breached, the mental apparatus is flooded with excitation, causing a feeling of helplessness.

Pavlov's (4) investigations continued the tradition of explaining the trauma response as the result of lasting physiological alterations. He and others employing his paradigm have coined the term "defensive reaction" for a cluster of innate reflexive responses to environmental threat. Many studies have shown how the response to potent environmental stimuli (unconditional stimuli, US) becomes a conditioned reaction. After repeated aversive stimulation, intrinsically nonthreatening cues associated with the trauma (conditional stimuli, CS) become capable of eliciting the defensive reaction by themselves (conditional response, CR). A war veteran may respond to conditioned stimuli, such as the sound of gunshots or a passing helicopter, as if he or she were in combat. Pavlov also pointed out that "constitutional factors" (i.e., individual differences in temperament) accounted for the variability in the human response to traumatic stimuli. Subsequent investigators such as Selye (5) have also viewed posttraumatic stress disorder (PTSD) mainly as a physiological disturbance.

The human response to trauma is relatively constant across traumatic stimuli: the central nervous system (CNS) seems to react to any overwhelming threatening and uncontrollable experience in a consistent pattern. Regardless of the precipitating event, traumatized people continue to have a poor tolerance for arousal. They tend to respond to stress in an all-or-nothing way: either unmodulated anxiety, often accompanied by motoric discharge that includes acts of aggression against the self or others, or else social and emotional withdrawal (6). Their difficulty in modulating affect leads them to respond to emotional stimulation barely at all, or with an intensity appropriate to the original trauma. As noted in Chapter 2, childhood experiences may profoundly affect adult reactivity to external stimuli. Children exposed to disruptions of attachment to their primary caregivers through separation, abuse, or neglect often develop extreme reactivity to internal and external stimulation; that is, they overreact to subsequent situations and have trouble modulating anxiety and aggression, both against others and against themselves. A high proportion of psychiatric patients have been found to have a history of severe childhood physical and sexual abuse (7–9) (Chapters 1, 2, 4, 5). Many have symptoms reminiscent of adult posttraumatic sequelae, such as physiological hyperreactivity, subjective loss of control, chronic passivity alternating with uncontrolled violence, and nightmares that may be poorly disguised relivings of earlier traumatic events. These patients carry a variety of psychiatric diagnoses. Among the most common are borderline and hysterical personality (see Chapter 5). In addition, many patients with a history of trauma use drugs and alcohol in an ill-fated attempt to relieve their posttraumatic symptoms (10).

PTSD as a "Physioneurosis": The Loss of Ability to Modulate Arousal

Kardiner (11) pointed out that many people with PTSD are emotionally constricted, but respond physically to certain stimuli as if there were a continuing threat of annihilation. Struck by this continuing physiological hyperreactivity, he coined the term "physioneurosis" to describe posttraumatic stress. He suggested that the autonomic nervous system (ANS) of people with PTSD appears to continue to prepare them for action. Several studies (12–14) have demonstrated an increase in ANS activity in veterans reexposed to combat stimuli; they reacted physically and affectively in the same way as they had in combat. During World War II, Wenger (quoted in 15) performed extensive tests on autonomic reactivity in Air Force combat flyers with "operational fatigue," comparing them with student pilots. On 9 of 20 tests of autonomic function, the combat veterans had a statistically higher reactivity; this supported his hypothesis that operational fatigue was accompanied by excessive sympathetic function. Recent measurements of urinary norepinephrine metabolites in Vietnam veterans with PTSD have shown a chronic elevation in noradrenergic activity, as compared to controls with other psychiatric diagnoses (16). It is still unclear whether hyperarousal following trauma is a conditioned response specific to the traumatic stimuli. Probably, there is considerable stimulus generalization: the trauma victim becomes somewhat habituated to the original traumatic stimuli, but associated events cause increased arousal (17). Hyperarousal in response to relatively minor stimuli occurs not only after adult traumatization, but also after disruptions of social attachment in childhood. The work of Field (18), Reite et al. (19), and others (22, see Chapter 2) has shown physiological disorganization in infants separated from their caregivers. In the absence of the mother, an infant may suffer extremes of under- and overarousal that are aversive and disorganizing. Field (18) postulated that an unresponsive or abusive early environment can stimulate the emergence of hyperarousal states that have long-term effects on the child's ability to modulate anxiety and aggression.

The Psychological Consequences of the Inability to Modulate Physiological Arousal

Autonomic activation is necessary to cope with major stress, so a diminished capacity to activate appropriate autonomic stress reactions causes impaired physiological adaptation to stress (20). In many traumatized people this adaptive mechanism has been disturbed by the trauma: they continue to respond even to minor stimuli with an intensity appropriate only to emergency situations (6, 11, 17). This interferes with their ability to assess situations calmly and appropriately and to achieve the psychological distance necessary for a measured response. Schachter and Singer (21) have shown that the degree of autonomic arousal determines the intensity of the emotional response, but that the subjective valence of the arousal is determined by social context and the subject's preexisting mood. Increased arousal leads to intensification of all emotional reactions: an injection of adrenaline heightens relaxation under pleasant circumstances, but it increases anger or anxiety under frustrating conditions. The degree of subjective mastery over the situation determines the response to the arousal (23, 24).

The intensity of autonomic arousal in traumatized people often causes them to go immediately from stimulus to response. The correlation between actual external threat and the physical emergency responses is lost. Autonomic arousal, no longer a preparation to meet external threat, becomes itself a precipitant of fear and emergency responses (17). This dissociation between the magnitude of the external stimulus and the size of the autonomic response needs to be a central focus in the treatment of posttraumatic states. At the end of this chapter we will discuss psychopharmacological agents that decrease reactivity. However, nonpharmacological interventions can also allow the patient to regain some control over his or her reactivity. Psychotherapy can make the patient aware of the historical roots of the emergency response and promote some cognitive distance from physiological arousal (see Chapters 8 and 9). Training in the correct assessment of ANS reactions decreases subjective experience of anxiety and decreases the intensity of autonomic activation (25). Relaxation techniques and biofeedback can also be helpful in controlling reactivity (26).

The Animal Model of Inescapable Shock

The animal model of inescapable shock is especially helpful for studying the behavioral and physiological effects of traumatization. This is the only biological model for a major psychiatric disorder; surprisingly, it has been applied principally to depression rather than traumatization. The effects of exposure to inescapable aversive events include 1) deficits in learning to escape novel adverse situations, 2) decreased motivation for learning new contingencies, 3) chronic subjective distress (27), and 4) increased tumor genesis and immunosuppression (28). The helplessness syndrome that follows inescapable shock is due to lack of control, rather than to the shock itself—in fact, the behavioral and biochemical sequelae of escapable shock are just the opposite of those of inescapable shock (29).

Hyperarousal, Constriction, and Altered Catecholamine Receptor Sensitivity

Inescapable stress depletes norepinephrine (NE) and dopamine, presumably because use exceeds synthesis. Escapable shock does not lower NE levels and may even increase them (30–32). Anisman and Sklar (31) found that shocks with no measurable effect on naive animals produced NE depletion and escape deficits in mice previously exposed to inescapable shock. Thus NE depletion seems to become a conditioned response; chronic recurrent depletion of CNS NE then renders the NE receptors in the brain, or at least in parts of the brain, hypersensitive to subsequent NE stimulation (30–32) in response to threat or other arousal. Investigators such as Anisman et al. (32), Redmond and Krystal (33), van der Kolk et al. (34), Kraemer et al. (35), and Kolb (15) have postulated that the physiological hyperarousal following trauma is due to chronic alterations in the central neurotransmitter systems. While direct proof of noradrenergic receptor hypersensitivity in these cases is still elusive, there is accumulating evidence of long-term changes in the noradrenergic system, possibly at both output and receptor levels (36).

There is a striking parallel between the animal response to inescapable shock and the human response to overwhelming trauma. Grinker and Spiegel (37) described many autonomic and extrapyramidal symptoms of catecholamine depletion following acute combat stress in World War II soldiers. These included masked facies, reduced eye blink, cogwheel rigidity, postural flexion, and coarse tremor of the extremities. Behavioral sequelae of catecholamine depletion following inescapable shock in animals closely parallel the negative symptoms of PTSD in humans. Van der Kolk et al. (34) proposed that the diminished motivation, the decline in occupational functioning, and the global constriction seen in PTSD are correlates of NE depletion. The symptoms of hyper-reactivity (i.e., startle responses, explosive outbursts, nightmares, and intrusive recollections) in humans resemble those produced by chronic noradrenergic hypersensitivity following transient cat-echolamine depletion after acute trauma in animals. As we will explain in detail later, psychotropic agents that alter NE metab-olism, such as tricyclic antidepressants and monoamine oxidase inhibitors, have a therapeutic effect on a variety of posttraumatic symptoms, possibly including hyperreactivity. Prolonged treat-ment with antidepressants is known to cause a down regulation of sensitivity to NE in the postsynaptic cell (38). Antidepressant drugs may blunt the severity of the trauma response by reducing supersensitivity of noradrenergic receptors.

Stress and Drugs Uncover Long-Term Physiological Posttraumatic Alterations: Kindling and Behavioral Sensitization

Goddard et al. (39) first described the phenomenon of electrical kindling: repeated intermittent stimulation of the brain with an electrical current that was initially too small to produce overt be-havioral effects can eventually produce major motor seizures. Kin-dling can be produced in the same way by repeated doses of various psychostimulant drugs (40–42). Kindling only follows intermit-tent stimulation: it is not produced by continuous or very frequent stimulation. Racine (43, 44) and Post (45) have demonstrated that kindling does not necessarily involve major motor seizures: re-peated electrical stimulation of the amygdala causes long-term alterations in neuronal excitability, even without such seizures. In animals, kindling produces long-lasting and possibly perma-nent changes in neuronal excitability (46). Post et al. (46) state that kindling to the point of convulsions is difficult to achieve in nonhuman and human primates: "Kindled seizures will only be one marker of the development of the sensitization process; many of the important characteristics of the kindling paradigm, in-cluding change in threshold and associated changes in behavior can be observed in the absence of seizures." It is possible that kindling phenomena leading to lasting neurobiological and be-havioral (characterological) changes are produced by repeated traumatization, as in child abuse, or by one trauma followed by intrusive reexperiences. Kindling may also account for the fre-quency of neurological abnormalities in trauma victims, especially child victims of physical or sexual abuse (see Chapters 1 and 2). Carbamazepine and lithium have been shown to interfere with kindling (47).

Behavioral sensitization is similar to kindling in some ways, but different in others. It does not produce convulsions, its effects decay over time, and, unlike kindling, it is activated by stress (46). Psychomotor stimulants and dopamine agonists may cause behavioral sensitization: instead of tolerance, repeated administration may produce a gradual increase in behavioral effects. Psychostimulant-induced hypersensitivity causes a progressively shorter interval between administration of the drug and peak behavioral effect (48). After repeated administration, the response may occur at the same time as the stimulus and even in anticipation of the stimulus cue (49, 50). Antelman et al. (51) have shown that environmental stress and amphetamines produce interchangeable sensitization effects in rats. Kraemer et al.'s (35) findings that both stress and *d*-amphetamine caused previously isolated monkeys to become acutely violent and kill their peers were discussed in Chapter 2. Stress and psychostimulants are thought to activate similar neurotransmitter systems. Repeated administration of psychomotor stimulants and dopamine agonists produces long-term alterations in neuronal receptor sensitivity; the same mechanisms may be involved in persisting heightened reactivity to stress after psychological trauma. Nonhuman primate studies (e.g., 35) show long-term physiological alterations following traumatization early in life. Compared with normally raised peers, previously deprived monkeys had significantly higher levels of cerebrospinal fluid (CSF) NE after low doses of amphetamines. Kraemer and his co-workers concluded that deprivation of early social experience may produce changes in CNS neurochemical systems that are later translated into altered behavior in challenge situations or in response to certain drugs that affect modulation of arousal and mood.

Intrusive Reexperiencing in PTSD: Flashbacks and Nightmares

In many traumatized individuals, the trauma is reexperienced in the form of nightmares and flashbacks, which are often an exact reliving of actual traumatic experiences. Immediately after the trauma they usually occur frequently. After a while they subside, but they often recur, sometimes after decades of latency, in response to psychologically or biologically important events such as puberty, marriage, the birth of a child, the onset of physical illness, or retirement (52).

Posttraumatic nightmares have been reported in stage II and III sleep as well as REM sleep (52–54). The sleep stage does not seem to determine the degree of emotional distress experienced during the nightmare, but it probably does account for the amount of visual imagery present. Although current evidence is far from conclusive, it appears that REM nightmares are dreamlike (oneiric), and often have admixtures of other experiences, whereas stage II and III nightmares are usually exact movie-like (eidetic) recreations of the traumatic experience itself.

The locus coeruleus (LC) is the primary source of noradrenergic innervation of the limbic system, the cerebral cortex, the cerebellum, and, to a lesser degree, the hypothalamus (55). The noradrenergic tracts emanating from the LC to the hippocampus and amygdala (56) also play a role in facilitating memory retrieval. On the basis of animal data, van der Kolk et al. (34) have hypothesized that the repetitive intrusive reliving of the trauma, particularly under stress, is caused by stress-induced reactivation of LC–hippocampus/amygdala pathways. Delaney et al. (57) described a rapidly established and relatively permanent augmentation of monosynaptic evoked responses after brief high-frequency stimulation of central noradrenergic pathways. They suggested that this long-term potentiation of neural circuits provides a "neurophysiological analogue of memory." We have proposed that LC-mediated autonomic arousal activates these potentiated pathways when conscious control over limbic system activity is diminished, as it is under stress and during sleep (34). This would account for the increase in both flashbacks and nightmares when a person with chronic PTSD experiences major subsequent stress. Stress activation of memory tracts may also explain the eidetic rather than oneiric quality of many posttraumatic nightmares (52).

The immediacy of intrusive recollections is familiar to all clinicians who work with traumatized populations (see Chapter 8). Vietnam veterans may misinterpret the movements of a sleeping bed partner as a Viet Cong attack and react accordingly; mild noises played into the rooms of sleeping people with posttraumatic stress may precipitate nightmares in which old traumatic events are recreated in exact detail (58). An illustration of the association between autonomic arousal and flashbacks is provided by the case of a former parachutist who had a 3-month period of posttraumatic symptoms after his second parachute failed to open during a jump until he was a few hundred feet above the ground. Five years later the only remaining symptom is a flashback of this event after autonomic arousal, such as occurs in a near accident on the road.

The noradrenergic system is intimately involved in short-term memory: noradrenergic depletion decreases memory storage, whereas enhancement of noradrenergic activity with NE-stimulating agents increases memory retention (59). Preliminary data from our laboratory indicate a marked decrease in short-term memory for emotionally neutral stimuli during the constricted phase of PTSD, as compared with the hyperarousal phase.

Trauma and Endogenous Opioid Peptides

Animals exposed to inescapable shock develop analgesia when exposed to another stressor shortly afterward. The analgesic response to prolonged or repeated stress is mediated by endogenous opioids and is readily reversible by naloxone (60). Prolonged stress, such as 20 to 30 minutes of intermittent foot shock, caused analgesia in rats which was blocked by naloxone (61); briefer, continuous stress, such as 3 minutes of continuous foot shock, caused equally strong analgesia that was not affected by the drug. Christie and Chesher (62) demonstrated that prolonged stress in animals activates brain opiate receptors in the same way as repeated application of exogenous opiates. In severely stressed animals, opiate withdrawal symptoms can be produced either by termination of the stressful stimulus or by naloxone injections. Thus severe, chronic stress in animals induces a physiological state that resembles dependence on high levels of exogenous opioids (63). Tolerance develops for the naloxone-sensitive form of stress analgesia, but not for the naloxone-insensitive form (64). Significant pain inhibition following stress has been observed not only in laboratory experiments such as foot shock, but also under real-life conditions, such as battlefield operations without anesthesia and athletic performances that continue despite serious injuries. Opioid-induced analgesia is observed following a variety of stresses that are intense, inescapable, and consciously perceived; other examples are fighting (65, 66), sexual arousal (67), food deprivation (68), and thermal stress (69).

In a series of experiments, Lewis et al. (70) demonstrated that the opioids that mediate stress analgesia are enkephalins secreted in response to sympathetic stimulation. Placing rats in a chamber where they were previously submitted to foot shock can elicit many responses resembling those caused by foot shock itself (71). A previously neutral environment paired with an adversive outcome becomes capable of stimulating fear responses in animals, which then serve as predictors of upcoming aversive events. Pain suppression is one response that persists on reexposure to an environment previously associated with aversive events. Recent studies (61, 72, 73) indicate that this conditioned analgesia is opioid mediated: it can be blocked with opioid antagonists and shows cross-tolerance with morphine.

Canon et al. (74) and Bolles and Fanselow (75) examined the evidence that fear activates the secretion of opioid peptides, which in turn inhibit pain. They found that under ordinary conditions, endorphin levels are too low to produce analgesia, or any other readily apparent psychoactive effects. Conversely, under ordinary conditions, naloxone has strikingly few psychophysiological effects on people or animals. Current data indicate that when an organism is severely stressed, the initial shock to the system produces a fear response that is accompanied by endorphin release. This response is not rapid enough to decrease the intensity of the pain caused by this shock, but subsequent fear and the accompanying opioid secretion attenuates the perceived intensity of subsequent shocks. Naloxone abolishes this attenuation of the pain response.

Addiction to Trauma

In human beings, elevation of plasma beta endorphins has been reported following stress (76), surgery (77), gambling (78), and marathon running (79). A recent study found elevated metenkephalins in some patients who habitually mutilate themselves (80). Another study reported that chronic self-mutilation in some patients can be arrested by opiate receptor blockers (81). In our experience, a variety of chronic self-destructive behaviors such as wrist cutting and anorexia nervosa have responded to clonidine, which also blocks the autonomic manifestations of opiate withdrawal (van der Kolk et al., unpublished data).

It is likely that after exposure to severe and prolonged environmental stress, reexposure to traumatic situations in humans can evoke an endogenous opioid response, producing the same effect as temporary application of exogenous opioids. Opioids have psychoactive properties such as anxiolytic and tranquilizing action, a reduction in rage and aggression, antidepressant action, and a decrease in paranoia and feelings of inadequacy (82). Opioids have been used historically to treat depression and as self-medication for painful or overwhelming affects (83).

Endogenous opioid release could account for the sense of calm on reexposure to stress that is reported by many traumatized individuals. Students since Freud have been struck by the tendency of trauma victims to reexpose themselves voluntarily to situations reminiscent of the trauma. Freud (3) thought that traumatic reexperiencing "decathects" the impact of the trauma, that trauma may be undone by re-doing. Although there is little evidence that repeating the trauma actually leads to a resolution of the trauma response, voluntary reexposure to trauma is very common. Veterans may enlist as mercenaries or seek other dangerous occupations; incest survivors may become prostitutes; abused children may expose themselves to dangerous situations or engage in physically self-destructive behaviors (see Chapter 1). In one survey of Vietnam veterans who sought treatment in a Veterans Administration hospital for PTSD, at least 20 percent reported that they often saw combat movies or exposed themselves to dangerous situations (van der Kolk, unpublished data). We are currently investigating the role of endorphins in their behavior. The best descriptions of this "addiction to trauma" are in such movies as "The Pawnbroker," the Russian roulette scene in "The Deer Hunter," and the opening scene of "Apocalypse Now."

The Reciprocal Relationship Between Opioid and Noradrenergic Systems

The interaction of the opioid and the noradrenergic systems is well established. Stimulation of the LC, for example, produces the behavioral and psychological signs of opiate abstinence in opiate-naive monkeys (33). Van der Kolk et al. (34) proposed that the physiological aspects of both opiate withdrawal and PTSD are related to central noradrenergic hyperactivity associated with a relative decrease in brain opioid receptor binding. The noradrenergic system is known to mediate the symptoms of opiate withdrawal; clonidine, an alpha 2 adrenergic agonist that diminishes postsynaptic noradrenergic activity is an effective treatment for the symptoms of opiate withdrawal (84). Recently Kolb et al. (85) found clonidine useful in treating hyperreactivity in PTSD as well. While endogenous opioid release following reexposure to traumatic stimuli may result in a temporary sense of control, this may be followed by withdrawal symptoms manifested by sleep disturbances, hyperreactivity, and explosive outbursts of aggression.

Thus reexposure provides transient relief but also perpetuates the addictive cycle, which leads to further loss of psychophysiological control (34). The hyperreactivity in PTSD is probably not entirely due to conditioned endogenous opiate withdrawal. More likely, massive trauma causes a vulnerability to excessive ANS reactivity, which could be further enhanced by fluctuations in endogenous opioid levels in response to reexposure to traumatic situations.

Treatment Implications of the
Animal Model of Inescapable Shock

Many studies show that the effects of inescapable shock in animals are variable and at least partly reversible. Some animals are much more vulnerable to the effects of inescapable shock than others. As noted above, animals who have been exposed to escapable shock prior to inescapable shock are much more stress resistant. This is consistent with the vulnerability issues spelled out in Chapter 1, which showed that people with an internal locus of control (i.e., people who can be presumed to have successfully overcome adversities) appear to be more stress resistant. Early traumatic experiences probably adversely affect locus of control, a crucial variable in the persistence or resolution of the trauma response.

The behavioral effects of inescapable shock can be reversed with both psychopharmacological and behavioral methods. Several drugs, including clonidine (86), benzodiazepines (29), and antidepressants (30) ameliorate the long-term effects of inescapable shock in animals. Some animals exposed to inescapable shock can be trained to avoid subsequent shock if they are dragged across the grid into a non-electrified area. This "putting through" procedure can even reverse some of the neurochemical changes due to inescapable shock (87). This finding may have applicability to humans: therapists may have to perform the psychotherapeutic equivalent of dragging the patient into a non-electrified area; that is, actively encourage the patient to take action in order to reexperience control. This can attenuate some of the chronic sense of helplessness and victimization so common in people with PTSD.

The psychological treatment of traumatization has emphasized reliving and abreaction of the trauma, a technique first elaborated by Lindemann (88). The clinical issues involved in uncovering, working through, and integrating the chronic effects of psychological trauma are illustrated in Chapters 8 and 9. Individual psychotherapy, hypnosis, and group psychotherapy have all been proposed for this purpose (89). Reliving, however, does not necessarily lead to resolution (90): unearthing the trauma often becomes just a reliving, rather than a resolution, of terror. Many patients are unable to integrate the trauma fully.

The concept of addiction to the trauma has very complex treatment implications. If reliving is followed by a conditioned endorphin release and subsequent hyperreactivity, bringing back memories of the trauma may actually make the symptoms worse. Clinical experience shows that uncovering of traumatic memories often causes clinical deterioration. Nevertheless, for integration of the trauma to occur, the details and meaning of the trauma need to be explored in psychotherapy; the central issue is whether exploring the trauma ultimately promotes or inhibits the patient's sense of mastery (see Chapters 7–9). The art of the psychotherapist consists in knowing when to press for the traumatic material and when to emphasize control over current experience.

The Psychopharmacological Treatment of Posttraumatic Stress

Psychotherapy is rarely helpful as long as the patient continues to respond to contemporary events and situations with a continuation of physiological emergency reactions as if reliving the trauma. Remembering, working through, and putting in perspective—the three tasks of psychotherapy—cannot proceed as long as the patient is unable to tolerate feelings associated with the trauma and continues to experience emotionally stimulating events as an unmodified recurrence of the trauma. Therefore psychotherapy often must be supplemented with medications that decrease the anxiety accompanying the recurrent intrusive reexperiencing of affective or cognitive elements of the trauma. Most medications proposed for the treatment of PTSD help in modulating arousal and alleviating the tendency to react in an all-or-nothing fashion.

Despite the marked recent interest in PTSD, there are no carefully controlled studies on the effects of medications. The sparse literature consists entirely of case reports and small open trials. Clinical reports have claimed success for every class of psychoactive medication, including benzodiazepines (91), tricyclic antidepressants (92), monoamine oxidase inhibitors (91, 93, 94), lithium carbonate (91), beta adrenergic blockers (85), clonidine (85), carbamazepine, and antipsychotic agents. As is explored further in Chapter 5, the similarities between the borderline syndrome and PTSD are striking. The psychopharmacological treatment of borderline patients is also uncertain at this time, but the recognition of a close relationship between these conditions may allow the understanding of pharmacological treatments of one condition to be applied to the other.

The animal model of inescapable shock suggests some ways to reverse the effects of trauma with drug treatment. We saw that a variety of psychopharmacological agents prevent or ameliorate the long-term effects of inescapable shock in animals (95). This knowledge has not yet been applied to trauma in humans.

We have suggested the involvement of the ANS in many symptoms of PTSD, including startle reactions, irritability, nightmares and flashbacks, and explosive outbursts of aggression. Drugs can reduce autonomic arousal at different levels in the nervous system by: 1) inhibiting noradrenergic activity (clonidine and beta adrenergic blockers), 2) increasing the inhibitory effect of the GABAergic system with gabaergic agonists (benzodiazepines), or 3) stabilizing the CNS with miscellaneous agents, such as lithium and carbamazepine. Positive results have been claimed for all of these medications, but there is no good evidence yet which patient, or even which symptoms, predictably respond to any of them.

Medications That Affect the Noradrenergic System

Clonidine is known to occupy alpha 2 receptors in the LC where certain cell bodies manufacture most of the CNS NE that is transported through neuronal axons to synaptic clefts in the hypothalamus, limbic system, and cerebral cortex. In contrast, the beta blockers have a selective sympatholytic action on the peripheral nervous system (along with a variable effect on the CNS), which reduces the somatic symptoms of anxiety. Kolb et al.'s (85) patients who received either clonidine or propranolol reported a decrease in startle responses, explosiveness, intrusive reexperiencing, and nightmares. They prescribed clonidine in doses of 0.2 to 0.4 mg per day and propranolol in doses of 120 to 180 mg per day. We sometimes have had to use very high doses, up to 640 mg, in hyperreactive Vietnam veterans who had not responded to other drugs. At these high doses patients ran the risk of becoming confused, although their heart rate and blood pressures were not markedly affected.

Benzodiazepines

The anxiolytic action of the benzodiazepines is due to their effect on the CNS GABAergic system, which has a central inhibitory effect (96). Benzodiazepines decrease new learning in animals and humans by blocking anxiety in response to aversive stimuli (97). Thus patients chronically maintained on these medications are less capable of learning from unpleasant experiences. Benzodiazepines also improve sleep, decrease nightmares, and may decrease self-medication with alcohol. Many traumatized patients prefer diazepam because of its rapid absorption, which leads to peak activity within 20 minutes after oral administration. However, this rapid subjective relief enhances the likelihood of abuse. Lorazepam and oxazepam, with their slower onset of action and shorter half-lives, have less abuse potential. Clonazepam may have special therapeutic advantages in modulating affective arousal. Many specialists warn against prescribing benzodiazepines for known alcohol abusers because cross-tolerance between benzodiazepines and ethanol may interfere with their attempts to abstain.

Lithium and Carbamazepine

Lithium carbonate is just beginning to find acceptance for the treatment of psychiatric conditions other than bipolar illness (98). It seems to exert some control over all the mechanisms that regulate affect (99), and thus may be helpful in a number of conditions involving dysregulation of affect. In a study in our clinic (91), we gave lithium to patients who felt out of control, constantly on the verge of exploding, and emotionally removed from their families. Many wished that they had died in Vietnam, and all had frequent nightmares and startle reactions. Of the 22 patients for whom we prescribed lithium, 14 reported improved control over their lives. Lithium decreased their tendency to react to stress as a recurrence of the original trauma. Autonomic hyperarousal was markedly diminished, and all responders reported much less alcohol use. Four patients stopped taking lithium because of side effects, and four did not respond. None of the lithium responders had a personal or family history of bipolar or cyclothymic illness.

Carbamazepine has also been used in patients with PTSD; the results are similar to those obtained with lithium. This is particularly interesting in light of recent evidence that carbamazepine may be as effective as lithium in the treatment of bipolar disorder

(100). In our experience, only those lithium and carbamazepine responders who remained in regular individual or group psychotherapy continued to take their lithium or carbamazepine as prescribed. Many patients said they preferred the excitement of reliving the trauma to the dull realities of everyday life. Thus in some men the desire for reexperiencing the trauma was greater than the desire for control of hyperreactivity.

Antidepressant Drugs

Tricyclic antidepressants are widely used for the treatment of chronic PTSD, and appear to be effective for many patients in the constricted phase. However, there is only one published uncontrolled case report (92). Amitriptyline is reputed to be particularly effective for posttraumatic nightmares. Monoamine oxidase inhibitors have received much attention ever since a report by Hogben and Cornfeld (93) that five chronically hospitalized PTSD sufferers with panic reactions improved considerably after phenelzine treatment. They claimed a decrease in nightmares, improved motivation, and increased availability of affect for psychotherapy. We have found both phenelzine and tranylcypromine helpful in patients who are primarily constricted. However, its effect on many patients with repeated outbursts of aggression or chronically high levels of anxiety was to increase their aggression and intrusive traumatic recollections. A recent study by Davidson et al. (101) reported similar findings.

Conclusions

Overwhelming trauma affects both the soma and the psyche. PTSD, perhaps more than any other mental disorder, demonstrates the degree to which psychological and physiological reactions are interrelated. Biochemical and behavioral studies of traumatized animals point to the basic processes underlying the hyperarousal, constriction, and compulsive reexperiencing typical of PTSD. Therapeutic application of this knowledge is only now beginning. Most treatment reports are anecdotal; there are almost no controlled studies. Yet, there is a slowly emerging body of knowledge about the core issues in the treatment of the trauma response. We know that we can suppress nightmares with medications and modulate hyperarousal with a combination of psychotherapy and pharmacotherapy. Controlled clinical trials, however, are needed to confirm the clinical impression that psychotherapy and other restorative experiences can positively affect posttraumatic hyperarousal and possibly "re-set" the nervous system at premorbid levels. Scientific confirmation of this clinical impression and an understanding of its mechanism of action are essential for more effective therapy of PTSD.

References

1. Veith I: Hysteria: History of a Disease. Chicago, University of Chicago Press, 1965

2. Southard E: Shell Shock and Neuropsychiatry. Boston, WM Leonard, 1919

3. Freud S: Beyond the pleasure principle (1920), in Complete Psychological Works. Standard Ed. Vol 18. Translated and edited by Strachey J. London, Hogarth Press, 1959

4. Pavlov IP: Conditioned Reflexes: An Investigation of the Physiological Activity of the Cerebral Cortex (1927). Edited and translated by Anrep GV. New York, Dover, 1960

5. Selye H: The Stress of Life. New York, McGraw-Hill, 1956

6. Krystal H: Trauma and Affects. Psychonal Study Child 33:81–116, 1978

7. Carmen EH, Reiker PP, Mills T: Victims of violence and psychiatric illness. Am J Psychiatry 141:378–379, 1984

8. Herman J: Histories of violence in an outpatient population. Am J Orthopsychiatry 57:137–141, 1986

9. Beck J, van der Kolk B: Histories of incest in chronically hospitalized women. Submitted for publication

10. Lacoursiere R, Godfrey K, Rubey L: Traumatic neurosis in the etiology of alcoholism. Am J Psychiatry 137:966–968, 1980

11. Kardiner A: The Traumatic Neuroses of War. New York, P Hoeber, 1941

12. Kolb L: The posttraumatic stress disorders of combat: a subgroup with a conditional and emotional response. Milit Med 149:237–243, 1984

13. Dobbs D, Wilson WP: Observations on the persistence of traumatic war neurosis. J Nerv Ment Dis 21:40–46, 1960

14. Malloy PF, Fairbank JA, Keane TM: Validation of a multimethod assessment of post traumatic stress disorders in Vietnam veterans. J Consult Clin Psychol 51:488–494, 1983

15. Kolb LC: A general systems hypothesis for PTSD (unpublished manuscript)

16. Kosten TR, Mason JW, Giller EL, et al: Sustained urinary norepinephrine and epinephrine elevation in post traumatic stress disorder. New Research, American Psychiatric Association Annual Meeting, Dallas, TX, May 1985

17. Strian F, Klicpera C: Die Bedeuting psychoautonomische Reaktionen im Entstehung und Persistenz von Angstzustanden. Nervenartzt 49:576–583, 1978

18. Field T: Attachment as psychobiological attunement: being on the same wavelength, in The Psychobiology of Attachment and Separation. Edited by Reite M, Field T. New York, Academic Press, 1985

19. Reite M, Short R, Seiler C, et al: Attachment, loss and depression. J Child Psychol Psychiatry 22:141–169, 1981

20. Nauta WJH: The central visceromotor system: a general survey, in Limbic System Mechanisms and Autonomic Function. Edited by Hockman DH, Moruzzi G. Springfield, Ill, Charles C Thomas, 1972, pp 31–38

21. Schachter J, Singer JE: Cognitive, social and psychological determinants of emotional state. Physiol Rev 69:379–399, 1962

22. McKinney WT: Separation and depression: biological markers, in The Psychobiology of Attachment and Separation. Edited by Reite M, Field T. New York, Academic Press, 1985

23. Carver CS, Blaney PH: Perceived arousal, focus of attention and avoidance behavior. J Abnorm Psychol 86:154–167, 1977

24. Nisbeth RE, Wilson T: Telling more than we know: verbal reports on mental processes. Psychol Rev 84:231–259, 1977

25. Bloemkolk D, Defares P, van Enckwert G, et al: Cognitive processing of information on varied physiological arousal. European Journal of Social Psychology 1:31–46, 1971

26. Keane TM, Fairbank JA, Caddell JM, et al: A behavioral

approach to assessing and treating post traumatic stress disorder, in Trauma and Its Wake. Edited by Figley C. New York, Brunner/Mazel, 1984, pp 257–294

27. Maier SF, Seligman MEP: Learned helplessness: theory and evidence. J Exp Psychol [Gen] 105:3–46, 1976

28. Visintainer MA, Volpicelli JR, Seligman MEP: Tumor rejection in rats after inescapable shock. Science 216:437–439, 1982

29. Weiss JM, Glazer HI, Pohorecky LA, et al: Effects of chronic exposure to stressors on subsequent avoidance-escape behavior and on brain norepinephrine. Psychosom Med 37:522–524, 1975

30. Weiss JM, Stone EA, Harrell N: Coping behavior and brain norepinephrine levels in rats. J Comp Physiol Psychol 72:153–160, 1970

31. Anisman HL, Sklar LS: Catecholamine depletion in mice upon exposure to stress: mediation of the escape deficits reduced by inescapable shock. J Comp Physiol Psychol 93:610–625, 1979

32. Anisman HL, Ritch M, Sklar LS: Noradrenergic and dopaminergic interactions in escape behavior. Psychopharmacology 74:263–268, 1981

33. Redmond DE, Krystal JH: Multiple mechanisms of opiate withdrawal. Annu Rev Neurosci 7:443–478, 1984

34. van der Kolk BA, Greenberg MS, Boyd H, et al: Inescapable shock, neurotransmitters and addiction to trauma: towards a psychobiology of post traumatic stress. Biol Psychiatry 20:314–325, 1985

35. Kraemer GW, Ebert MH, Lake CR, et al: Hypersensitivity to d-amphetamine several years after early social deprivation in rhesus monkeys. Psychopharmacology 82:266–271, 1984

36. Anisman H: Vulnerability to depression: contribution of stress, in Neurobiology of Mood Disorders, Edited by Post RM, Ballenger JC. Baltimore, Williams & Wilkins Co, 1984, pp 407–431

37. Grinker RR, Spiegel JJ: Men under Stress. New York, McGraw-Hill, 1945

38. Sulser F, Vetulani J, Mobley PL: Mode of action of antidepressant drugs. Biochem Pharmacol 27:257–261, 1982

39. Goddard CV, McIntyre DC, Leech CK: A permanent change in brain functioning resulting from daily electrical stimulation. Exp Neurol 25:295–330, 1969

40. Post RM, Kopanda RT: Progressive behavioral changes during lidocaine administration: relationship to kindling. Life Sci 17:943–950, 1975

41. Post RM, Kopanda RT: Cocaine, kindling and psychosis. Am J Psychiatry 133:627–634, 1976

42. Post RM, Ballenger JC, Uhde TW, et al: Kindling and drug sensitization: implications for the progressive development of psychopathology and treatment with carbamezapine, in The Psychopharmacology of Anticonvulsants. Edited by Sandler M. Oxford, Oxford University Press, 1981, pp 27–53

43. Racine RJ: Modification of seizure activity by electrical stimulation I: after seizure threshold. Electroencephalogr Clin Neurophysiol 32:269–279, 1972

44. Racine RJ: Modification of seizure activity by electrical stimulation II: motor seizures. Electroencephalogr Clin Neurophysiol 32:281–294, 1972

45. Post RM: Clinical implications of a cocaine kindling model of psychosis. Clin Neuropharmacol 2:25–42, 1977

46. Post RM, Rubinow DR, Ballenger JC: Conditioning, sensitization and kindling: implications for the course of affective illness, in Neurobiology of Mood Disorders. Edited by Post RM, Ballenger JC. Baltimore, Williams & Wilkins Co, 1984, pp 432–466

47. Bunney WE, Garland BL: Lithium and its possible mode of action, in Neurobiology of Mood Disorders. Edited by Post RM, Ballenger JC. Baltimore, Williams & Wilkins Co, 1984, pp 731–743

48. Burchfield SR: The stress response: a new perspective. Psychosom Med 41:661–672, 1979

49. Segal DS, Mandell AJ: Long term administration of d-am-

phetamine: progressive augmentation of motor activity and stereotypy. Pharmacol Biochem Behav 2:249–255, 1974

50. Segal DS, Weinberger SB, Cahill J, et al: Multiple daily amphetamine administration: behavioral and biochemical alterations. Science 207:904–907, 1980

51. Antelman SM, Eichler AJ, Black CA, et al: Interchangeability of stress and amphetamine in sensitization. Science 207:329–331, 1974

52. van der Kolk B, Blitz R, Burr W, et al: Nightmares and trauma: a comparison of nightmares after combat with lifelong nightmares in veterans. Am J Psychiatry 141:187–190, 1984

53. Schlossberg A, Benjamin M: Sleep patterns in three acute combat fatigue cases. J Clin Psychiatry 39:546–548, 1978

54. Lavie P, Hefez A, Halperin G, et al: Long term effects of traumatic war related events on sleep. Am J Psychiatry 136:175–178, 1979

55. Grant SJ, Redmond DE Jr: The neuroanatomy and pharmacology of the nucleus locus coeruleus, in Pharmacology of Clonidine. Edited by Lal H, Fielding S. New York, Alan R Liss, 1981

56. Foot SL, Bloom FE, Aston-Jones G: Nucleus locus ceruleus: new evidence of anatomical and physiological specificity. Physiol Rev 63:844–914, 1983

57. Delaney R, Tussi D, Gold PE: Long-term potentiation as a neurophysiological analog of memory. Pharmacol Biochem Behav 18:137–139, 1983

58. Kramer M, Schoen LS, Kinney L: The dream experience in dream disturbed Vietnam veterans, in Post Traumatic Stress Disorder: Psychological and Biological Sequelae. Edited by van der Kolk BA. Washington, DC, American Psychiatric Press, 1984

59. Gold PE, Zornetzer SF: The mnemon and its juices: neuromodulation of memory processes. Behav Neural Biol 38:151–189, 1983

60. Kelly DD: The role of endorphins in stress-induced analgesia. Ann NY Acad Sci 398:260–271, 1982

61. Maier SF, Davies S, Grau JW: Opiate antagonists and long-

term analgesic reaction induced by inescapable shock in rats. J Comp Physiol Psychol 94:1172–1183, 1980

62. Christie MJ, Chesher GB: Physical dependence on physiologically released endogenous opiates. Life Sci 30:1173–1177, 1982

63. Terman GW, Shavit Y, Lewis JW, et al: Intrinsic mechanisms of pain inhibition: activation by stress. Science 226:1270–1277, 1984

64. Lewis JW, Cannon JT, Liebeskind JC: Opioid and non-opioid mechanisms of stress analgesia. Science 208:623–625, 1980

65. Miczek KA, Thompson ML, Shuster L: Opioid-like analgesia in defeated mice. Science 215:1520–1521, 1982

66. Rogers RJ, Hendrie CA: Naloxone partially antagonizes post-encounter analgesia and enhances defensive responding in male rats exposed to attack from lactating cospecifics. Physiol Behav 30:775–778, 1983

67. Hill RG, Ayliffe SJ: The antinociceptive effect of vaginal stimulation in the rat is reduced by naloxone. Pharmacol Biochem Behav 14:631–633, 1981

68. McGivern R, Berka C, Berntson GG, et al: Effect of naloxone on analgesia induced by food deprivation. Life Sci 25:885–888, 1979

69. Bodnar RJ, Sikorsky V: Naloxone and cold water swim analgesia: parametric considerations and individual differences. Learning and Motivation 14:223–237, 1983

70. Lewis JW, Tordoff MG, Sherman JE, et al: Adrenal medullary enkephalin-like peptides may mediate opioid stress analgesia. Science 217:557–560, 1982

71. Cassens G, Roffman M, Kuruc A, et al: Alterations in brain norepinephrine metabolism induced by environmental stimuli previously paired with inescapable shock. Science 209:1138–1140, 1980

72. Maier SF, Sherman JE, Lewis JW, et al: The opioid/non-opioid nature of stress induced analgesia and learned helplessness. J Exp Psychol 9:80–90, 1983

73. Drugan RC, Maier SF: Analgesic and opioid involvement in

the shock-elicited activity and escape deficits produced by inescapable shock. Learning and Motivation 14:30–47, 1983

74. Canon JT, Liebeskind JC, Frenk H: Neural and neurochemical mechanisms of pain inhibition, in The Psychology of Pain. Edited by Sternbach RA. New York, Raven Press, 1978

75. Bolles RC, Fanselow MS: A perceptual-defensive-recuperative model of fear and pain. The Behavioral and Brain Sciences 3:291–323, 1980

76. Bortz WM, Angevin P, Mefford IN, et al: Catecholamines, dopamine, and endorphin levels during extreme exercise. N Engl J Med 305:466–469, 1981

77. Cohen MR, Pichas D, Dubois M, et al: Stress induced plasma beta endorphin immunoreactivity may predict postoperative morphine usage. Psychiatry Res 6:7–12, 1982

78. Blaszczynski AP, Winter SW, McConaghy X: Plasma endorphin levels in pathological gambling. Paper presented at the Sixth National Conference on Gambling and Risk Taking, Atlantic City, NJ, 1984

79. Colt, EW, Wardlaw SL, Frantz AG: The effect of running on plasma beta endorphin. Life Sci 28:1637–1640, 1981

80. Coid J, Allolio B, Rees LH: Raised plasma metenkephalin in patients who habitually mutilate themselves. Lancet 2:545–546, 1983

81. Richardson JS, Zaleski WA: Naloxone and self-mutilation. Biol Psychiatry 18:99–101, 1983

82. Verebey K, Volavka J, Clouet D: Endorphins in psychiatry. Arch Gen Psychiatry 35:877–888, 1978

83. Khantzian E: The self medication hypothesis of the addictions. Am J Psychiatry 142:1259–1264, 1985

84. Gold MS, Redmond DG, Kleber HD: Clonidine blocks acute opiate withdrawal symptoms. Lancet 2:599–601, 1978

85. Kolb LC, Burris BC, Griffiths S: Propranolol and clonidine in the treatment of post traumatic stress disorders of war, in Post Traumatic Stress Disorder: Psychological and Biological Sequelae. Edited by van der Kolk BA. Washington, DC, American Psychiatric Press, 1984

86. Sherman AD, Allers GL, Petty F, et al: A neuropharmacologically relevant animal model of depression. Neuropharmacology 18:891–893, 1979

87. Seligman MEP, Maier SF, Geer J: The alleviation of learned helplessness in the dog. J Abnorm Psychol 73:256–262, 1968

88. Lindemann E: Symptomatology and management of acute grief. Am J Psychiatry 101:141–148, 1944

89. Horowitz MJ: Stress Response Syndromes. New York, Jason Aronson, 1976

90. Lidz T: Psychiatric casualties from Guadacanal. Psychiatry 9:143–213, 1946

91. van der Kolk BA: Psychopharmacological issues in post-traumatic stress disorder. Hosp Community Psychiatry 34:683–691, 1983

92. Burstein A: Treatment of post traumatic stress disorder with imipramine. Psychosomatics 25:681–686, 1984

93. Hogben GL, Cornfeld RB: Treatment of traumatic war neurosis with phenelzine. Arch Gen Psychiatry 38:440–445, 1981

94. Levenson H, Lanman R, Rankin M: Traumatic war neurosis and phenelzine. Arch Gen Psychiatry 39:1345, 1982

95. van der Kolk BA, Boyd H, Krystal J, et al: Post traumatic stress disorder as a biologically based disorder: implications of the animal model of inescapable shock, in Post Traumatic Stress Disorder: Psychological and Biological Sequelae. Edited by van der Kolk BA. Washington, DC, American Psychiatric Press, 1984

96. Tyrer PJ, Lader MH: Response of propranolol and diazepam on psychic and somatic anxiety. Br Med J 2:14–16, 1974

97. Carlton PL, Siegel JL, Murphree HB: Effects of diazepam on operant behavior in man. Psychopharmacology 73:314–317, 1981

98. van der Kolk BA: The use of lithium in patients without major affective illness. Hosp Community Psychiatry 37:675–682, 1986

99. Sheard MH, Marini JL: The effect of lithium on impulsive aggressive behavior in man. Am J Psychiatry 133:1409–1413, 1976

100. Ballenger JC, Post RM: Carbamezapine in manic depressive illness: a new treatment. Am J Psychiatry 137:782–790, 1980

101. Davidson J, Walker JI, Kilts C: Phenelzine in chronic post traumatic stress disorder. Br J Psychiatry (in press)

CHAPTER 4

Evolving Ideas: The Effect of Abuse on Children's Thought

Caroline C. Fish-Murray, Ed.D.
Elizabeth V. Koby, M.D.
Bessel A. van der Kolk, M.D.

Children's understanding of their inner and outer world changes qualitatively as they grow up. In this chapter we will explore how a child tries to make sense of experiences of abuse, loss, and neglect over time. We will attempt to combine ideas from the fields of dynamic personality and cognitive development to contribute to a deeper understanding of how trauma impairs cognition, an understanding that will be needed for more effective diagnosis and treatment.

Domains of Cognitive Competencies

The psychiatric literature has devoted little attention to the development of distinct cognitive competencies (cognitive domains). Cognitive status has been determined mainly by broad, all-inclusive measurements, such as IQ, "g" factor (general intelligence), or tests for Piagetian stages. Nevertheless, long before the recent explosion of knowledge of brain structure and chemistry, Janet understood that consciousness was not unitary but flowed in streams that did not intersect (1). Psychologists are now recognizing that cognitive development involves a variety of discrete mental aptitudes that are not necessarily interrelated. Great mathematical abilities can exist without advanced language skills, or high verbal ability without a capacity of understanding oneself.

Gardner (2) defined seven discrete domains of intelligence, each of which he assumes to be grounded in a particular neurobiological substrate: linguistic, musical, logical-mathematical, spatial, bodily-kinesthetic, and two personal intelligences, knowing oneself and knowing others. Each of these domains may have its own symbolic coding and representational systems. There is now an extensive body of knowledge about the nature of domains and their relationship to normal human development.

Normal Cognitive Development

Before trying to understand pathological behavior, we should review what is understood about normal cognitive development. Cognitive development, like emotional development, unfolds sequentially with assumed correlates in central nervous system (CNS) maturation.

According to Piaget (3), the growth of the mind requires two *functional invariants* of thinking: assimilation and accommodation. Assimilation means the incorporation of new experiences into existing schemas and structures. It is seen best in free play, where a child practices relationships and correspondences according to his or her level of cognitive organization, distorting reality at will to fit the needs of the moment. Accommodation occurs when the child readjusts and transforms these assimilated structures to correct discrepancies between the play and the demands of reality. The child tries to anticipate new situations, making the play more attuned to his surroundings. The child constantly imitates and matches schemas to reality. Assimilation and accommodation are in a continuous process of equilibration, a dynamic dialectic necessary to ensure adaptation. They help to maintain affiliative bonds and allow for subjective control and mastery over experiences.

Cognitive structures play a central role as the child completes age-appropriate social tasks. They become increasingly complex, differentiated, and efficient systems of adaptation. This growth in problem-solving ability causes a slow evolution in the child's capacity to make subjective sense of his experiences. The operations, schemas, and structures involved are partly conscious but largely unconscious. These mental systems are not just elements or aggregates of experience but condensations and transformations of experiences resulting from the child's interaction with his world.

A developing child organizes information according to an increasingly complicated set of inferential relationships, using domain-specific *representational systems* such as action codes, visual imagery, and verbal symbols. When the newborn baby imitates its mother sticking out her tongue, the excitement of communication and the experience of tender affection are greatly increased. The infant continues to communicate by gestures and actions, showing its wishes by moving, grasping, dropping things, crawling, and so on. By the age of 1 year, the child is using iconic, or picture-like, symbols to store information. His behavior is governed by what he sees. For instance, he will not cross a solid glass sheet bridging two boxes because he has developed depth perception and looks down and sees a cliff and a drop that he "knows" to be unsafe. A few months earlier, he had fearlessly crossed the glass to his mother. At about 2 years, language begins to put a whole new symbol and memory system at his disposal.

Building on innate reflexes, the infant establishes a repertoire of *cognitive operations* such as identity (that is my mother), negation (that is not my mother), and comparison (she is different from my father). These operations organize and condense information; they join fragments of experience into meaningful schematas, scenarios, and narratives. Early experiences are thus constantly transformed from simple memory traces into ways of understanding and controlling the inner and outer world. When schemas are incorporated into larger structures, they become the basis of future mental operations. For example, object permanence is achieved at about 8 months. The ability to preserve a memory of persons and things when they are out of sight provides a sense of competency and a security that promotes further exploration and experimentation. In a similar way, each new cognitive grouping is accompanied by an increased sense of mastery over somatic sensations of fear, anxiety, and anger.

Piaget and his successors have identified four relatively independent sequential stages of development: sensorimotor, preoperational, concrete operational, and formal operational logic. This is, of course, a theoretical idealization: it does not take into account the vagaries of individual growth and talents (4).

The *sensorimotor period* lasts from birth to about age 2. The baby uses innate rhythms and reflexes to interact with the world, and this interaction is the origin of functions and structures that underlie later thinking. For instance, the sucking and grasping reflexes combine to form a new schema, thumb-sucking, used for self-soothing. The infant's knowledge of the world comes from his actions upon objects. The baby knows the mother by how she looks, smells, tastes, and feels, and how she responds to his smiling, crying, holding, kicking, and biting. Later in this period the semiotic or symbolic function begins, culminating in language. Memory codes are now being differentiated.

The *preoperational stage* is divided into two periods. In the *preconceptual stage* (ages 2 to 4), representational systems are fixed and classes have immutable boundaries. A little girl was asked whether her toy horse and man were alike in any way. She answered, "No, because this person is not brown and shaped like a horse." When presented with assorted toys, she excluded a costumed animal from the class of animals because "animals don't wear clothes."

At the next level of cognitive development, the *intuitive stage* (ages 4 to 7), children begin to let imaginative representations shift in and out of their classification systems using flexible groupings. They now realize that animals and men are alike because they are alive. But as yet these intuitions are not coherent or practiced enough to be called operations. Children by now have a sense of cardinal and ordinal numbers. They can count, seriate, and put things in ordered ranks, but they are unable to understand mathematical formulas for addition, subtraction, multiplication, and division of numbers or objects. They can understand that two lines have an equal number of objects if the objects are arranged in one-to-one correspondence; but if one line is stretched out, they think the long one is "bigger" and therefore has more objects in it. In other words, they almost have the operation of reversibility, but not enough to hold the concept of the whole in mind when physical changes are made.

"Will" and a hierarchy of cognitively shaped motives become a potent force for organization during this period of development, coordinating cognition with the emotional system. Motives are actions. The child in this preoperational period is self-centered. Human activities seem to cause natural events. The world revolves around the child; he is not only the master of the world but guilty if anything goes wrong.

After this stage a child thinks the whole world is made up of interrelated parts that are known to grown-ups. He constantly asks "Why?" He wants to be sure of all those links, and the omnipotent adult certainly must know. His questions go from particular to particular, with limited understanding of inferences or causality. He attends only to single features of objects. If he sees a ball of clay elongated, he believes the amount of clay has changed because he cannot keep amount and length in his mind at the same time. He also links unrelated things just because they are next to each other in space and time.

Inanimate objects at this stage seem to be alive and to have intentions. Clouds are alive because they move. A lamp intends to give you light, a furnace to give you heat. Psychological events are quasi-tangible entities. A thought is a voice in the mouth. When the child is supposed to be tired and go to bed, a large black cloud called night fills the sky (5).

At the *concrete operational level*, the child acquires the operation of reversibility and the consequent ability to conserve. This major transformation in cognitive organization occurs between the ages of 7 and 11. The essence of operational thinking is the dominance of thought over appearance. Children are no longer limited to single aspects of a problem and they can make logical inference. Thus when the shape of a lump of clay is changed, the child knows if nothing has been added or subtracted, the amount of clay must logically remain the same.

In personal domains, conservation allows the child to move from self-centeredness to a recognition of reciprocal roles using multiple simultaneous perspectives. A child needs conservation in the personal domains to comprehend motivations and intentionality in others. He is able for the first time to enact Oedipal themes. By age 7, the major aspects of personality are firmly entrenched. Now time and energy are spent on getting to know others, understanding their intentions, learning right and wrong, and becoming competent in newly acquired cognitive operations and structures (6). Play is no longer self-centered but involves genuine role divisions. Reversibility allows the mental reconciliation of opposing forces; the capacity to tolerate ambivalence emerges (7). Children also experience genuine guilt for the first time because they know they could have acted otherwise (6).

Formal operational thought begins around age 12 with propositional thinking and the ability to think about thinking. An adolescent can now do hypothetico-deductive thinking and comprehend probability. For the first time, a true ego is active, self-known, self-observed, and self-contained. The exciting period of shaping ideals and testing of possibilities begins.

Cognitive Dysfunction in Pathological Development

Cognitive dysfunction, as defined in the Piagetian developmental tradition, has been studied in many types of psychiatric pathology. Children with neurotic disturbances show an unusual amount of oscillation between stages of thought (8). Bemporad et al. (9), studying latency-aged borderlines, found similar fluctuation of functioning and noted the children's failure to master developmental tasks.

More severely disturbed children demonstrate an inadequate assimilation of reality. What they take in, digest, and change depends on their idiosyncratic history and biology and on their specific fears and needs, not on real world demands. Consequently, their use of symbols is idiosyncratic, and they have a hard time envisaging and anticipating changes (8).

Voyat and his group at City University, New York (10–13), found that the cognitive organization of psychotic children was qualitatively different from that of normal children. They were unable to conserve and could not use the operation of reversibility at an appropriate age; thus they could not properly assess other people's intentions. They could manipulate materials but not explain what they had done. The children lacked playful imagination and an ability to interact with the examiner. These children did not seem to go through the usual invariant stages of development.

Working with Piaget and the Geneva group, Inhelder (14) found that older psychotic children were preoperational and could not understand the concept of chance. They had more difficulty with logical relations than logical classes. They also had poor linguistic skills and disturbed symbolic and semiotic functions; their understanding of relationships with others was also disturbed. Schmid-Kitsikis (15), another Genevan, looked specifically at assimilation and accommodation in psychotic children, finding them to be nonfunctional and disequilibrated. Her psychotic children had particular difficulty with seriation and could not move beyond the search stage in solving problems. In other words, they accepted the materials presented and seemed to understand the problem but could not anticipate or come up with solutions. Thus there was little feedback for self-correction and stabilization. They could verbalize the instructions but could not complete the task largely because of interference from visual clues. There were also serious spatial and motor disturbances. The coexistence of operational and preoperational reasoning led to avoidance, insecurity, self-doubt, and fear of participation.

Breslow and Cowan (16) also found that psychotic children were delayed in developing the ability to seriate. Psychotic children were unable to use anticipatory imagery. This suggested that "thought disorder" might result from a mismatch between higher level logical structures and lower level functions such as perception, attention, and imagery. The authors concluded that deficits in imagery were central to the disordered thinking of the psychotic.

The psychotic children studied by Caplan and Walker (17) also had marked delays in acquiring logical structures. Their mental representations were static and they lacked conservation even in their late teens. Lerner et al. (18) found that adolescent psychotic children could learn through drill and memorization but lacked operatory structures that would allow them to comprehend the problems they were working on.

Mentally retarded children pass through cognitive stages much as normal children do, but at a slower rate, and they usually reach a ceiling at the preoperational level or earlier (19). Dysphasic, dyspraxic, and dyslexic children have specific deficiencies in symbolic abilities. Blind children develop elementary logic without difficulty, although they are slow on spatial logic. They are delayed in achieving conservation as seriation is hard for them to master (20). Deaf children acquire operatory logic without the benefit of language (21). Other studies show characteristic delays, depending on the pathological category (22).

To summarize, children in the research studies reviewed above demonstrated developmental delays in several of Gardner's (2) domains. The ability to use mental imagery to solve problems is particularly affected, indicating defects in the visual domain (although this is not so true of the deaf population). Verbal abilities and social skills are also notably affected. The children coped with change by relying on sensorimotor action instead of creating meaning through imagery or logical thought. Aside from these structural limitations, their functions of assimilation and accommodation are clearly not in a healthy balancing adaptive relationship.

The Cognitive Processing of Traumatic Events

While the study of cognitive impairment in abused children is still in its initial stages, current evidence indicates these children interpret the meaning of their pain and anxiety according to their cognitive structural level. Research confirms developmental delays in verbal abilities in the ability to accomplish age-appropriate tasks of personality development (23–26).

A debate on the primacy of initial cognitive over emotional response at times of psychological crises continues (27, 28). As Piaget pointed out, affective and cognitive changes are complementary and simultaneous; behavior always has elements of both

(29). Trauma or memory of trauma interrupts development, another element of "fixation on the trauma" (see Chapter 1).

When habitual and previously adaptive actions and strategies fail, the autonomic nervous system is activated and a search through the memory systems of different domains begins. In children this search is heavily weighted toward visual memory. Normally the child makes a rapid unconscious cognitive evaluation of the situation to find a way out (27). When the system is overloaded because of unassimilated fear and pain, the child loses the ability to shift easily through sets and to previously assimilated signs and symbols. He has lost the function of accommodation, the ability to self-correct, to anticipate, to admit ranges of possibilities. Earlier coping mechanisms are activated and repeated to ensure the safety of sameness (30).

Numbing, denial, and constriction of personality functioning follow traumatization in adults (30, 31). This numbness may be the result of confrontation with discrepancies that present an indigestible amount of data. It involves unconscious concentration on available data processing schemas and a rapid construction, combining, and testing of combinations to deal with the overwhelming discrepancies. A person who appears stunned and immobile to the outside observer may be processing data, calculating relationships, and working to build novel and manageable structures to deal with information overflow.

Krystal (32) noted how traumatized individuals use stimuli, depending not so much on the degree or duration of the trauma as on the ability to fit the experience into existing mental structures (i.e., to make it meaningful). This in turn depends on the child's level of development and the preferred memory systems. For similar reasons, Schneider-Rosen and Cicchetti (33) could not find a strong relationship between behavior and type of neglect or abuse.

Cognitive Dysfunction in Abused Children

There is a long history of studies on the effects of abuse on cognition. A burst of interest followed Kempe's (34) 1968 book on the "battered child syndrome," which called attention to the extent and pervasiveness of child abuse. Bowlby (35) had already demonstrated that sexually or physically abused children lag behind nontraumatized children in both intellectual and emotional development. Other research showed cognitive, language, and motor skill delays (36), and deficiencies on auditory and visual reception and verbal reception and expression (31, 36–40).

Some of the best longitudinal research is being done by Cicchetti and colleagues (41, 42) at the Harvard Child Maltreatment Project. They have found a wide range and variability in the way abused children react to their deviant caregivers. An early reliable attachment system in these children was vulnerable to disruption in the first two years of life. They stress the complexity of each child's development and warn against taking a simplistic view of cause and effect. Delays in socioemotional development were noted at all ages, with lags in both motor and social behavior in infants. Abused infants show a kind of attachment to caregivers that is less secure than that of nonabused children. Abused children are not as good at self-recognition, although they have acquired object permanency (i.e., they can remember objects but not themselves). Possibly they already have different levels of development among domains, normal for age-appropriate scientific logical inference but immature in understanding of self and others. The preoperational and operational abused children showed a cognitive delay in flexible use of operations. The abused childrens' verbal abilities were also not as good as those of controls.

Bemporad et al. (9) found a high frequency of organic impairment, physical abuse, and family disturbance in a study of borderline children. These children had trouble forming relationships with peers, stabilizing successful defenses, expanding cognitive ability, and pursuing social activities.

Terr (43–45), using psychiatric interviews in a follow-up of the children buried in the bus at Chowchilla, noted the following cognitive dysfunctions: distorted concepts of time, selective encoding of memory, transfer of perceptual memories to other modalities, and verbal restrictions. She also noted distortions of visual and auditory perception, visual hallucinations, elaboration and condensation of early memories, and compulsive scanning of trauma.

In a review of the literature (31, 34, 37–39, 46–52) on the effect of abuse on the cognition of children, there are continual references to the delay in development of the self and in the ability to get along with and understand others. These papers described behavior similar to Bowlby's (35) children who suffered separation and loss. Abused children were reported to be withdrawn, apathetic, but hypervigilant, with a "frozen watchfulness."

While many of these studies suffer from a lack of controls, poor definition of trauma, lack of follow up, weak instrumentation, and overemphasis on psychodynamic interpretations, they provide important leads for further examination of the effects of trauma on cognitive development (46, 53). More sophisticated theory and methodology are needed to understand the development of traumatized children.

Ongoing Research

In the past three years the Trauma Clinic at the Massachusetts Mental Health Center has been exploring specific cognitive deficits of abused and neglected children. Aber and Cicchetti (41) had begun the essential study of social and emotional development. We focused more directly on the functions, operations, and structures within cognitive domains, attempting to determine whether abused children develop systematic strategies of response and avoidance within these domains.

The number of subjects under study is not yet large enough for definitive conclusions, but preliminary observations are generating hypotheses for future examination. Our population consists of children between the ages of 6 and 11 with documented histories of physical and/or sexual abuse and/or severe deprivation. They have been matched for sex, age, race, and socioeconomic status with well-functioning, and as far as we know, nonabused children. Five of the experimental group were hospitalized in an inner city mental hospital. One boy had been repeatedly beaten by his mother; one girl was a victim of incest at the age of 4. Another boy came from a chaotic home where he was tied to a chair and whipped. Another was beaten by his father. One boy had been abandoned in early childhood. One girl's mother, a prostitute, was raped, dismembered, burned, and put into the trunk of a car when the patient was 5. The mother's pimp was suspected of sexually abusing the girl.

In our studies we have not distinguished among sexually abused, physically abused, and grossly neglected children on the general assumption that the immediate response of the CNS does not distinguish among these sources of trauma.

We devised a wide range of tests to examine three domains: scientific inferential thinking, knowledge of self, and understanding of others. Data were obtained on 1) cognitive functions (assimilation, accommodation), 2) operational processes (identity, negation, seriation, conservation, etc.), and 3) the organization of schemata and structures within and among the three domains.

The Domain of Scientific–Mathematical Logic

In all but two tests of scientific–mathematical logic, abused children scored lower than controls. The abused children's poor responses in the domain of early scientific thinking might account for some of their difficulties in school, where the succession of tasks generally follows the normal cognitive developmental path. All of these children had average IQs. The tests of logical stages within domains were more discriminating than IQ in spotting functional and structural disabilities and lags.

The Domains of Knowledge of Self and Others

Abuse clearly affected the personal domains more than the scientific one. In self-knowledge and sense of others, the abused group was decidedly at a lower level than the nonabused. They had a markedly impaired ability to shift roles. The controls made more requests and spontaneously told more stories than the abused. Their stories were usually about themselves. The nonabused group also made spontaneous exclamations of pleasure.

None of the abused children had trouble relating to new examiners. They assimilated and accommodated these new persons into their ongoing lives. Yet when they saw pictures of children like themselves, with parents or siblings, and were asked to associate to these images, memories of their own traumatic experiences returned and held them captive. Piaget holds that the key to multiple paths of cognitive organization is flexibility and variability (4). If emotional charges cause the return and reenactment of scenes, the child is pulled toward predominantly visual and less developed and interactive structures of thought. If vision remains the central organizing force, the child has to go step-by-step over the immediate visual field. Time sequencing is difficult because of the concentration on the here and now. This type of visual thinking keeps a child centered on his own world and preoperational in logic.

All children have standards that serve as motivating cognitive schemas, reflecting the culture and family of the child. The standards of the abused children were very different from the controls; for example, they did not have the same concepts of justice and responsibility for rules. They tended to think that rules were made by the largest male in the place, and physical punishment was the reason for not breaking them. The control children were more apt to see authority and rules as necessary for social order; they were beginning to understand the idea of the social contract.

The abused children could not go beyond seeing themselves at the center of the universe. They found it hard to shift sets, not only with physical objects but with self/other categories. Reciprocal role playing was especially hard for them. They found it difficult to use flexible, mobile imagery to work out problems, to anticipate solutions, and to visualize what alternatives would look like. They found it particularly hard to encounter the uncertainty and unpredictability of some of the tests.

According to Gardner (2), cognitive domains develop at different rates, and operations and structures do not generalize across domains. This was illustrated in one study of an abused child and his control. The abused child had a solid sense of conservation in the scientific–mathematical domain but did not have conservation in dealing with himself and others. His matched control had just the opposite capabilities: no conservation in the mathematical–scientific domain, but the highest scores of the whole group in moral standards, personal and interpersonal skills, and taking other people's points of view.

Like researchers who study adult trauma victims (54), we have found that the abused children's traumatic experiences determine their apperception of stimuli presented by the examiner. Their vivid pictorial memories seemed ineradicable. A 7-year-old abused girl who had been an incest victim at age 4 was presented with a picture of a pregnant woman. She saw images of penises, vaginas, and uteruses and repeatedly asked about sexual functions, her own and the examiner's. Her matched control, seeing the same card, told a matter-of-fact story about a widowed lady sadly looking out the window looking for a husband. The story concluded with the lady finding her man.

The Effect of Abuse on Accommodation

The capacity to accommodate, to self-correct, is markedly impaired in the abused group. When telling stories to the Thematic Apperception Test (TAT), or photographs similar to the TAT, some of the abused children simply lost all coherence and testing had to be terminated. Those who did manage to get their stories straightened out told gruesome tales of murder, kidnapping, beating, and abandonment, with few happy endings. The controls introduced some nasty subjects but could bring someone to the rescue, or get distance by turning the story into a television program or commercial or a late-night movie. They tacked on happy endings even if they were unrelated to the main story. When the adequate assimilation of the abused children was not equilibrated by the function of accommodation, their response to a new situation seemed automatized and the equivalent of fixation.

The "All or None" Response

Like Vietnam veterans with posttraumatic stress disorder (54), abused children tended to react in an all or none fashion to projective tests. Refusal to respond or extremely limited responses were characteristic, even though the child looked carefully at each card, studying it, taking it in. If the child did respond, it was with an intensity appropriate to the traumatic experience, approaching the catastrophic.

The lack of response on projective tests may not be a question of repression, as Freud suggested; it may be caused by fixation at a level where information could not be processed. The trauma is so overpowering that the child had inadequate organizing perceptions to make sense of it. The memory of trauma is registered in the CNS, but is not yet digestible by the existing structures of logic. Therapy helps the child assimilate the experiences into adaptive thinking processes.

Inflexibility

Thus far, our strongest finding in these abused children has been the inflexibility of organized schematas and structures in all domains. When we studied them, they were at an age when rigid classification boundaries of early preoperational thought should have been loosened. Instead, function and structure were frozen so that dynamic change could not take place. Accommodation was not operating efficiently, apparently because autonomic nervous system arousal and steady state anxiety caused by conditioned fear and anticipatory frustration inhibited the ability to make guiding plans, to play with alternative approaches, or to anticipate probabilities at age-appropriate levels. Yet, as we noted, some domains, such as the mathematical–scientific, were less affected than personal knowledge.

Effect of Abuse on Verbalization

Although we did not test the verbal domain specifically, reviewing protocols supported other research showing verbal abilities compromised by abuse. Our abused children spoke fewer sentences and used fewer words than controls. Abused children did not enjoy inventing stories, whereas the controls did. The storytelling of abused children showed a lack of the essential curiosity that leads to exploratory behavior.

Abuse and Dissociation

Since personality development depends on a continuous rethinking of boundaries, abused children are at a distinct disadvantage; they are stuck and unwilling to experiment. If domains are restricted by fixed boundaries and if thought within them is repetitive, domain repertoires may become so independent that they increase dissociation in functioning. In support of this notion, Hilgard (55) and Mounoud and Vinter (56) found that dissociation depended on separate cognitive structures and activities.

Piaget (57) pointed out that

> It is precisely because there is no immediate accommodation that there is complete dissociation of the inner activity from the external world. As the external world is represented solely by images, it is assimilated without resistance to the unconscious ego, and it is in this respect that oneiric [dream] symbolism is a continuation of ludic [play] symbolism.

Van der Kolk et al. (58) found such unaccommodated material in the dreams of traumatized adults. Their dreams contained scenarios of their actual traumatic events, generally unmodified by other circumstances of their lives.

Abused children are sometimes described as "splitting" representations of love objects into good and bad characters. This may be misleading because splitting suggests an original whole. It is more likely that an abused child, fixated at a preoperational stage in the personal domains, knows two different sides of himself or others as distinct individuals. Without conservation, there is no superordinate self, no one person with many characteristics. If this state lasts because of fixation (i.e., if it is encapsulated through lack of accommodation), the child may go on thinking of himself as many selves, unrelated to one another, like any normal child in the preoperational stage, while other cognitive domains continue to develop at normal rates.

Abused children at the preoperational stage are often accused of lying; they deny this vigorously. Another child did the bad things—one not related to the presenting good child. As the child grows up, these multiple personalities may take on powerful identities, especially if the trauma is continuous. As the child loses competence in the world of peers, he turns to the multifarious group inside himself for challenge, growth, assimilation, and accommodation.

If the child is no longer accommodating himself to his environment, his energies are directed toward building a self from within. For children at the height of hypnotizability (ages 7 to 11) (1), self-hypnotizing can become an escape from being an abused object. They learn to leave their bodies to the abuser, to become invisible and let a part of themselves float free (59, 60), thus laying the groundwork for dissociative disorders, including multiple personalities.

Children using self-hypnosis concentrate on a narrow field where contrast, comparison, and critical judgment are not operative. This state is comparable to preoperational thinking. During alert, aroused concentration, the child does not, and cannot, conceive of randomness and multiple causality. Delusional thinking is often the adult equivalent and possibly the encapsulated remnant of an early thought process that occurred during traumatization. When an adult handles a problem with the childish simplicity of preoperational thought, he is designated "delusional" or "thought disordered."

Relation of Abuse to Attentional Deficit Disorder

Four of six abused children had diagnoses of attention deficit disorder (ADD), three with hyperactivity; four were either taking or about to take methylphenidate hydrochloride (Ritalin). The relation of cause and effect here is hard to establish. In the first place, although it seems real, the construct of ADD has not yet been robustly validated (61). In this connection it is interesting to note that ADD and posttraumatic stress disorder, as defined in the *Diagnostic and Statistical Manual of Mental Disorders*, Third Edition (DSM-III) (62), have many symptoms in common, such as hyperarousal, hypervigilance, and impulsivity. These symptoms are present not only in abused children but also in children and animals separated from their mothers (see Chapter 2).

Common sense suggests that a child who has trouble paying attention and can't stay still to learn will also have secondary cognitive deficits. In fact, ADD is often accompanied by learning disorders and conduct disturbances, such as socially disruptive, aggressive, or antisocial behavior (63), indicating low peer and self-esteem. Children with ADD do not have deficiencies with perception or memory, but they do have difficulty processing and storing information and organizing it into available chunks for retrieval (63).

At this point in research, measures of covariance would be more useful than trying to find simple causality. Situational as opposed to generalized ADD is a major complicating variable. We need to explore whether abused children are more likely to show situational ADD, and whether the situations that evoke hyperactive behavior are related to their past experiences. Do abused children have domain-specific ADD, and if so, in which domain?

Deprivation

All the children we studied came from one of the most depressed areas of Boston, all living in poverty. Deprivation is a constant in the lives of these children. During the study, in the school attended by the control children, one boy doused another with gasoline and set him on fire. During the time of testing, a boy in the school, walking with his father and a young friend, was caught in a cross-fire gun battle and was wounded in the groin. His friend was killed. Both abused and control children told tales of horror. They had all witnessed violence, but the controls were protected by not having been the direct recipients of sexual or physical abuse. They still had trust in their environment; they could imagine ways out of bad situations and could practice displacement. They also seemed to have strong attachment bonds, which made them secure enough to continue to learn.

Implications for Diagnosis and Treatment

Diagnosis and treatment can be tailored to the child's special needs by taking into account the impact of traumatic memories on specific cognitive domains. Since personal, verbal, and scientific—mathematical domains are affected, it is useful to determine the level of cognitive development in these domains. Therapeutic intervention could then make use of appropriate stage tasks involving anticipation, self-correcting expectations, contradiction, and recognition of discrepancies. Competency in any domain could be encouraged to help the child feel strong and in control of some areas of his life.

Special attention should be given to equilibrating the functions of assimilation and accommodation. The unprocessed memories of trauma have to be gradually drawn into the child's cognitive life. Imitation, trying to match inner assimilated structures to models, can be practiced to stabilize accommodation. Well-practiced cognitive operations and structures can help the child resist intrusion and reenactment of traumatic memories.

References

1. Braun BG, Sachs RG: The development of multiple personality disorder: predisposing, precipitating, and perpetuating factors, in Childhood Antecedents of Multiple Personality. Edited by Kluft RP. Washington, DC, American Psychiatric Press, 1985

2. Gardner H: Frames of Mind. New York, Basic Books, 1983

3. Piaget J: Structuralism. New York, Basic Books, 1970

4. Gruber HE, Voneche JJ: The Essential Piaget. New York, Basic Books, 1977

5. Kagan J: The Nature of the Child. New York, Basic Books, 1984

6. Ginsburg H, Opper S: Piaget's Theory of Intellectual Development: An Introduction. Englewood Cliffs, NJ, Prentice-Hall, 1969

7. Selman R, Jaquette D, Lavin DR: Interpersonal awareness in children: toward an integration of developmental and clinical psychology. Am J Orthopsychiatry 47:264–274, 1977

8. Inhelder B: Some pathologic phenomena analyzed in the perspective of developmental psychology, in Piaget and His School: A Reader in Developmental Psychology. Edited by Inhelder B, Chipman HH. New York, Springer-Verlag, 1976

9. Bemporad JR, Smith HF, Hanson G, Cicchetti D: Borderline syndromes in childhood: criteria for diagnosis. Am J Psychiatry 139:596–602, 1982

10. Voyat G: Psychosis: a cognitive and psychodynamic perspec-

tive, in Piagetian Theory and Implications for Helping Professions. Edited by Poulson M. Los Angeles, Calif, University of Southern California Press, 1979

11. Sloate PL, Voyat G: Cognitive and affective features in childhood psychosis. Am J Psychother 37(3):376–386, 1983

12. Oram K: Developmental aspects of "childhood schizophrenia": A structural analysis using a Piagetian and psychoanalytic approach. Unpublished doctoral dissertation, City University, New York, 1978

13. Shackelford MD: The structure of thought in schizophrenic children: a Piagetian analysis. Unpublished doctoral dissertation, City University, New York, 1977

14. Inhelder B: Operatory thought processes in psychotic children, in Piaget and His School: A Reader in Developmental Psychology. Edited by Inhelder B, Chipman HH. New York, Springer-Verlag, 1976

15. Schmid-Kitsikis E: The cognitive mechanisms underlying problem-solving in psychotic and mentally retarded children, in Piaget and His School: A Reader in Developmental Psychology. Edited by Inhelder B, Chipman HH. New York, Springer-Verlag, 1976

16. Breslow L, Cowan PA: Structural and functional perspectives on classification and seriation in psychotic and normal children. Child Dev 55:226–235, 1984

17. Caplan J, Walker HA: Transformational deficits in cognition of schizophrenic children. J Autism Dev Disord 9:161–177, 1979

18. Lerner S, Bie I, Lehrer P: Concrete-operational thinking in mentally ill adolescents. Merrill Palmer Quarterly 18:287–291, 1972

19. Inhelder B: The Diagnosis of Reasoning in the Mentally Retarded. New York, John Day, 1968

20. Schmid-Kitsikis E: Piagetian theory and its approach to psychopathology. Am J Ment Defic 79:694–705, 1973

21. Furth HG: Piaget and Knowledge. Theoretical Foundations. Englewood Cliffs, NJ, Prentice-Hall, 1969

22. Greenspan SI, Lourie RS, Nover RA: A developmental ap-

proach to the classification of psychopathology in infancy and early childhood, in Handbook of Child Psychiatry. Vol 2. Edited by Noshpitz J. New York, Basic Books, 1979

23. Cicchetti D: The emergence of developmental psychopathology. Child Dev 55:1–7, 1984

24. Cicchetti D, Rizley A: Developmental perspectives on the etiology, intergenerational transmission and sequelae of child maltreatment. New Directions for Child Development 11:31–55, 1981

25. Hoffman-Plotkin D, Twentyman JT: A multimodal assessment of behavior and cognitive deficits in abused and neglected children. Child Dev 55:794–802, 1984

26. Orzek AM: The child's cognitive processing of sexual abuse. Child and Adolescent Psychotherapy 2:110–114, 1985

27. Mandler G: The generation of emotion, a psychological theory, in Emotion: Theory, Research and Experience, Theories of Emotion, Vol 1. Edited by Plutchik R, Kellerman H. Orlando, Florida, Academic Press, 1980

28. Zajonk RB: Feeling and thinking: preferences need no inferences. Am Psychol 35:151–175, 1980

29. Decarie TG: Intelligence and Affectivity in Early Childhood: An Experimental Study of Jean Piaget's Object Concept and Object Relations. New York, International Universities Press, 1965

30. Krystal H: Trauma and affects. Psychoanal Study Child 33:81–116, 1978

31. Martin HP, Rodeheffer M: Learning and intelligence, in The Abused Child: A Multidisciplinary Approach to Developmental Issues and Treatment. Edited by Martin HP. Cambridge, Mass, Ballinger, 1976

32. Krystal H: View of information processing. Paper presented at Symposium on Psychological Trauma in Children and Adults: Implications for Diagnosis and Treatment in Psychiatry, Boston, Mass, 30 November–1 December 1984

33. Schneider-Rosen K, Cicchetti D: The relationship between affect and cognition in maltreated infants: Quality of attach-

ment and the development of visual self-recognition. Child Dev 55:648–658, 1984

34. Kempe CH, Helfer RE: The Battered Child. Chicago, University of Chicago Press, 1968

35. Bowlby J: Attachment and Loss. Vol 2: Separation: Anxiety and Anger. New York, Basic Books, 1973

36. Cohn AH: An evaluation of three demonstration child abuse and neglect treatment programs. J Child Psychiatry 18:283–291, 1979

37. Morgan SR: Psycho-educational profile of emotionally disturbed abused children J Clin Child Psychol 8:3–6, 1979

38. Soeffing M: Abused children are exceptional children. Except Child 42:126–133, 1975

39. Sandgrund A, Gaines RW, Green AH: Child abuse and mental retardation: a problem of cause and effect. Am J Ment Defic 79:327–330, 1974

40. Helfer RE, Kempe CH (Eds): Child Abuse and Neglect. The Family and Community. Cambridge, Mass, Ballinger, 1976

41. Aber JL, Cicchetti D: The socio-emotional development of maltreated children: an empirical and theoretical analysis, in Theory and Research in Behavioral Pediatrics. Edited by Fitzgerald H, Lester B, Yogman M. New York, Plenum, 1984

42. Cicchetti D, Rosen KS: Theoretical and empirical considerations in the investigation of the relationship between affect and cognition in an atypical population of infants, in Emotion, Cognition and Behavior. Edited by Izard C, Kagan J, Zajonc R. New York, Cambridge University Press, 1984

43. Terr L: Chowchilla revisited: the effects of psychic trauma four years after a school bus kidnapping. Am J Psychiatry 140:1543–1550, 1983

44. Terr L: Time sense following psychiatric trauma: a clinical study of ten adults and twenty children. Am J Orthopsychiatry 53:244–261, 1983

45. Terr L: Chowchilla: The aftermath of a kidnapping. Paper presented at Symposium on Psychological Trauma in Children and Adults: Implications for Diagnosis and Treatment in Psychiatry. Boston, Mass, 30 November–1 December 1984

46. Torro PA: Developmental effects of child abuse: a review. Child Abuse Negl 6:423–431, 1982

47. Green AH: Generational transmission of violence in child abuse. Paper presented at Symposium on Psychological Trauma in Children and Adults: Implications for Diagnosis and Treatment in Psychiatry, Boston, Mass, 30 November–1 December 1984

48. Green AH: Dimension of psychological trauma in abused children. J Am Acad Child Psychiatry 22:231–237, 1983

49. Green AH: Psychopathology of abused children. J Am Acad Child Psychiatry 17:92–101, 1978

50. Helfer RE, McKiney JP, Kempe RE: Arresting or freezing the developmental process, in Child Abuse and Neglect, The Family and the Community. Edited by Helfer RE, Kempe CH. Cambridge, Mass, Ballinger, 1976

51. Oates RK: Child development after physical abuse. Arch Dis Child 59:147–150, 1984

52. Galdston R: Observations on children who have been physically abused and their parents. Am J Psychiatry 122:440–443, 1965

53. Newberger EH, Newberger CM, Hampton RL: Child abuse: the current theory base and future research needs. J Am Acad Child Psychiatry 22:262–268, 1963

54. van der Kolk BA, Ducey C: Clinical implications of the Rorschach in post traumatic stress disorder, in Post Traumatic Stress Disorder: Psychological and Biological Sequelae. Edited by van der Kolk BA. Washington, DC, American Psychiatric Press, 1984

55. Hilgard ER: Divided Consciousness. Multiple Controls in Human Thought and Action. New York, John Wiley & Sons, 1977

56. Mounoud P, Vinter A: A theoretical developmental model: self-image in children, in The Future of Piagetian Theory. The Neo-Piagetians. Edited by Shulman VL, Restaino-Baumann CR, Butler L. New York, Plenum Press, 1985

57. Piaget J: Play, Dreams and Imitation in Childhood. New York, WW Norton & Co, 1962

58. van der Kolk BA, Blitz R, Burr W, Sherry S, Hartmann E:

Nightmares and trauma: a comparison of nightmares after combat with lifelong nightmares in veterans. Am J Psychiatry 141:187–190, 1984

59. Noyes R, Hoenk PR, Kuperman S, Slyman DJ: Depersonalization in accident victims and psychiatric patients. J Nerv Ment Dis 164:401–407, 1977

60. Bliss EL: Multiple personality: a report of 14 cases with implications for schizophrenia and hysteria. Arch Gen Psychiatry 37:1388–1397, 1980

61. Rutter M (Ed): Developmental Neuropsychiatry. New York, Guilford Press, 1983

62. American Psychiatric Association: Diagnostic and Statistical Manual of Mental Disorders, 3rd ed. Washington, DC, American Psychiatric Association, 1980

63. Douglas VI: Attentional and cognitive problems: hyperkinetic/ attentional deficit syndrome, in Developmental Neuropsychiatry. Edited by Rutter M. New York, Guilford Press, 1983

CHAPTER 5

Traumatic Antecedents of Borderline Personality Disorder

Judith L. Herman, M.D.
Bessel A. van der Kolk, M.D.

In the past two decades, borderline personality disorder has become the subject of intensive theoretical and clinical investigation. Early descriptive formulations (1, 2) have been successively refined, culminating in the development of *Diagnostic and Statistical Manual of Mental Disorders*, Third Edition (DSM-III) (2a) criteria for a reliably identifiable syndrome (3, 4), stable over time (5), with quite serious morbidity (6, 7). The prevalence of this disorder in the general population is unknown; however, patients with this diagnosis represent between 10 and 25 percent of psychiatric inpatients (8–11). It is generally agreed that patients with borderline personality disorder are difficult to treat because of the intensity of their engagement with caregivers, the sometimes overwhelming nature of their demands for care, and the intense emotions and conflicts that they provoke in others (7, 12).

Most clinical descriptions of patients with borderline personality disorder identify disturbances in five major areas of functioning: 1) affect regulation, 2) impulse control, 3) reality testing, 4) interpersonal relationships, and 5) self-concept or identity formation (2, 7, 12–21). Consistent difficulties in affect regulation include unstable affect, intense affective reactivity to relatively

111

mild stimuli (including pervasive, apparently inappropriate anger and episodic severe anxiety), poor tolerance for unpleasant affect, chronic dysphoric mood with feelings of emptiness or boredom, and intermittent episodes of major depression. Consistent difficulties in impulse control and self-care often result in behaviors that are destructive to self or others, including substance abuse, risk-taking, promiscuous or perverse sexual activity, and violent outbursts. Self-mutilation, especially wrist-cutting, is very common in borderline patients and is considered by some authors to be almost pathognomonic for the disorder (7). Suicide attempts are also common.

Patients with borderline personality disorder generally demonstrate intact reality testing; under particular types of stress, however, brief lapses in reality testing occur and psychotic symptoms emerge. These symptoms generally involve alterations of perception, dissociative episodes, or paranoid ideas, and are usually reported as ego-dystonic. On psychological testing, borderline patients demonstrate generally intact functioning on structured tests but may show evidence of idiosyncratic and disorganized thinking on projective testing. Their fantasy productions on projective testing are described as either overly constricted (coarcted) or floridly bizarre (overideational) (22). Singer (23) attributes this characteristic test performance to the intrusion of highly personalized and affectively laden associations: "Borderline persons, as seen by testers, tend to add too much and too specific affect to simple perceptions."

Borderline patients are often described as unable to tolerate being alone and to seek emotional involvement with others actively (7, 18, 19). However, the relationships they establish are intensely conflictual and unstable. Desperate searching for a relationship of symbiotic closeness results in periods of brief intense attachment in which the other is idealized, alternating with rage or despairing withdrawal when the borderline patient's wishes for care are frustrated or disappointed (15). In these latter periods, the other person is furiously denigrated and devalued. Thus borderline patients are often described both as dependent and masochistic in their relations with others, and as exploitative, manipulative, and lacking in empathy.

Finally, borderline patients are generally described as having a diffuse, unstable, and poorly integrated sense of self (13, 14, 24). Such patients may have a deep conviction of utter badness, disguised by a persona that is not only poorly integrated but in fact perceived by the patient as a false self (7). Moreover, under certain types of stress, borderline patients are described as experiencing disintegration of the self and "annihilation panic" (12).

Attempts to conceptualize the underlying pathology of the borderline personality have generally invoked either a biologic, implicitly genetic model of affective disorder, or a psychodynamic model of developmental arrest. Investigators such as Klein (25), Akiskal (26), Akiskal et al. (27), Soloff and Millward (10), and Perry (28) have emphasized the strong association between borderline personality disorder and affective disorders. Perry (28) pointed out that the borderline patient's persistent difficulty in experiencing and regulating affect could be considered in itself a form of affective disorder. The lifetime likelihood for development of at least one episode of major depression is extremely high in borderline patients; the syndrome might best be considered an atypical variant of affective disorder (26–28). This biologic formulation, with its underlying assumption of genetic transmission, has inspired a number of studies of affective disorder in the first-degree relatives of borderline patients. The results of such studies indicate, however, that personality disorder, not affective disorder, is unusually common in such relatives, whereas affective disorder is found disproportionately in the relatives of patients with primary affective disorder (6, 10, 29, 30).

Psychodynamic formulations of the pathology of the borderline personality take as their point of reference the works of the British school of object-relations theorists, especially Mahler and colleagues (31, 32). The primary defect in the borderline patient is conceptualized as a relative failure to complete the tasks of self- and object-representation ordinarily accomplished in the second and third years of life, in the stage of separation–individuation. These developmental tasks include the achievement of object constancy: a stable inner representation of a comforting person that is sufficient to sustain ordinary periods of separation from a primary caretaker. Kernberg (13, 14) described the primary defect as an inability to synthesize good and bad internalized objects. Gunderson (7) conceptualized the defect as an arrest at the level of transitional object-relatedness, and Adler (12) described the fundamental psychopathology as a failure to achieve solid evocative memory in the area of object relations. While psychoanalytically oriented investigators are in broad agreement on the nature of the developmental arrest underlying the disorder, they differ in their hypotheses about the reasons for this arrest. Kernberg postulated constitutional factors such as an innate lack of anxiety tolerance and a heightened intensity of aggressive drives. Others postulated a pathological disturbance in the relationship between the child and primary caretakers. Maternal overinvolvement, clinging, and a punitive attitude toward the child's attempts at autonomous behavior are cited by Masterson and Rinsley (33) and by Zinner and Shapiro (34). These studies are generally anecdotal in nature and are not confirmed by more systematic investigations. Parental neglect and unprotectiveness are cited by Walsh (35), Frank and Paris (36), Gunderson (7), and Feldman and Guttman (37). Early, prolonged separation from or permanent loss of primary caretakers is described anecdotally by Adler (12) and demonstrated in a significant proportion of patients in retrospective studies by Bradley (38) and Akiskal et al. (27).

Curiously, the role of actual parental abuse in the development of this disorder has never been systematically investigated. Occasional case examples that include severe physical or sexual abuse in the background of borderline patients are found throughout the literature; generally these are reported without any comment on the possible impact of the trauma. In the main, the idea that borderline patients may in actuality have been severely abused tends to be discounted or dismissed as part of the patient's self-serving distortion of reality. Gunderson (7), for example, writes: "It is commonplace for the borderline patients to see themselves as having been repeatedly victimized and mistreated in a long series of previous relationships, often beginning with their parents." The possibility that this perception might have some validity is not considered.

Child abuse has been overlooked even by those investigators who have made the most painstaking and thorough explorations of the families of borderline patients. For example, Gunderson et al. (39) reviewed extensive case records from direct observations of families of 12 hospitalized borderline patients. Their 72-item rating scale included such items as marital discord, poor enforcement of rules, and parental neglect, but scrupulously avoided the mention of physical or sexual abuse. This perplexing omission may be attributable to the influence of the author's psychoanalytic paradigm, within which the reality of parental aggressions against children has traditionally been minimized, while the content of childhood fantasy has been the main focus of inquiry (40–45).

Clinical descriptions of borderline personality disorder, however, are remarkably congruent with descriptions of chronic post-traumatic stress disorder (PTSD), and especially with the form of the disorder described in patients who have been subjected to repeated trauma over a considerable period of time. In both syndromes, major disturbances are found in the areas of affect regulation, impulse control, reality testing, interpersonal relationships, and self-integration. Disturbances in affect regulation in patients with PTSD include poor affect tolerance (46–48), heightened aggression (46, 47), heightened reactivity to mild stimuli (46, 49, 50), irritability (46), chronic dysphoric mood, emptiness and inner deadness (48), and recurrent depression (51). Difficulties in impulse control include risk-taking behavior, self-mutilation, and drug and alcohol abuse. These behaviors are often interpreted as reenactments of trauma or as attempts to defend against the extreme distress associated with recurrent intrusive memories of trauma (50). Brief episodic disturbances in reality testing include dissociative episodes and paranoid ideas of reference. On projective psychological testing, patients with combat-induced PTSD give responses similar to those described for borderline patients: their protocols are either barren and constricted, or filled with florid, affectively laden material. Alternations between these two extreme types of response may be observed in individual patients over time (52). Disturbances in interpersonal relations may be seen in PTSD after a single trauma, such as street rape (53–60), and become increasingly common and pervasive in patients who have been subjected to repeated, prolonged victimization, such as battered women (61, 62) or abused children (43, 63–67) (Chapter 4). Adults with a history of childhood sexual victimization show persistent disturbances in interpersonal relations that result in high rates of marital failure and repeated victimization (42, 68, 69). Their relationships are characterized by alternating periods of intense searching for closeness with an idealized other person, during which they may put themselves at risk for further exploitation, and angry or despairing withdrawal, with furious denigration of others (42, 70–74). Finally, loss of an integrated sense of self is observed transiently in well-functioning adults after a single acute trauma (53–56). Disturbance in identity formation is observed as a persistent problem in patients known to have been subjected to chronic recurrent trauma in childhood. Such patients display identity diffusion, splitting of the good and bad self, and a relentless sense of inner badness essentially indistinguishable from the phenomena described in borderline patients (42, 72–75).

Indeed, the most significant descriptive discrepancy between borderline personality disorder and chronic PTSD is the absence in the criteria for borderline personality disorder of a recognizable stressor in the patient's history. We contend that traumatic stressors may indeed figure significantly in the etiology of borderline personality disorder. Such stressors may not have been previously identified for several reasons. First, and most importantly, no research specifically addressing this question has ever been done. Second, questions regarding childhood experiences of abuse are not generally integrated into standard clinical assessment of patients. Third, even when such histories are obtained, the connection between trauma and symptomatology is often unexplored. For example, Kernberg (personal communication, 1985) acknowledged that histories of physical or sexual abuse are common in his borderline patients but states that it is "hard to know what to make of it." Finally, without careful probing by clinicians who are sensitive to the emotional impact of childhood abuse, many patients do not disclose such experiences, either because they find them deeply shameful or because their memories for such experiences are repressed.

The hypothesis that childhood trauma plays a significant role in the development of borderline personality disorder offers a possible explanation for the overwhelming predominance of this disorder in women. Every major study reports a significant majority of female patients with this diagnosis, ranging from 67 to 87 percent (6, 10, 19, 20, 27, 30). This gender difference in prevalence of the disorder is usually reported without comment, and most attempts at conceptual formulation offer no explanation of this finding. Some (6, 7) have suggested that male patients with this diagnosis may be more likely to express their anger in overt violence against others, and as a result to be diagnosed as having an antisocial rather than borderline personality disorder. We propose, alternatively, that the observed gender difference in borderline personality disorder may be a real phenomenon, related to the greater vulnerability of girls to prolonged, sustained abuse in childhood. The prevalence data on child abuse indicate that while boys and girls are at approximately equal risk for physical abuse, girls are at two to three times greater risk for sexual victimization (76, 77). Moreover, sexual abuse is apparently more prevalent, and often more prolonged, than physical abuse (78). If childhood abuse should prove to be an important antecedent to the development of borderline personality disorder, the greater frequency of such abuse experiences in girls might explain the higher prevalence of borderline personality disorder in women.

Suggestive clinical evidence in support of our hypothesis may be found in descriptive studies of abused and borderline children, in studies documenting the traumatic antecedents of multiple personality disorder, and in pilot data from three clinical sites on adult borderline patients. Clinical studies of borderline children (79, 80) described extreme sensitivity and physical reactivity to stimulation, inability to modulate anxiety, a preoccupation with themes of mutilation and death, and fear of annihilation. Borderline children are also described as emotionally constricted in their thinking and their play. With authority figures they are described as either eager to please or withdrawn, while they may bully and torment younger and weaker children. Essentially identical observations are reported by investigators who have studied children with an identified history of abuse (63–67, 81, 82). Bowlby (43), in an extensive review of clinical and experimental studies of abused children, described the same constellation of heightened anxiety and aggression, ego constriction, and disturbed relationships with caretakers and peers. A particularly poignant consequence of this syndrome is the response that abused children arouse in others. Because of their ambivalent, approach–avoidance behavior and their unprovoked hostile attacks, such children often provoke intense negative reactions even in the most well-intentioned caregivers. These reactions are quite similar to those experienced by clinicians who attempt to work with adult borderline patients. Pertinent also are Green's (66) observations of self-mutilating behavior in abused children, which may be an early precursor of the wrist-cutting seen in adolescent and adult borderline patients. Finally, in one study of borderline children, a history of physical abuse was in fact documented in 10 of the 24 children. Of the 24, 22 were thought to come from a "chaotic" household in which the threat of violence was regularly present (80).

Recent studies of adult patients with multiple personality disorder have established the etiological role of severe childhood abuse in the development of this syndrome (83, 84). Using hypnosis, Bliss (85) was able to document the role of specific traumatic events such as sexual and physical abuse in the formation of alter personalities in nine patients with multiple personality disorder. Patients with multiple personality disorder resemble borderline patients in many respects: indeed Horevitz and Braun (86) found that 70 percent of patients with an established diagnosis of multiple personality disorder also qualified for the diagnosis of borderline personality disorder by DSM-III criteria. Like borderline patients, patients with multiple personality disorder have extreme reactions (often including the emergence of alter personalities) to relatively mild environmental stimuli. The inability to make a connection between current anxiety states and repressed historical events leaves these patients unable to modulate their affective response to mild environmental stressors. The use of dissociation and the fragmentation of self commonly observed in borderline patients is carried to the extreme in patients with multiple personality disorder.

Data from three pilot studies offer suggestive evidence that histories of childhood abuse may be found in the majority of borderline patients, and that this finding, although common in the general patient population, is significantly more common in patients with a borderline diagnosis. In a study of 190 consecutive psychiatric outpatients at an urban teaching hospital, Herman (87) found that 8 of 12 patients (67 percent) diagnosed as borderline according to DSM-III criteria had a history of abuse in childhood or adolescence. Such histories were found in only 22 percent of the patient population as a whole. A study of 12 hospitalized borderline patients reported by Stone (88) indicated that 75 percent had a history of incest. Finally, in the most methodologically rigorous study completed to date, Nelson and her colleagues (unpublished manuscript) identified 14 borderline patients by DSM-III criteria among 100 consecutive inpatients in a private psychiatric hospital. Of these 14, 12 (86 percent) had a history of sexual abuse prior to age 16. The comparable figure for the entire patient population was 34 percent. While all of these studies involve small numbers of patients, their findings are quite consistent and provide sufficient suggestive evidence in favor of our hypothesis to warrant further, more systematic investigation.

Our hypothesis implicating childhood traumatic events in the development of borderline personality disorder, if confirmed, offers the potential for further development and refinement of the current psychodynamic understanding of borderline personality disorder. It also offers the possibility of developing a biological model of the disorder that does not rely on an implicit genetic premise, but rather on known models of trauma-induced psychophysiologic changes (89). It draws from ethologic concepts of Bowlby (43) and others who conceptualize human attachment and caregiving systems as biologically based as well as socially learned, and recognizes the possibility that early experiences of violence, especially those that occur within the developing child's system of primary attachments, may produce both psychological and psychophysiologic disorders (see Chapter 2). Thus our formulation offers the potential for integrating psychodynamic and biological understanding of this difficult and troubling syndrome.

Finally, our hypothesis has direct clinical implications for the treatment of borderline personality disorder. Clinical literature on the treatment of PTSD repeatedly cites the importance of recovery and integration of traumatic memories with their associated affects, and the necessity for validation of the patient's traumatic experiences. The integration of the trauma is a precondition for development of improved affect tolerance, impulse control, and defensive organization; the validation of the trauma is a precondition for restoration of an integrated self-identity and the capacity for appropriate relationships with others (42, 48, 50, 90–96). PTSD is often undiagnosed in cases in which secrecy or stigma prevent recognition of the traumatic origins of the disorder. Such patients often improve dramatically when the connection between symptoms and trauma is recognized and appropriate treatment is instituted. We believe that some of the negative therapeutic reactions so frequently observed in borderline patients might be avoided by early and appropriate recognition of the relationship between the patient's current symptomatology and its origins in a traumatic history.

References

1. Knight R: Borderline states. Bull Menninger Clin 17:1–12, 1953

2. Grinker R, Werble B, Drye R: The Borderline Syndrome: A Behavioral Study of Ego Functions. New York, Basic Books, 1968

2a. American Psychiatric Association: Diagnostic and Statistical Manual of Mental Disorders. 3rd ed. Washington, DC, American Psychiatric Association, 1980

3. Spitzer R, Endicott J: Justification for separating schizotypal and borderline personality disorders. Schizophr Bull 5:95–104, 1979

4. Frances A, Clarkin JF, Gilmore M, et al: Reliability of criteria for borderline personality disorder: a comparison of DSM-III and the diagnostic interview for borderline patients. Am J Psychiatry 141:1080–1084, 1984

5. Barasch A, Frances AJ, Hurt S, et al: Stability and distinctness of borderline personality disorder. Am J Psychiatry 142:1484–1486, 1985

6. Pope H, Jonas J, Hudson J, et al: The validity of DSM-III borderline personality disorder. Arch Gen Psychiatry 40:23–30, 1983

7. Gunderson JG: Borderline Personality Disorder. Washington, DC, American Psychiatric Press, 1984

8. Kroll J, Sines L, Martin K, et al: Borderline personality disorder: construct validity of the concept. Arch Gen Psychiatry 38:1021–1026, 1981

9. Andrulonis P, Glueck B, Stroebell C, et al: Borderline personality subcategories. J Nerv Ment Dis 170:670–679, 1982

10. Soloff P, Millward J: Psychiatric disorders in the families of borderline patients. Arch Gen Psychiatry 40:37–44, 1983

11. McGlashan T: The Chestnut Lodge follow-up study. II: long-term outcome of borderline personalities. Arch Gen Psychiatry 41:586–601, 1984

12. Adler G: Borderline Psychopathology and Its Treatment. New York, Jason Aronson, 1985

13. Kernberg O: Borderline personality organization. J Am Psychoanal Assoc 15:641–685, 1967

14. Kernberg O: Borderline Conditions and Pathological Narcissism. New York, Jason Aronson, 1975

15. Grinker R, Werble B (eds): The Borderline Patient. New York, Jason Aronson, 1977

16. Rinsley D: An object-relations view of borderline personality, in Borderline Personality Disorders: The Concept, the Syndrome, the Patient. Edited by Harticollis P. New York, International Universities Press, 1977

17. Rinsley D: Borderline and Other Self Disorders. New York, Jason Aronson, 1982

18. Spitzer R, Endicott J, Gibbon M: Crossing the border into borderline personality and borderline schizophrenia: the development of criteria. Arch Gen Psychiatry 36:17–24, 1979

19. Perry JC, Klerman G: Clinical features of the borderline personality disorder. Am J Psychiatry 137:165–173, 1980

20. Sheehy M, Goldsmith I, Charles E: A comparative study of

borderline patients in a psychiatric outpatient clinic. Am J Psychiatry 137:1374–1379, 1980

21. Mack J (ed): Borderline States in Psychiatry. New York, Grune & Stratton, 1975

22. Rapaport D, Gill MM, Schafer R: Diagnostic Psychological Testing. Chicago, Year Book, 1945–1946

23. Singer M: The borderline diagnosis and psychological tests: review and research, in Borderline Personality Disorders: The Concept, the Syndrome, the Patient. Edited by Harticollis P. New York, International Universities Press, 1977

24. Searles HF: Dual- and multiple identity processes in borderline ego functioning, in Borderline Personality Disorders: The Concept, the Syndrome, the Patient. Edited by Harticollis P. New York, International Universities Press, 1977

25. Klein D: Psychopharmacology and the borderline patient, in Borderline States in Psychiatry. Edited by Mack J. New York, Grune & Stratton, 1975

26. Akiskal HS: Sub-affective disorders, dysthymic, cyclothymic and bipolar II disorders in the borderline realm. Psychiatr Clin North Am 4:25–46, 1981

27. Akiskal HS, Chen SE, Davis GC, et al: Borderline: an adjective in search of a noun. J Clin Psychiatry 46:41–47, 1985

28. Perry JC: Depression in borderline personality disorder: lifetime prevalence at interview and longitudinal course of symptoms. Am J Psychiatry 142:15–21, 1985

29. Stone M, Kahn E, Flye B: Psychiatrically ill relatives of borderline patients: a family study. Psychiatr Q 53:71–84, 1981

30. Loranger AW, Oldham JM, Tulis EH: Familial transmission of DSM-III borderline personality disorder. Arch Gen Psychiatry 39:795–799, 1982

31. Mahler MS, Pine F, Bergman A: The Psychological Birth of the Human Infant. New York, Basic Books, 1975

32. Mahler M, Kaplan L: Developmental aspects in the assessment of narcissistic and so-called borderline personalities, in Borderline Personality Disorders: The Concept, the Syndrome, the Patient. Edited by Harticollis P. New York, International Universities Press, 1977

33. Masterson J, Rinsley D: The borderline syndrome: the role of the mother in the genesis and psychic structure of the borderline personality. Int J Psychoanal 56:163–177, 1975

34. Zinner J, Shapiro E: Splitting in families of borderline adolescents, in Borderline States in Psychiatry. Edited by Mack J. New York, Grune & Stratton, 1975

35. Walsh F: The family of the borderline patient, in The Borderline Patient. Edited by Grinker R, Werble B. New York, Jason Aronson, 1977

36. Frank H, Paris J: Recollections of family experience in borderline patients. Arch Gen Psychiatry 38:1031–1034, 1981

37. Feldman RB, Guttman HA: Families of borderline patients: literal-minded parents, borderline parents, and parental protectiveness. Am J Psychiatry 141:1392–1396, 1984

38. Bradley SJ: The relationship of early maternal separation to borderline personality in children and adolescents: a pilot study. Am J Psychiatry 136:424–426, 1979

39. Gunderson JG, Kerr J, Englund D: The families of borderlines: a comparative study. Arch Gen Psychiatry 37:27–33, 1980

40. Herman JL, Hirschman L: Father-daughter incest. Signs: Journal of Women in Culture and Society 2:735–756, 1977

41. Rush F: The Best Kept Secret: Sexual Abuse of Children. Englewood Cliffs, NJ, Prentice-Hall, 1980

42. Herman JL: Father-Daughter Incest. Cambridge, Mass, Harvard University Press, 1981

43. Bowlby J: Violence in the family as a disorder of the attachment and caregiving systems. Am J. Psychoanal 44:9–27, 1984

44. Masson JM: The Assault on Truth: Freud's Suppression of the Seduction Theory. New York, Farrar, Straus & Giroux, 1984

45. Miller A: Thou Shalt Not Be Aware: Society's Betrayal of the Child. New York, Farrar, Straus & Giroux, 1984

46. Kardiner A: The Traumatic Neuroses of War. New York, P Hoeber, 1941

47. Krystal H: Trauma and affects. Psychoanal Study Child 33:81–116, 1978

48. Horowitz MJ: Stress Response Syndromes. New York, Jason Aronson, 1976

49. van der Kolk BA: Psychopharmacological issues in post-traumatic stress. Hosp Community Psychiatry 34:683–691, 1983

50. van der Kolk BA: The trauma response as a biopsychosocial entity, in Long-Term Effects of Violence: Cross-Cultural, Treatment, and Research Issues in PTSD. Edited by Garrison J. Washington, DC, National Institute of Mental Health, 1986

51. Niederland WG: An interpretation of the psychological stresses an defenses in concentration camp life and the late aftereffects, in Massive Psychic Trauma. Edited by Krystal H. New York, International Universities Press, 1968

52. van der Kolk BA, Ducey CP: Clinical implications of the Rorschach in post-traumatic stress, in Post Traumatic Stress Disorder: Psychological and Biological Sequelae. Edited by van der Kolk BA. Washington, DC, American Psychiatric Press, 1984

53. Burgess AW, Holmstrom LL: Rape: Victims of Crisis. Englewood Cliffs, NJ, Prentice-Hall 1974

54. Burgess AW, Holmstrom LL: Adaptive strategies and recovery from rape. Am J Psychiatry 136:1278–1282, 1979

55. Burgess AW, Holmstrom LL: Rape trauma syndrome and post traumatic stress response, in Rape and Sexual Assault: A Research Handbook. Edited by Burgess AW. New York, Garland, 1985

56. Hilberman E: The Rape Victim. Washington, DC, American Psychiatric Association, 1976

57. Kilpatrick DG, Veronen LJ, Resick PA: The aftermath of rape: recent empirical findings. Am J Orthopsychiatry 49:658–669, 1979

58. Kilpatrick DG, Resick PA, Veronen LJ: Effects of the rape experience: a longitudinal study. Journal of Social Issues 37:105–122, 1981

59. Nadelson C, Notman M, Zackson H, et al: A follow-up study of rape victims. Am J Psychiatry 139:1266–1270, 1982

60. Becker J, Skinner L, Abel G: Sequelae of sexual assault: the survivor's perspective, in The Sexual Aggressor: Current Perspectives on Treatment. Edited by Greer J, Stuart I. New York, Van Nostrand Reinhold Co, 1983

61. Walker LE: The Battered Woman. New York, Harper & Row, 1979

62. Hilberman E: Overview: the "wife-beater's wife" reconsidered. Am J Psychiatry 137:1336–1347, 1980

63. Gaensbauer TJ, Sands K: Distorted affective communication in abused/neglected infants and their potential impact on caretakers. J Am Acad Child Psychiatry 18:236–250, 1979

64. George C, Main M: Social interactions of young abused children: approach, avoidance, and aggression. Child Dev 50:306–318, 1979

65. Lynch M, Roberts J: Consequences of Child Abuse. London, Academic Press, 1982

66. Green A: Child abuse: dimensions of psychological trauma in abused children. J Am Acad Child Psychiatry 22:231–237, 1983

67. Gomes-Schwartz B, Horowitz J, Sauzier M: Sexually Exploited Children: Service and Research Project. Washington, DC, US Office of Juvenile Justice and Delinquency Prevention, 1984

68. Herman JL, Russell DE, Trocki K: Long-term effects of incestuous abuse in childhood. Am J Psychiatry (in press)

69. Russell DEH: The Secret Trauma: Incest in the Lives of Girls and Women, New York, Basic Books, 1986

70. Meiselman K: Incest. San Francisco, Jossey-Bass, 1978

71. Goodwin J: Sexual Abuse: Incest Victims and Their Families. Boston, John Wright, 1982

72. Summit R: Beyond belief: the reluctant discovery of incest, in Women's Sexual Experience. Edited by Kirkpatrick M. New York, Plenum, 1982

73. Gelinas DJ: The persisting negative effects of incest. Psychiatry 46:312–332, 1983

74. Carmen EH, Rieker PP, Mills T: Victims of violence and psychiatric illness. Am J Psychiatry 141: 378–383, 1984

75. Goodwin J: Post-traumatic symptoms in incest victims, in Post-Traumatic Stress Disorder in Children. Edited by Eth S, Pynoos RS. Washington, DC, American Psychiatric Press, 1985

76. Finkelhor D: Sexually Victimized Children. New York, Free Press, 1979

77. Finkelhor D: Child Sexual Abuse: New Theory and Research. New York, Free Press, 1984

78. Pagelow M: Family Violence. New York, Praeger, 1984

79. Frijling-Schreuder EC: Borderline states in children. Psychoanal Study Child 24:307–327, 1970

80. Bemporad JR, Smith HF, Hanson G, et al: Borderline syndromes in childhood: criteria for diagnosis. Am J Psychiatry 139:596–602, 1982

81. Burgess AW, Groth AN, Holmstrom LL, et al: Sexual Assault of Children and Adolescents. Lexington, Mass, DC Heath & Co, 1978

82. Adams-Tucker C: Proximate effects of sexual abuse in childhood: a report on 28 children. Am J Psychiatry 139:1252–1256, 1982

83. Putnam FW, Post RM, Guroff JJ, et al: One hundred cases of multiple personality disorder. J Clin Psychiatry 47:285–293, 1986

84. Sachs R, Goodwin J, Braun B: The role of childhood abuse in the development of multiple personality, in Multiple Personality and Dissociation. Edited by Braun B, Kluft R. New York, Guilford, 1986

85. Bliss EL: Multiple personalities: a report of 14 cases with implications for schizophrenia and hysteria. Arch Gen Psychiatry 37:1388–1397, 1980

86. Horevitz RP, Braun BG: Are multiple personalities borderline? Psychiatr Clin North Am 7:69–87, 1984

87. Herman JL: Histories of violence in an outpatient population. Am J Orthopsychiatry 57:137–141, 1986

88. Stone MH: Borderline syndromes: a consideration of subtypes and an overview, directions for research. Psychiatr Clin North Am 4:3–13, 1981

89. van der Kolk BA, Greenberg M, Boyd H, et al: Inescapable shock, neurotransmitters, and addiction to trauma: toward a psychobiology of post traumatic stress. Biol Psychiatry 20:314–325, 1985

90. Niederland WG: The role of the ego in the recovery of early memories. Psychoanal Q 34:564–571, 1965

91. Blank AS: Lessons learned from treatment of combat veterans. Paper presented at NIMH Services Research and Evaluation Colloquium: The Aftermath of Crime: A Mental Health Crisis. Washington, DC 1985

92. Danieli Y: The treatment and prevention of long-term effects and intergenerational transmission of victimization: a lesson from holocaust survivors and their children, in Trauma and Its Wake. Edited by Figley CR. New York, Brunner/Mazel, 1985

93. Donaldson MA, Gardner R: Diagnosis and treatment of traumatic stress among women after childhood incest, in Trauma and Its Wake. Edited by Figley CR. New York, Brunner/Mazel, 1985

94. Frederick CJ: Post-traumatic stress reactions of victims of violence and crime. Paper presented at NIMH Services Research and Evaluation Colloquium: The Aftermath of Crime: A Mental Health Crisis. Washington, DC, 1985

95. Scurfield RM: Post-trauma stress assessment and treatment: overview and formulations, in Trauma and Its Wake. Edited by Figley CR. New York, Brunner/Mazel, 1985

96. van der Kolk BA: The drug treatment of post-traumatic stress. Psychiatr Med (in press)

CHAPTER 6

Trauma in the Family: Perspectives on the Intergenerational Transmission of Violence

Steven Krugman, Ph.D

The human response to sudden and overwhelming events is increasingly recognized as a stable psychological entity (see Chapter 1). Horowitz (1), Burgess and Holmstrom (2), Figley (3), Green et al. (4), and van der Kolk (5) have described a consistent psychological and physiological pattern, the posttraumatic stress response, which involves intense feelings of vulnerability and rage. This pattern is remarkably constant across a great range of extremely stressful situations (e.g., life-threatening combat, criminal victimization, natural disasters). Some elements of the trauma response are likely to occur in most people, regardless of previous level of adjustment (6).

The trauma syndrome is actually a continuous range of reactions (7). In addition to the classic biphasic alternation of denial and intrusion described by Horowitz (1), there are two other long-term effects: secondary elaboration (8) and posttraumatic decline (9). Secondary elaboration is a characterological adaptation to traumatization that includes depression, avoidance of intimacy,

The author wishes to acknowledge the contribution and support of Bessel van der Kolk, M.D., and Pat Reiker, Ph.D.

and "relational distortions." These features are most evident when the trauma has been neither acknowledged nor treated as such. Posttraumatic decline is an impoverishment of activity and role functioning secondary to psychological constriction and phobic avoidance.

The trauma model now being developed includes hypothesized links to basic biological and neurohormonal processes (see Chapter 3), learning theory (10, 11), and attribution theory (12). It also recognizes the crucial role played by contextual variables (13, 14).

Contemporary studies of trauma and its aftermath have largely emphasized individual, intrapsychic responses, although most researchers recognize that contextual factors are important in determining the meaning of the traumatic event and in promoting or impeding recovery. The limitations of this individual approach become clear on consideration of the role of the family and the community. Traumatization often begins in the family with wife battering and the physical and sexual abuse of children (15). The family can also be crucial in protecting its members from traumatization and helping them recover (16–19). Thus the family is critical to vulnerability, recovery, and resilience. Clinicians must also keep in mind that the family as a whole suffers traumatization when one or more of its members is overwhelmed by outside events.

Traumatic Violence Within Families

The signs of posttraumatic stress disorder in battered women and sexually or physically abused children are unmistakable. Hilberman (20) and Hilberman and Munson (21) reported that the battered women in their sample "were a study in paralyzing terror that was reminiscent of the rape trauma syndrome, except that the stress was unending and the threat of assault ever present." They go on to describe a full array of posttraumatic symptoms, including agitation and anxiety, startle, chronic apprehension and vigilance, sleep disturbance and nightmare, depression, and passivity. Green (14) wrote,

> During the initial stages of treatment of the abused child, when the violent and assaultive behavior of the parents is still occurring . . . anxiety states, in which the children experience feelings of panic and helplessness, are often manifested. . . . Ego functioning is frequently paralyzed with a marked regression in behavior.

Over a longer term, particularly when untreated, victims of intrafamilial violence often suffer from delayed or chronic posttraumatic stress disorder. For example, Donaldson and Gardner (22) reported that 25 of 26 women who requested treatment for the effects of childhood incest fit the *Diagnostic and Statistical Manual of Mental Disorders*, Third Edition (DSM-III) (6) criteria for posttraumatic stress disorder, delayed or chronic.

The developmental impact of traumatic abuse on a family is complex. Traumatic experience is only one major factor shaping the lives of victims of battering, abuse, or incest. The families in which these events occur are never otherwise normal; there are usually high levels of stress (e.g., poverty, unemployment, single parents alone with large families), poor interpersonal boundaries, character disorders, alcoholism, and other serious problems. The violence erupts from distorted family relations in a disturbed, frequently pathological emotional and social context. To add to the complexity, abuse rarely occurs only once. Usually, there are many incidents, sometimes involving more than one perpetrator and more than one victim. The developmental age of the victim and stage of the relationship with the perpetrator must also be considered in determining whether and in what way a particular incident or experience is or is not traumatic. Above all, the meanings assigned the abuse by the victim, the family, and the community largely determine how the experiences are encoded in memory.

Traumatic experience is central in organizing, structuring, and reproducing the emotional, interpersonal, and systemic features common to abusive and intrusive families. Despite some important differences between abuse, incest, and battering, the family dynamics, structures, and intergenerational features are common to all three types of abuse. All cause victims, perpetrators, and others in the family to rely heavily on denial, avoidance, projection, and splitting. All three disorders place victims at risk of being victimized again, victimizing others, or transmitting vulnerability to their children. All three are characterized by secrecy, reluctant disclosure, disguised presentation, and resistance to treatment; all have serious social and legal consequences and require social and legal remedies. Finklehor et al. (23) pointed to another similarity: intrafamilial abuse is an abuse of power, flowing generally from the stronger to the weaker, older to younger, male to female, in which abusers compensate for their perceived lack or loss of power in the family as well as in the outside world.

The trauma model, while not pretending to be a complete explanation (24), must integrate many of these psychological, interpersonal, and cultural data connecting traumatization with the structure and character of physically abusive and sexually intrusive families. For example, how does a child's victimization make revictimization or growing into an abusive adult more likely? How does witnessing abuse of one's mother increase the risk of becoming an abusive parent or husband?

To use the construct of trauma fully, two conditions must be met. First, the definition of a traumatic event must be specific (6, 7). Second, the impact of trauma as it radiates through all levels of the victim's biopsychosocial system must be elaborated. Thus one must consider not only the individual's symptoms, but also the way in which the event colors the individual's experience of the ecosphere (25) and organizes his or her interpersonal world, including the behavior of significant others. Further, some explanation must be given for secondary elaboration. The traumatic experience shapes and is shaped by the family's interpersonal dynamics (26) and its relationship with the larger community (11, 25, 27). The trauma model makes certain assumptions about the developmental history of family members.

1. *A formative traumatic experience.* A parent or child in this generation or the previous one has experienced or witnessed traumatic violations of attachment, such as battering, physical abuse, or sexual abuse. This experience has caused a posttraumatic stress response that includes flooding affect, helplessness and vulnerability, shattered trust, and the use of emergency defenses to cope with intolerable thoughts and feelings.

2. *The trauma conditions the microsystem.* The initial trauma is an extraordinary event. Abuse victims often retain vivid, eidetic images of violent incidents. The experience is so intense that certain interpersonal situations, feelings, voice tones, topics, locations, and so on become associated with traumatization and become subject to defensive organization and control. The impact of trauma may be linked or heightened by variables such as the intensity and duration of the assault, the relationship of the assailant to the victim, and the presence of others who are protective and soothing. The self, the organization of interpersonal behavior, and the ecosphere are all affected, although not necessarily equally affected.

3. *Emotional life organized to avoid traumatic memory and feeling.* The traumatized person often develops a chronic character disorder in defense against recurrence of the traumatic memory. The unresolved and unintegrated traumatic experience

affects cognitive functioning, object relations, and interpersonal skills, leaving the victim with maladaptive first-order defenses (8, 9), constricted ego functioning, and distorted role relations. This secondary elaboration of posttraumatic responses into chronic character pathology is most likely to occur when either the abuse is repetitive or neither parent is capable of rapproachment and soothing, leaving the protective function of the family chronically disabled.

4. *Normalizing maltreatment.* As the individual becomes inured to the abuse, the extraordinary becomes more ordinary, more predictable, and therefore easier to defend against. New abusive or intrusive incidents cause varying degrees of posttraumatic stress that, along with family conflict and ecological stress, reinforce maladaptive behavior patterns. More and more of the self comes to be organized in ways designed to ward off further vulnerability.

5. *Vulnerability of traumatized systems.* When two previously traumatized adults marry, defensive adaptations to traumatic experience shape and limit the relational structure of the new family. Trauma-driven deficits in cognitive, emotional, and interpersonal skills limit frustration tolerance, problem solving, and conflict resolution. Such families lack many basic social skills, avoid anxiety-arousing situations, and rely heavily on alcohol and drugs. They have poor boundaries and difficulty separating. They are often socially isolated, psychologically impoverished, and vulnerable to stress of all kinds.

Traumatic Intrafamilial Violence: A Multilevel Analysis

The Intrapsychic Consequences of Traumatic Abuse

Like other human-borne trauma, intrafamilial abuse damages the human bond. Greene (14) wrote that "it is hard to imagine anything more terrifying to an infant or young child than to be punched, kicked, burned, or hurled across the room without warning by an uncontrolled parental figure from whom nurturance and protection are usually expected." As Steele (28) observed, such children feel fundamentally unprotected. The parent no longer serves as an "auxiliary stimulus barrier" (29), and the child must find ways to preserve the integrity of the self in the face of profound vulnerability and narcissistic injury. Emergency measures are needed in defense, but these attempts to cope often become maladaptive. Child victims of abuse try to maintain the connection to the parent even at great cost to themselves. Basic trust, secure attachment, and self-esteem are among the casualties. The problems are compounded by the resulting irritability, hypervigilance, nightmares, learning disabilities, and passivity and withdrawal or hyperactivity and aggression.

Many sexually abused children respond to overwhelming feelings and forced silence (30) with dissociation and depersonalization (31, 32). Depression, reenactment, and self-destructive behavior are common in girls (8, 13, 31). Other consequences are hypersexuality and sexual dysfunction, along with phobic avoidance and somatization. Boy victims tend to become aggressive and to victimize children (33, 34). Research data and clinical experience suggest that witnessing violence between parents causes the child to develop deficits in empathy, behavior problems, and diminished self-esteem, while fostering premature caretaking of the parent by the child (35, 36).

Parent–Child Dyad

Abusive and intrusive behavior is transmitted primarily from parent to child (37–39). Mother–child interactional patterns have their origins in the mother's experience in her own family. A history of traumatization producing ego deficits, developmental deviations, and insecure interpersonal relations sets the stage for a maladaptive family environment in the next generation. "Although abusive parents are diagnostically heterogeneous, they are homogeneous with respect to certain traits that cut across diagnostic classes" (40). Bowlby (37) observed that while abusive parents vary in personality, they share a "proneness to intense anxiety punctuated by outbursts of violent anger."

Arousal and Empathy

Studies comparing abusive mothers with neglectful and control mothers (41–43) show that abusive mothers are more irritable and physiologically aroused, respond less to changes in infant signals, and find crying more aversive. They are deficient in the ability to use fantasy to engage the child in play, and in "mastering the stresses of parenting" (44). Although most of the reported data do not indicate whether these mothers were themselves maltreated as children, their behavior suggests a posttraumatic adaptation. Van der Kolk (5) suggested that the hyperarousal, irritability, and an easily evoked startle response are basic physiological features of the trauma response. He also pointed out that traumatized individuals tend to have reduced capacity for fantasy and a poor discrimination of arousing stimuli.

A critical link in the transmission sequence is the damaged capacity for empathy, a consistent finding in the literature (24, 40, 44). In my own clinical experience, abusive parents often show a bewildering lack of remorse and failure to feel the child's pain. Belsky (27) argued that they are not affected by the child's suffering, partly because they themselves never received the warmth and caring necessary to develop the capacity to put themselves in the child's position. Boszormenyi-Nagy and Spark (45) explained abusive rage as the result of a cycle of exploitation, deprivation, and entitlement. Parents who have been exploited as children feel entitled to gratification and caretaking from their own children. If the child is ungratifying or does not meet developmentally inappropriate demands, parental rage is unleashed with little or no remorse. Steele (28) noted that abused parents, under stress, "give priority" to their own needs, "as if responding to the need to ward off traumatic anxiety." In the face of repeated narcissistic injury without protection, containment, and caring, abused children are unlikely to develop the capacity for empathy. Rohner (46) suggested that it is "the general experience of parental rejection" in childhood, and not "exposure or subjection to violence and aggression per se," that is associated with later abusive and neglectful behavior. In other words, it may be the absence of parental soothing and of an opportunity to repair the broken connection that encodes abuse as traumatic.

Anxious Attachment

Bowlby (37) suggested that the diminished capacity for empathy, low self-esteem, heightened dependency, and low frustration tolerance of abusive parents engenders feelings of insecure attachment in children, particularly traumatized children. Insecure attachment arises when the parent is unable or unwilling to respond to the child's needs. Although it may have many different causes, the most common are commensurate with a traumatic history. It is associated not only with ongoing spouse abuse and other trauma, but also with narcissistic unavailability, depression, alcoholism, and somatic preoccupation, all of which may themselves be the results of traumatization. Anxious attachment becomes critical in structuring family relations. The terrible inconsistency in this type of parent–child relationship creates anxiety over separation and abandonment alternating with avoidance of closeness and outright rejection. Bowlby noted that "careseeking" behavior is heightened by pain and distress. Van der Kolk (5) stated that "people, in fear, attach to anyone, even bad attachments." Abuse engenders this condition in children. Like their parents, they develop an intense need for closeness and support, combined with a fear of being hurt and abandoned. The clinging vigilance often displayed by abused children results from this dilemma. The abusing mother, irritable, intensely self-critical, and ungratified, pushes the demanding child away and punishes. Some effects in the child are fear of parents or other adults, withdrawal, listlessness, hyperactivity or repetitive motor activity, and persistent irritability among abused children (47). When the anxiously attached child seeks care, it is likely to be subject to further rejection and abusive violence.

Identification and Reenactment

The abused child, feeling helpless, frustrated, and impotently enraged, diminishes its vulnerability by splitting the image of the abusive parent into "good" and "bad" parts. The good parent introject is maintained as a protective and nurturant object, while the child sees himself as bad and therefore to blame for the abuse. At the same time, the child identifies with the aggressor and transforms its "fears of helplessness and annihilation . . . replacing them by feelings of power and omnipotence" (8).

In sexual abuse, especially when the sexual contact is traumatic, the child protects its sense of self by means of a profound splitting of its inner world. Not only are the protective and abusive parts of the parent split off and incorporated as "part objects," but the self object is also subject to dissociative defenses (32, 48). In the most extreme instance, multiple personalities arise to cope with the intensity of the feelings. Gender is a critical variable. Hilberman (20), Carmen et al. (13), and Galdston (49) observed that abused boys are more aggressive and more likely to identify with the aggressor. Girls are found to be more isolated and clinging, and are more likely to form a conscious identification with the victim, becoming depressed and self-destructive. On becoming parents, they experience these identifications with their own parent as abuser and as victim. "Flipping of the identification" then makes them abuse their own children (28).

Traumatic repetition does not occur only in parent–child relationships. Traumatized individuals have a more general tendency to re-create situations that resemble the original traumatic event, both within the family and in the world at large. This has been explained as undoing, as an attempt at mastery (1), and as acute physiological "addiction to the trauma" (5). The pattern results from sensation-seeking, a traumatic derivative that involves the excessive use of motor activity in the absence of a capacity for affect modulation or linguistic problem solving. The recreation of high-risk situations is part of the sequence by which abusive behavior is transmitted.

The Role of the Child

Although children cannot be said to "cause" their abuse, researchers and clinicians have nevertheless noted "abuse-eliciting behavior" in some of them (27, 50, 51). Green (52) found that abused children were hyperactive, impulsive, aggressive, destructive, self-destructive, and accident-prone. It is true that hyperactive children are at greater risk of becoming victims of abuse, but there is now growing evidence that abuse itself is a cause of hyperactivity (5). Johnson and Morse (53) reported that 70 percent of 268 children showed physical and behavioral abnormalities. Gil (54) also reported increased rates of behavioral deviance, particularly in the first year after the abuse. Martin (55) distinguished two types of abused children: most are apathetic and unresponsive, but some are aggressive. George and Main (56) observed increased aggression toward age mates and caretakers. These findings are consistent with the trauma model.

The Impact of Trauma at the Marital Level

The victims and witnesses of familial violence must come to terms with the knowledge that a person who loves you will also physically hurt you. Solutions to this profound dilemma include fusion, reenactment, and disengagement. Alcohol and drugs are often used to medicate anxiety and depression and to deaden the impact of affectively charged situations.

Interpersonal Fusion

Abused children who have developed anxious attachment often form symbiotic relationships as adults in order to avoid reexperiencing the anxieties and vulnerabilities of childhood. Barnhill et al. (57) suggested that feelings of helplessness, inadequacy, and low self-esteem drive them toward this symbiotic merging. Any disruption of the symbiosis causes rage. Any thought, feeling, or action that suggests autonomy is a reminder of separateness, which reawakens memories of trauma and renders the traumatized individual to experience intolerable feelings of abandonment and helplessness. In such relationships, violence serves to punish the other for being autonomous, while also allowing intense emotional contact and the fantasy of repairing the damage bond.

Two patterns are particularly common in abusive marriages. In the first, one partner with needs for dominance and counterdependence chooses a submissive and passive mate. Often both grew up in traumatic environments: he has identified with the aggressor and uses rigid perfectionistic standards developed as a means of avoiding the wrath of punitive parents; she is more passive and withdrawn, perhaps with pronounced learned helplessness (10). Their unspoken pact is that "I'll protect and take care of you if you depend on me and never leave." As time goes on it turns out from his point of view she cannot ever do enough of the right things. She shows her anger by emotional withdrawal and diminished role functioning. Feeling disappointed, betrayed, and abandoned, he becomes even more intensely critical and self-righteous, eventually directing emotional terror and physical abuse not only at his wife but also at his children.

A second scenario begins with what Bowen (58) called the "emotional cut-off." An adolescent, vulnerable and enraged by a traumatic upbringing, flees from home and cuts off all contact with the family of origin. Having learned self-protection through emotional constriction and avoidance of emotionally charged issues, the adolescent now chooses a partner who shares these characteristics and can be relied on to avoid painful matters. Since both partners are cut off from families of origin and isolated by virtue of constricted lives, the marriage becomes the sole source of support and nurturance. The relationship must meet all social and emotional needs; the pull toward fusion and symbiosis is strong. Since they lack the ability to communicate and manage conflict, they fight both to make contact and to keep the other at a distance when fusion becomes threatening. When a child is born, fears of abandonment and competition for scarce emotional resources often precipitate violence, which may be directed at the needy and abandoning mother or at an unborn or newborn child. The growing child is later inducted into a parentified role or becomes a scapegoat.

Object Relations and Identification

Traumatization distorts the object world of the victim. Love and violence, sexuality and aggression become fused. Having witnessed or experienced violence at home, the child has only maladaptive alternatives in the effort of mastering the terrifying feelings: identification with the aggressor and the denial of vulnerability, or identification as a victim desperately in need of protection but too vulnerable to be intimate. In the latter case, rage is split off, dissociated, and turned against a self regarded as bad, inadequate, or worthless. The choice of a partner motivated by efforts to resolve these splits often recreates the original traumatic situation. Green (14) remarked that the repetitive quality of these kinds of violent and abusive relationships "suggests that identification with the aggressor is embedded in the compulsion to repeat the trauma." Repetitive patterns in intrafamilial violence are well known: the woman who returns again and again to her abusive mate; the man who reenacts his own childhood sexual victimization by molesting his own children or by being victimized in homosexual encounters; the sexually abused adolescent girl who turns to promiscuity and prostitution.

Other factors reinforce the power of identification. Traumatic bonding results from the utter dependency of a terrorized person on an assailant, and the resulting pathological identification wherein the victim feels benignly toward the perpetrator. In families where maltreatment is common, dependency is intensified because the child or adolescent has been deprived of the opportunity to develop skills and to function effectively in the world at large. Many battered women are prevented from leaving their abusive husbands and lovers by learned helplessness and low self-esteem, as well as economic dependency and social isolation.

The following case illustrates altered object relations and pathological identifications.

Robert grew up with a violent alcoholic father who often beat his mother and brothers. Although he knew he was his father's favorite, he too was terrorized and slapped around, often at random and with no explanation except "because I love you." Robert was close to his mother. He identified with her "goodness" and swore he'd never be like his father. He married Susan, a "sweet" (i.e., passive and patient) woman who embodied many of his ideals. He worked hard and, in return, expected to be taken care of and appreciated. The harder he worked to "make things right," the more critical he became of what he regarded as Susan's perceived shortcomings. When she disputed his criticism, challenged his efforts to control her, and asserted her autonomy, he became deeply upset. Susan became more overtly compliant while inwardly distant and evasive. Recognizing that she was harboring secret critical thoughts and feelings, he became anxious, somewhat paranoid, and increasingly jealous. More and more Susan began to remind Robert of his hapless mother. Her emotional withdrawal reminded him of his mother's inability to protect him as a child. Beset by these terrible feelings, he became enraged and abusive toward his wife, another failed protector. During one fight he called her a "whore," the same epithet his father had hurled at his mother.

The Impact of Trauma at the Systemic Level

To understand the cross-generational transmission of risk and vulnerability (39, 59) and to clarify the role of the family system and community in worsening, preventing, or healing traumatic injury, a systemic perspective on trauma in the family is needed. The ecological systems perspective conceptualizes the family as an interactive, hierarchically and generationally organized series of relationships (60, 61). These relationships take on the properties of a relatively open cybernetic system (62, 63) that is nested within a larger context (25) and interfaces with an interpersonal surround (mesosystem) that includes extended kinship and friendship systems, as well as formal institutions such as schools, day care, workplace, churches, and protective services.

Unless childhood trauma is resolved through reparative experiences, including psychotherapy, components of the trauma will be incorporated into the pattern of family life in the next generation. At the systemic level, trauma derivatives may manifest themselves in disorders of hierarchy and boundaries. Trauma also creates problems of communication and coordination within the family microsystem and between the family and the surrounding mesosystem (25, 27, 64). Research on this topic is still limited. Danielli (65) examined family defensive style in response to surviving the Nazi holocaust. Alexander (66) applied family systems theory to her analysis of incestuous families. Elder (39), using longitudinal data, studied the intergenerational transmission of behavior disturbance as a function of family characteristics. McCubbin and Patterson (67) used Hill's ABCX model of family coping to study the responses of families with a chronically ill child.

Intergenerational Aspects

At the first level of the family system is the phenomenon of triangulation across generations (68). This pattern is basic in the organization and transmission of family violence. In effect, it means that adults take it out on children when they cannot manage tension and conflict among themselves. Belsky (27) noted: "to the extent that physical punishment of children is considered more socially acceptable than the exercise of physical force against one's spouse, child abuse may result from displaced aggression." In one pattern, the classic scapegoating sequence, parents maintain their alliance and stabilize the family system by blaming and punishing the child. In another pattern, commonly associated with sexual abuse, the child is elevated into the parental hierarchy and the system stabilized through role reversal. The child may thus be either covertly allied with one parent against the other, or parentified and obliged to care for a parent suffering from alcoholism, depression, or another disability. The child may also be assigned the role of surrogate parent for other children or, in the case of father-daughter incest, the role of surrogate wife.

In one three-generation pattern commonly encountered in single-parent families, the child becomes a pawn or a player in the cross-generational conflict. The grandmother and her daughter fight over the daughter's child, reenacting an unresolved, often abusive relationship. The child, initially the pawn but eventually a player, is subject to shifting alliances and vulnerable to abuse, usually from the parent.

Triangulation occurs because protective and care-taking functions are weak, direct marital conflict is avoided, and the adults meet these needs by the indirect manipulation of vulnerability and loyalty. The child is used to ward off feelings, to discharge unintegrated parental impulses, or to substitute for the disabled parent. These systemic demands distort the child's experience of generational hierarchies. When interpersonal boundaries are regularly violated (as in alcoholic and abusive families), the child never learns how to set and maintain his or her own boundaries. The child does not receive the care and protection necessary for secure individuation and maturation. Parentified children are also exposed to developmentally inappropriate demands that impair their understanding of their own needs vis-à-vis those of others.

The extraordinary coping mechanisms that the child may rely on (discussed above) include constriction, isolation, dissociation, hyperaggression, hypersexuality, sensation seeking, and entitlement. Each of these maladaptations may eventually help to make the child an abusive or exploitative parent or mate, or a vulnerable and victimized adult.

Impact on Family Organization

The posttraumatic experience of adult family members is likely to affect the family system in one of three ways: constriction leading to enmeshment, avoidance leading to disengagement, and impulsive behavior leading to chaos (69, 70).

Enmeshed systems. Abusive and maltreating families are usually closed and socially isolated systems (27, 64). They are poorly connected with the outside world and "too richly" connected internally (61). Intergenerational boundaries are often porous and the family is "highly resonant" to minor shifts in homeostatic equilibrium (66). From a trauma perspective, such closed, enmeshed systems are based on the reparative fantasy that a family in which nobody ever leaves or develops autonomous strivings and competing loyalties will provide the safety that was absent in the family of origin. In certain respects this process is an elaboration of anxious attachment and traumatic bonding at a systemic level, but it also has its own dynamic and systemically driven imperatives.

In the prototypical incestuous family (31, 71, 72), the father finds it safer to obtain sexual gratification and nurturance through the conditioning or coercion of one or more of his children. The father himself may have been sexually abused or suffered other developmental deviations. His behavior is related to characteristics of the closed systems. Family life is organized around trauma-driven beliefs: the world out there is dangerous and will hurt you; it is safe here; I am the only one you can trust and depend on; tell no one about your family. Danielli's (65) discussion of "victim families" captures this mentality from another perspective. The family is largely cut off from the community (66), and the marital dyad is often disabled. The wife is frequently avoidant and tired of the excessive demands from her own family of origin, her husband, and her children. Her wish not to deal with emotional demands leads to the parentification of her children. She denies her own traumatic past and therefore denies that her children are at risk. Thus the husband feels entitled; the mother distant and disengaged; and the children confused, angry, and vulnerable. Despite parental distance, these families are often exquisitely sensitive to changes in levels of tension and need. One client related that as an 8-year-old she was taught by her mother to recognize her father's angry moods and offer him a backrub to forestall a violent outburst. Despite this high emotional resonance, intolerance of open disagreement makes internal communication difficult, especially when it concerns incest or sexual exploitation. Incest victims often report their mothers denied and avoided the reality, either stigmatizing and blaming them for the incest (23), or enforcing silence (30). It is no surprise that incest often ends when the child, wishing more autonomy and peer friendship, breaks the family secret and reveals what has been going on. The disclosure brings intervention and often ends the incestuous relationship.

Battering also depends on the victim's isolation and sense of being trapped (20, 73). Anxious attachment, traumatic bonding, poor self-esteem, and lack of economic and social resources often make battered women virtual prisoners in their marriages. The abuse is likely to end only if the battered woman can gain support through links on the outside.

Open systems respond to stress and outside influence by differentiation and skill development. In closed systems any outside influence is seen as intrusive and disorganizing. To maintain homeostasis and prevent change, they keep it to a minimum. The closed family system must inhibit growth because growth means change, change means differentiation, and differentiation implies distance and apparent abandonment. Self-development and the development of cognitive and social skills suffer where disagreement breeds intimidation and conflict is resolved with violence. Violence also maintains hierarchies based on fear. The power of the system comes, in part, from the wish to avoid reawakening of traumatic memories. Such systems are therefore remarkably stable and engender loyalties even in the face of crisis, abuse, and exploitation.

Disengaged family systems. These families are not consistently disengaged, but are effectively shaped by the disengaged stance of one of the adults. At least one spouse has been exploited in childhood and does everything possible to avoid letting it happen again. The marriage is based on a wish to be taken care of with no demands. At times both partners have this, but eventually a struggle for care taking ensues and one partner loses the struggle to be taken care of and is forced once again to overfunction (74). The disengaged partner, often depressed or alcoholic, is distant and unavailable. He or she avoids contact, closeness, and responsibility as much as possible. The system's rules are set by this avoidant stance, with the collusion of the overfunctioning partner. There is little mutuality or accountability. External boundaries are poorly maintained and not well monitored. Children's whereabouts are often unknown. The disengaged parent's personal boundaries are dense, often impenetrable. It may be hard to get their attention and to involve them in family tasks in a sustained manner.

The rest of the system—spouse, children, other relatives—may not be particularly well differentiated. Children in such families are often pressed into service to compensate for the unavailable parent. They are vulnerable to neglect and sexual abuse by outsiders because of poor supervision, incest by virtue of a surrogate wife role, and child abuse. Many hyperactive children seem to grow up in homes with depressed, inaccessible, and inattentive mothers. Their hyperactivity is often an attempt to stimulate the withdrawn parent into activity and to arouse her interest, but instead it earns punishment.

Chaotic systems. A family is acutely traumatized if there is intense fighting between spouses, or between an abusive parent and the children. Such families are impulse-ridden and highly reactive to changes in the environment and disagreements among members. Often there is an impulsive, explosive man (possibly a veteran) and a depressive woman. The family is repeatedly in crisis brought on by trauma-related cues (e.g., anger, jealousy, loss). The explosive partner self-medicates (with alcohol and street drugs) to avoid trauma-related anxiety and the boredom of emotional constriction. He is fixated on earlier trauma and unable to modulate affect so small problems become big ones and pathological action substitutes for deliberation. External as well as internal boundaries are fluid; each moment is governed by the press of impulses and the wish to ward off intrusive imagery and affect. The family system as a protective container and auxiliary stimulus barrier is damaged or had never been intact. Since delay and modulation are impossible, stresses like emigration, dislocation, poverty, and unemployment become catastrophic, often destroying the family as a unit. Organized family functioning, protection, supervision, and future orientation are among the casualties. The remaining family fragments are decidedly unsafe for children. There is high risk for repetition of abuse and transmission to the next generation, often by an unwed teenage mother.

The Family's Interface with the Community

The relation between the family system and the community is important from an ecological perspective. This is especially so in dealing with incest, child abuse, and battering, where action by public agencies is mandated by law (in child cases) and often necessary for protection, prevention, treatment, and prosecution.

Ecological stressors such as unemployment (54), the lack of social resources, and the presence of dysfunctional networks interact with vulnerable family systems. Lack of integration with the larger community is in itself a source of stress and disorganization. At this interface the unsafe and disturbing intrapsychic and interpersonal world of the trauma victim is frequently externalized. The environment becomes crisis-ridden. Family members often see themselves as being victimized by the environments (e.g., a persecutory school system, a heartless utility company). This distracts them from the underlying pain and terror of their family life.

An impoverished relationship to the community perpetuates vulnerability (64). Mothers have few opportunities to gain information and support when anxiety and stress exhaust their own resources. Men without skills and stable employment lack social sources of self-esteem and support as well. Their rage about their social ineffectiveness is taken out on overwhelmed wives who do not have the emotional reserves to shore up their self-esteem. Many abusive families are not only isolated from prosocial family and community networks, but also tend to be connected to dysfunctional networks where traumatic reenactment is common.

Community attitudes and values also potentiate family violence, particularly the belief that physical punishment is appropriate discipline for children (15) and acceptable for women (73, 75). These values, when supported by the surrounding community or subculture, reinforce the role of violence in the home. They may make it harder for victims to feel that they can change the situation or to get help stopping the abuse from other family members. Such values are also reflected in the availability of programs for battered women and abused children and in the attitudes of the police and the courts in dealing with perpetrators and victims.

Treatment Implications

Treating and preventing violence has become a government priority during the past decade. Extending our growing understanding of the impact of traumatization on psychological functioning into the realm of the family and larger systems has important implications for the development and organization of social policy and human services. The trauma model offers human service providers dealing with violent and abusive families some helpful perspectives and suggestions.

Physically abusive and sexually intrusive families share a commitment to secrecy and denial. In families where new trauma continuously mixes with old, it is not abuse or violence per se that causes a crisis. The crisis comes when outsiders find out. Disclosure threatens to disrupt the homeostatic equilibrium (however destructive) and deprive family members of their accustomed means of dealing with tension and conflict. Because disclosure, not abuse, is seen as the main danger, such families either strongly resist intervention or quickly form clinging dependent relations with providers.

Clinicians know how hard it is to establish that someone has been hit or sexually abused, how vigorously families resist disclosure and engagement, how brittle the treatment alliance often is, how often the effects of treatment are overwhelmed by a secondary crisis, and how complicated it can be to work with the many service providers who are often involved in such cases.

To summarize, traumatized families rely heavily on denial, minimization, and avoidance to protect themselves from traumatic memories, intrusive imagery, and affective flooding. Secrets, silence, coercion, and a fear of outsiders serve to protect the homeostasis from disruption. Fear of disclosure is a fear of change and loss. Engagement in treatment creates a risk of disorganization and exposure to intolerable feelings. Clients often break off treatment either because external controls are lifted or because affect threatens the family's fragile equilibrium. When emergent affects threaten the homeostasis, family members take refuge in sensation seeking, pathological action, and traumatic reenactment. Children respond to parental and systemic distress by becoming symptomatic. If they too have been abused, their symptoms are likely to follow the aggressive and self-destructive pathways described above. Secondary crises overwhelm the system, including the provider network. Clients, caught between intolerable feelings and impending chaos, will pressure and split the providers into familiar rescuer, victim, and persecutor roles. Helping agencies may have an ambivalent response, leaving the victim and the family vulnerable to collective denial and iatrogenic abuse.

Effective intervention and treatment of intrafamilial violence begins with the recognition of the primacy of traumatic events. The aim of treatment is to restore a modicum of safety and control and begin to heal damaged or shattered bonds. The direction of work is from the family–community interface toward the intrapsychic self. Since the family's protective and containing functions have failed, the initial task is to reestablish physical and emotional safety. When the environment and social sphere has served as a projective field for disowned thoughts and feelings, the therapeutic alliance can be built by reconstructing functional boundaries and links between the immediate family and those in the community who can offer support and other resources. To diminish isolation and reduce stress, links with other systems such as schools, day care, and social service should be encouraged and coordinated as part of the treatment plan.

Traumatized families, like traumatized individuals, tend to flee from therapeutic experiences that reproduce the experience of being out of control. Thus treatment should be organized around the most vulnerable member. The therapist should challenge the family system's tendency to minimize the problem and affirm the right of family members not to be hit, hurt, or otherwise abused or exploited. As in other group treatment situations, once the family is reassured that the therapist will protect the most vulnerable member, and thereby symbolically contain and modulate the family's aggression, it becomes safe to begin disclosing what is really going on.

The first phase involves helping the family establish as much safety as is necessary (where children are at risk) or possible (where adults are involved), and empowering the responsible adults to gain a modicum of control over the environment. The second phase is a slow reconstruction of the family system accomplished by establishing effective interpersonal and generational boundaries and hierarchies and repairing damaged parent-child and marital dyads. Developmental deficits in the cognitive and social domains secondary to traumatization and growing up in an impoverished emotional environment must be identified and remedied as much as possible.

In the second phase, the therapist must be aware of the danger of too rapid disclosure of traumatic material, of the limits of the family's tolerance for affect, and of the systemic management of tension and discharge within the family. The slow reconstruction of traumatic events must be buttressed by structural changes and increased competence in the management of concrete realities. Therapeutic encouragement of gradual change and the prediction of occasional regression help keep the family in control of the pace. A touch of hope, a trustworthy attachment, growing self-esteem, and a sense of being in control make the unbearable somewhat less so.

References

1. Horowitz M: Stress Response Syndromes. New York, Jason Aronson, 1976

2. Burgess A, Holmstrom L: The rape trauma syndrome. Am J Psychiatry 131:981–986, 1974

3. Figley C: Stress Disorders among Vietnam Veterans. New York, Brunner/Mazel, 1978

4. Green B, Wilson J, Lindy J: Conceptualizing post-traumatic stress disorder: a psychosocial framework, in Trauma and Its Wake. Edited by Figley C. New York, Brunner/Mazel, 1985

5. van der Kolk B: Post Traumatic Stress Disorder: Psychological and Biological Sequelae. Washington, DC, American Psychiatric Press, 1984

6. American Psychiatric Association: The Diagnostic and Statistical Manual of Mental Disorders. 3rd ed. Washington, DC, American Psychiatric Association, 1980

7. Figley C: Trauma and Its Wake. New York, Brunner/Mazel, 1985

8. Gelinas D: Persistent negative effects of incest. Psychiatry 46:312–332, 1983

9. Titchener JL, Kapp FT: Family and character change at Buffalo Creek. Am J Psychiatry 133:295–299, 1976

10. Seligman ME, Garber J: Human Helplessness. New York, Academic Press, 1980

11. Keane T, Fairbank JA, Caddell JM, et al: A behavioral approach to assessing and treating post-traumatic stress disorder in Vietnam veterans, in Trauma and Its Wake. Edited by Figley C. New York, Brunner/Mazel, 1984

12. Janoff-Bulman R, Frieze IH: A theoretical perspective for understanding reactions to victimization. Journal of Social Issues 39:1–19, 1983

13. Carmen E, Reiker P, Mills T: Victims of violence and psychiatric illness. Am J Psychiatry 141:378–379, 1984

14. Green A: Child abuse: dimensions of psychological trauma in abused children. J Am Acad Child Psychiatry 22:231–237, 1983

15. Straus M, Gelles R, Steinmetz S: Behind Closed Doors: Violence in the American Family. New York, Doubleday, 1980

16. Quarantelli EL: A note on the protective function of family in disasters. Marriage and Family Living 22:263–264, 1960

17. Drabek TE, Key WH, Erickson PE, et al: The impact of disaster on kin relationships. Journal of Marriage and the Family 37:481–494, 1975

18. White PN, Rollins JC: Rape: a family crisis. Family Relations 30:103–109, 1980

19. Pruett KD: Home treatment for two infants who witnessed their mother's murder. Presented at 24th Annual Meeting of the American Academy of Child Psychiatry, Houston, October 1977

20. Hilberman E: Wife beater's wife reconsidered. Am J Psychiatry 137:1336–1347, 1980

21. Hilberman E, Munson M: Sixty battered women. Victimology 2:460–471, 1977–1978

22. Donaldson M, Gardner R: Diagnosis and treatment of post traumatic stress among women after childhood incest, in Trauma and Its Wake. Edited by Figley C. New York, Brunner/Mazel, 1984

23. Finklehor D, Gelles RJ, Hotaling GT, et al: The Dark Side of Families. Beverly Hills, Calif, Sage Publications, 1983

24. Gelles RJ, Straus MA: Determinants of violence in the family: toward a theoretical integration, in Contemporary Theories About the Family. Edited by Burr WR, Hill R, Nye FI. New York, Free Press, 1979

25. Bronfenbrenner U: The Ecology of Human Development. Cambridge, Harvard University Press, 1979

26. Russell CS, Olson DH, Sprenkle DH, et al: From family symp-

tom to family system: a review of family therapy research. American Journal of Family Therapy 11:3–14, 1983

27. Belsky J: Child maltreatment: an ecological integration. Am Psychologist, 35:320–335, 1980

28. Steele BF: Parental abuse of infants and small children, in Parenthood: Its Psychology and Psychopathology. Edited by Anthony EJ, Benedict T. Boston: Little, Brown and Co, 1970

29. Furst S: Psychic Trauma. New York, Basic Books, 1967

30. Bowlby J: On knowing what you are not supposed to know and feeling what you are not supposed to feel. Can J Psychiatry 24:403–408, 1979

31. Herman J, Hirschman L: Father-Daughter Incest. Cambridge, Harvard University Press, 1981

32. Putnam FW, Post RM, Guroff JJ, et al: One hundred cases of multiple personality disorder. New Research Abstract #77. Washington, DC, American Psychiatric Association, 1983

33. Knopp FH: Remedial Intervention in Adolescent Sex Offenses: Nine Program Descriptions. (New York State Council of Churches) Syracuse, New York, Safer Society Press, 1982

34. Johnson R, Shrier D: Sexual victimization of boys: an adolescent medicine clinic population. Unpublished paper, New Jersey Medical School, Newark, New Jersey, 1986

35. Hinchey F, Gavalek JR: Empathy in children of battered mothers. Paper presented at the National Conference for Family Violence. University of New Hampshire, Durham, New Hampshire, 1984

36. Wolfe D, Jaffe P, Wilson S, et al: Predicting children's adjustment to family violence. Paper presented at the National Conference for Family Violence, University of New Hampshire, Durham, New Hampshire, 1984

37. Bowlby J: Violence in the family as a disorder of the attachment and caregiving systems. Am J Psychoanal 44:9–27, 1984

38. Bowlby J: Attachment and Loss, II. Separation: Anxiety and Anger. London, Hogarth Press, 1973

39. Elder G: Problem behavior and family relationships: life course and intergenerational themes, in Human Development: Mul-

tidisciplinary Perspectives. Edited by Sorensen A, Weinert F, Sherrod L. Hillsdale, NJ, Lawrence Erlbaum Associates, 1985, pp 293–340

40. Berger A: The child abusing family, I: methodological issues and parent related characteristics of abusing families. American Journal of Family Therapy 8(3):53–66, 1980

41. Disbrow M, Doerr H, Caufield C: Measuring the components of parents' potential for child abuse. Child Abuse Negl 1:279–296, 1977

42. Melnick B, Hurley JR: Distinctive personality attributes of child abusing mothers. J Consult Clin Psychol 33:746–749, 1969

43. Frodi AM, Lamb ME: Psychophysiological responses to infant signals in abusive mothers and mothers of premature infants. Paper presented at the Society for Psychophysiological Research, Madison, Wisconsin, 1978

44. Canick E: An exploration of the capacity for fantasy in mothers with a history of abusive behavior. Doctoral dissertation, Massachusetts School of Professional Psychology, 1985

45. Boszormenyi-Nagy I, Spark G: Invisible Loyalties. New York, Harper and Row, 1973

46. Rohner R: Parental Acceptance and Rejection. New Haven, Conn, Human Relations Area Files, 1978

47. Baldwin J, Oliver J: Epidemiology and family characteristics of severely abused children. British Journal of Preventive Social Medicine 29:205–221, 1975

48. Hymer S: Integrating the splits in crime victims' self images: toward the reparation of the damaged self, in Psychotherapy and the Terrorized patient. Edited by Stern ME. New York, Haworth Press, 1985

49. Galdston R: Observations on children who have been physically abused and their parents. Am J Psychiatry 122:531–540, 1965

50. Reid JB, Taplin PS: A social interactional approach to the treatment of abusive families. Paper presented to the American Psychological Association, Washington, DC, 1975

51. Patterson G: The aggressive child: victim and architect of a

coercive system, in Behavior Modification and Families. Edited by Hammerlyck L, Marsh E, Handy L. New York, Brunner/Mazel, 1976

52. Green A: Self-destructive behavior in battered children. Am J Psychiatry 135:579–582, 1978

53. Johnson B, Morse HA: Injured children and their parents. Children 15:147–152, 1968

54. Gil D: Societal violence and violence in families, in Child Abuse and Violence. Edited by Gil D. New York, AMS Press, 1979

55. Martin MP: Which children get abused: high risk factors in the child, in The Abused Child: A Multidisciplinary Approach to the Developmental Issues and Treatment. Edited by Martin HP. Cambridge, Ballinger, 1976

56. George C, Main M: Social interactions among young abused children: approach, avoidance, and aggression. Child Dev 50:306–318, 1979

57. Barnhill L, Bloomgarden R, Berghorn B, et al: Clinical and community interventions in violence in families, in Group and Family Therapy. Edited by Wolberg L, Aronson M. New York, Stratton, 1980

58. Bowen M: Family Therapy in Clinical Practice. New York, Jason Aronson, 1978

59. Herrenkohl E, Herrenkohl R, Toedter L: Perspectives on the intergenerational transmission of abuse, in The Dark Side of Families. Edited by Finklehor D, Gelles RJ, Hotaling GT, et al. Beverly Hills, Calif, Sage Publications, 1983

60. Minuchin S: Families and Family Therapy. Cambridge, Harvard University Press, 1974

61. Hoffman L: Foundations of Family Therapy. New York, Basic Books, 1981

62. Bateson G: Steps Toward an Ecology of Mind. New York, Ballantine Books, 1972

63. Brodey WM: A cybernetic approach to family therapy, in Family Therapy and Disturbed Families. Edited by Zuk GH, Boszormenyi-Nagy I. Palo Alto, Science and Behavior Books, 1967

64. Garabino J, Gilliam G: Understanding Abusive Families. Lexington, Mass, Lexington Books, 1980

65. Danielli Y: The treatment and prevention of long term effects and intergenerational transmission of victimization, in Trauma and Its Wake. Edited by Figley C. New York, Brunner/ Mazel, 1985

66. Alexander P: A systems theory conceptualization of incest. Fam Process 24:79–88, 1985

67. McCubbin H, Patterson J: The family stress process: the double ABCX model of adjustment and adaptation, in Social Stress and the Family. Edited by McCubbin H, Sussman MB, Patterson JM. New York, Haworth Press, 1983

68. Minuchin S, Fishman C: Family Therapy Techniques. Cambridge, Harvard University Press, 1981

69. Kantor D, Lehr W: Inside the Family. San Francisco, Harper and Row, 1975

70. Olson DH, Russell CS, Sprenkle DH: Circumplex model of marital and family systems, II: empirical studies and clinical intervention, in Advances in Family Intervention, Assessment, and Theory. Vol 1. Greenwich, CT, JAI Press, 1980, pp 129–176

71. Anderson LM, Shafer GS: The character disordered family: a community treatment model for family sexual abuse. Am J Orthopsychiatry 49:436–445, 1979

72. Finklehor D: Child Sexual Abuse: New Theory and Research. New York, Free Press, 1984

73. Gelles R: An exchange/social control theory, in The Dark Side of Families. Edited by Finklehor D, Gelles RJ, Hotaling GT, et al. Beverly Hills, Calif, Sage Publications, 1983

74. Gillis-Donovan J: Workshop presentation on child abuse. Leonard Morse Hospital, Framingham, Mass, 21 May 1981

75. Walker LE: The Battered Woman Syndrome. New York, Springer, 1984.

CHAPTER 7

The Role of the Group in the Origin and Resolution of the Trauma Response

Bessel A. van der Kolk, M.D.

I borrow myself from others; man is a mirror for man.

Merleau-Ponty

The trauma response has generally been studied as an intrapsychic, or at least individual, experience. However, it is unrealistic to separate the individual's psychological state from the multiple social forces by which it has been shaped, and in which it continues to be embedded. Psychological trauma invariably occurs in a social context involving either the loss of attachment figures or the destruction of the basic sense of security and continuity that results from accumulated secure experiences with others. Lindemann (1) defined trauma as "the sudden uncontrollable severance of affective ties." Krystal (2) stated that "in the acute traumatic state one stands alone and abandoned by all sources of feelings of security." The essence of the trauma response is the severance of secure affiliative bonds.

The psychiatric symptoms of post-traumatic stress disorder (PTSD) are always accompanied by impoverished interpersonal relationships. Following trauma, social attachments may become anxious and clinging, with idealization and a loss of psychological autonomy, or the trauma victim may suffer from interpersonal numbing: "a giving up of hope for satisfactory human contact,

153

which is the result of the destruction of basic trust" (3). Either way, trauma results in a disorder of hope; the capacity of others to provide emotional gratification and security is either under-valued or overvalued.

The Loss of Communality Following Trauma

In her study of the dam burst at Buffalo Creek, Erikson (4) stated that collective trauma is "a blow to the tissues of social life that damages the bonds linking people together and impairs the pre-vailing sense of communality." This leads to demoralization, dis-orientation, and loss of connection. Ashamed of their own vulnerability and often enraged about the lack of help from out-side, many victims lose faith in the possibility of meaningful and mutually beneficial human relationships. Even the nuclear acci-dent at Three Mile Island, which did not involve the direct loss of life, led to serious and sometimes lasting disagreements among friends and families about who to blame and what to do (5). Ac-rimonious debates were common even 4 years after the event. Baum (6) found more social conflict and neighborhood distrust than in a comparison community. Feelings of vulnerability, sur-vival guilt, and rage often cause a search for scapegoats; if the community does not band together against an external enemy or rally around a common goal, victims often turn against one an-other. Lindy (7) pointed out that, following disasters, a commun-ally held perception about who or what to blame gradually emerges, and the nature of this communal myth has a major impact on the ultimate posttrauma adaptation. A case in point is the attempts to "explain" the problems of Vietnam veterans: they had no busi-ness being in Vietnam in the first place; they lost the war; they were "babykillers"; or they all had preexisting character disorders. There were few forces to counter these negative myths. The war was unpopular. There was no "victory," and there was a loss of communality among returning veterans because discharges were individual and because there were no veteran groups (except Viet-nam veterans against the war) to celebrate the homecoming, or at least to give the experience meaning. These myths devised to explain away what happened to Vietnam veterans may in fact have contributed to the severity and persistence of PTSD among them.

Sociological research shows that a cohesive survivor support network strongly militates against the development of long-term symptoms of PTSD (8). Most people need some form of social support to overcome the effects of trauma, but victims may shun their natural social supports out of shame, fear, and distrust. In addition, their feelings of anger and vulnerability may make them think that they are dangerous to the community. Vietnam veterans often stay away from people for fear of inflicting harm. Victims of childhood sexual abuse often fear that they may inflict similar abuse on the next generation.

As we saw in Chapter 6, the family, although potentially the best form of support, often shares in this shame and guilt and cannot deal with the traumatization of one of its members (5). One of the most urgent therapeutic tasks facing therapists of traumatized individuals is the re-creation of a sense of human interdependence and community. Often fellow victims provide the most effective short-term bond because the shared history of trauma can form the nucleus for retrieving a sense of communality. Sharing a common experience in the "there and then" may lead to active sharing of mutual concerns, including feelings of ambivalence, in the "here and now."

The Role of the Group in Surviving Extreme Conditions

In a study of group phenomena in concentration camp survivors, Davidson (9) wrote: "It has become increasingly evident that co-operation for survival among members of the same species is a basic law of life. Throughout the history of man, sharing relationships have been the central mode of coping with and adapting to the environment." In Chapter 2 it was noted that in many animal species danger causes increased attachment to available caregivers, regardless of how much safety they actually provide. When faced with an external threat, people tend to band together in groups to protect themselves against external enemies. The degree to which individuals seek this kind of protection depends on both their internal sense of security and the intensity of the external threat. Becker (10), discussing submergence in the group, said that "transference [i.e., allegiance to the group] is the taming of terror." He quoted Freud's (11) essay on group psychology to support his observation that the more terrifying the external threat, the stronger this allegiance becomes.

Eitinger (12) noted that even in concentration camps, group formation had a significant influence on the chance of survival. People survived either because others helped them or because they themselves had to think of others: "Even though this help was often minimal and/or symbolic, it seems to have contributed in a decisive way towards the individual's ability to retain part of his personality and self-respect, and this is given considerable importance in relation to the capacity for survival." In a study of Holocaust survivors, Klein (13) described "cohesive pairing" as a specific psychosocial coping response in concentration camps. He noted that "these individuals attribute their survival to the existence of a tightly knit supportive group during the Holocaust. Survival is intimately linked with community." In another study of Nazi concentration camp survivors, the sociologist Des Pres (14) concluded that "the struggle of life in extremity depends on solidarity, on social bonding and interchange," and that "even in Auschwitz and Buchenwald life was intensely social . . . based on an awareness of the common predicament and the need to act collectively."

In a study of 52 concentration camp survivors, Luchterhand (15) noted that all had had a mutually sharing relationship with one or more other prisoners. Even under these extreme conditions, the inmates formed stable pairs; companions were quickly replaced when one partner died or was removed. Other survivors reported that they had formed stable, intensely loyal groups of up to seven or eight people, based on common origins or interests, with selfless mutual devotion to each other and apparent total disregard for all outsiders (9). Group cohesion occurred even among children and adolescents, who often formed closely knit bands that persisted after liberation (16). The Holocaust literature describes group activities among both children and adults that ranged from provision of basic needs, such as collecting and sharing food, to storytelling, reminiscing, singing, and joking (9). Through interpersonal bonds these survivors kept alive the essential qualities of human existence: belonging, being useful to others, and sharing a common culture and past. Davidson (9) stated that:

> Women who knew Anne Frank in Bergen Belsen in the month before she died believed that neither the hunger nor the typhus killed her, but the death of her sister Margot. One of these women said "It was frightening to see how easy it was to die for someone who had been left all alone in a concentration camp.". . . From our survivor studies it has become clear that interpersonal support, by buffering and protecting the psyche in the face of even catastrophic stress situations, can mitigate the traumatic process, and the progression to the final state of apathetic resignation and surrender may be prevented and even averted. In this way social bonding could mitigate the destructive process that led to the overwhelming and paralysis of the coping and recuperative resources of the psyche.

Adolescent Individuation and Group Formation

Group formation is an essential part of adolescence: adolescents need to leave their parents' milieu to establish psychological autonomy. Sullivan (17) proposed that peer relationships in adolescence allow the affirmation of self-worth necessary to break dependent ties with parents. The peer group plays a central role even in lives of preadolescent children, but the family still functions as the principal safe base from which the child can explore other interpersonal ties. As a child enters adolescence, peer bonding becomes increasingly important to deal with fearful emotions and events. Adolescence has been described as "the great second chance" (18): at this age experiences of intimacy and competence within the peer group can to some degree compensate for a family's inability to provide safety and proper role models.

Adolescents use the peer group as an intermediate stage between dependence on the family and emotional maturity (18). It provides a sense of belonging and acceptance that is no longer possible in the family of origin. Identification with the power of the group protects them against infantile dependencies and guilt feelings (10, 18). Offer and Offer (19) have shown that adolescents with secure homes are better able to make use of this restitutive function than those from more disturbed environments; but the peer group offers all adolescents opportunities for identification and belonging that were not available at an earlier age. According to Erikson (20), the ability to develop intimacy with peers during adolescence is related to subsequent capacity for closeness and intimacy.

Identification with the peer group fosters a primitive narcissistic gratification and a sense of power. Blos (18) noted that, while passing from infantile dependence to adult autonomy, adolescents temporarily view the world in absolutes: good versus evil, activity versus passivity, and love versus hate. Kernberg (21) pointed out that "the violence of groups under such psychological conditions reflects the need to destroy any external reality that interferes with this group illusion. The loss of any individuality within such a group is compensated for by the shared sense of omnipotence in all its members." Under normal conditions, this intense and sometimes destructive adolescent peer bonding can be a useful transitional experience. However, if psychological trauma occurs during this phase, confirming a view of the world as bad and the self as helpless, the adolescent may attempt to restore a sense of integrity by fantasies of omnipotence: "should the process of individuation stop at this stage, then we encounter all sorts of narcissistic pathology of which the withdrawal from the object world represents the gravest impasse" (18).

This second separation/individuation stage is resolved by late adolescence. Haley (22) stated that two elements are essential for this resolution: 1) clearly defined societal/familial values, ethics, and rules, and 2) consistent, caring, and supportive family and peers. Offer and Offer (19) have shown that youngsters who enter adolescence with a distrust of the adult world develop more intense and tumultuous peer relationships than those who come from more secure environments. Exclusive dependence on the peer group for affirmation makes them vulnerable to either self-destructive conformism or social isolation. Unable to return safely to the parental fold, they tend to develop clinging and dependent relationships, either with someone of the opposite sex or with gang members of the same sex. Conscious awareness of dependency needs is threatening for many adolescents, particularly those who have had to accommodate a pathological home environment to satisfy earlier dependency needs (23). As Aichorn (24) first showed, adolescent males often cover up underlying feelings of emptiness, loneliness, and fear with acts of bravado, including antisocial behavior, which serve the need for acceptance by and dependence on the peer group. Girls often deal with their dependency needs by taking care of a troubled male on whom they try to exert a restitutive influence that was not possible in their family of origin (see Chapter 6).

According to Erickson (20), identity is fully formed at the resolution of adolescence.

> Man, to take his place in society, must acquire a conflict free habitual use of a dominant faculty, to be elaborated in an occupation: a limitless resource, a feedback, if it were, from the immediate exercise of this occupation, from the companionship it provides, and from its tradition; and finally, an intelligible theory of the processes of life.

Traditionally, the military has served many adolescents with an avenue to achieve this resolution.

Adolescence, Military Service, and Trauma

In a large follow-up study of World War II veterans, Elder (25) found that for many men with disadvantaged backgrounds, the military was a way to escape and succeed: "Over the years, the Armed Forces have offered an alternative for youth who lost out in education and employment and for those who lacked a sense of direction and goals." The military fosters self-esteem and a sense of efficacy in many young males, possibly by providing them with strong role models and group support (26). Nevertheless, Elder (27) found that a group of World War II veterans ranked well below nonveterans on a variety of measures of personal competence. The military had recruited many men with little educational promise, particularly those who entered at an early age. However, the vast majority of these veterans used the GI bill to enhance their chances in life. Although they did not do nearly as well occupationally as nonveterans and veterans who entered the service later in life, they achieved a degree of personal stability that was remarkable given their earlier disadvantages. Elder ascribed this change to personal growth fostered by the service.

Emotional closeness in response to clear external stress is normal. People who share periods of great stress, such as the London Blitz, continue to regard these times as the best of their lives, and often prize the friendships formed at tense times above all others. Nevertheless, the quality of these relationships under stress varies considerably, depending in part on a person's developmental level and prior experiences. The army, particularly in combat, maximizes the impact of peer group cohesion. Basic training, especially in the Marine Corps, successfully exploits the adolescent need to substitute peer group for family ties. Shatan (28) pointed out that the Marine Corps basic training aims at abandonment of individual values in favor of total submergence in the group: the drill instructor becomes "one's mother, father and friend." All ties to home, parents, and girlfriends are ridiculed and temporarily severed, and the drill instructor is placed in total control over even the minutest details of a fresh recruit's life.

In clinical observations of World War II combat soldiers, Lidz (29) and Fairbairn (30) compared those who developed chronic PTSD with those who did not. They both concluded that men with persistent symptoms had disrupted early family relationships and were prone to develop intensely dependent relationships with a single person. Both found that war neuroses developed after disruption of such a relationship. Moses (31) showed that in Israeli combat soldiers group cohesion was largely a function of early life security, and its disruption was directly related to the development of PTSD. Fox (32) also saw the loss of group cohesion as a major contributor to the development of PTSD. He noted that U.S.

combat Marines in Vietnam developed difficulties in managing hostile and aggressive impulses after the loss of a buddy with whom they had intensely identified. He argued that this buddy relationship is a "mirror relationship" as defined by Kohut (33). Haley (22), discussing the same phenomenon, quoted Modell (34) as follows: "these dyadic relationships have the capacity for magical thought to mitigate the danger of catastrophic anxiety through the creation of a lack of separateness between self and object." Clinical accounts of Vietnam veterans describe how adolescent combat soldiers under extreme stress exchanged articles of clothing and carried belongings of dead comrades around until after their return home. Haley stated that:

> Another indicator of the magical quality of the buddy-soldier relationship is that following their military service, most veterans did not contact their buddy. It is as though that special, magical, and idealized relationship would be shattered were the soldier to really know the mundane realities of his buddy's life: what his buddy loves and values, independent of the soldier. The buddy's death in combat served as a premature loss of an essential and life sustaining transitional object.

Elder (personal communication, 1986) confirmed that this idealized relationship with combat buddies seems to be in part age-dependent; men who entered the service after adolescence were more likely than the younger recruits to have frequent and meaningful relationships with members of their combat units 40 years later. It is likely that the ties of older recruits with other men in their combat units were more personal, whereas adolescent soldiers had more narcissistic bonds that tended to dissolve after the combat experience ended.

In a study of Vietnam veterans with persistent PTSD 10 and more years after combat, van der Kolk (35) found that they avoided expressing aggression and, regardless of their level of social adjustment, felt a profound loss of the ability to affect their destinies. He also found a significant age effect: the average age of combat in those with PTSD was 18.3 years, compared with 21.5 for the control group without PTSD. The younger men had developed an intense attachment to other men in their combat unit. When this was disrupted by the death of a buddy, the loss often led to retaliation and subsequent profound feelings of helplessness. The Vietnam veterans with PTSD had felt particularly close to their combat units; most had become vengeful and committed atrocities after a buddy was killed in action. Laufer et al. (36) also found significant correlations between participation in abusive violence and the persistence of stress responses in Vietnam veterans. These results were consistent with Fox's (32) finding that soldiers with PTSD had reacted to the death of a friend as a narcissistic injury rather than an object loss. In other words, they had experienced their friends as extensions of themselves rather than as separate individuals. This resulted in a need to avenge the friend's death, which persisted "despite the passage of time and even after specific acts of revenge had been committed against the enemy" (32).

These men had become fixated on the trauma and continued to respond to subsequent slights with intense rage (35). Events and relationships both before and after the trauma had lost their affective significance (2). Subsequent social functioning depended principally on premorbid adjustment: many successful high school students had entered the professions, while others found occupations that were within expectations for their class standing and other premorbid variables. All subjects were married. Despite this outwardly good social adjustment, they were just "going through the motions" of a normal life. Regardless of personality, the affective experience appropriate to intimacy and accomplishment was lacking. All subjects with PTSD complained of difficulty in feeling emotionally close to their families. One former Vietnam Marine sergeant who had become a lawyer suffered severe and recurrent nightmares on the anniversaries of the deaths of comrades in the field. He refused to take drugs to control these nightmares; he felt that he needed to have them as a memorial to his dead comrades "lest they have died in vain." This concern did not extend to the significant others in his present life. He rarely spent time with his children; emotional demands such as childbirth or illness in the family caused further emotional withdrawal and preoccupation with the deaths of his comrades.

Haley (22) noted the similarities between these reactions to the loss of a combat buddy and the reaction described by Bowlby (37) following the separation of a child from its mother, namely protest, despair, and detachment. Bowlby (37) observed that protest is eventually replaced by a despairing grief for the lost attachment figure, resulting in numbed detachment. This psychic numbing following catastrophic life experiences has been extensively documented by Lifton (38) and Krystal (2, 3).

Haley (22) noted that "because of the ambiguous nature of the

Vietnam war, one of the most damaging effects . . . was the strip-
ping away of their adolescent illusions and the tarnishing of their
ego ideals." She goes on to quote Blos (18), who wrote that:

> Under stress, a revival of childhood traumas takes place at a higher
> level of action without any restraining environmental forces. The
> revived trauma becomes more devastating than the original because
> the child had a supportive system that took responsibility for the
> child. The second edition of the trauma, where one has not only
> murderous fantasies, but murderous actions, is much more dev-
> astating to the psychic organization.

Many cultures have cleansing rituals for returning warriors,
which allow them to restore the integrity of the self, to be accepted
by the community, and to form a survival support network that
promotes the establishment of what Lindy and Titchener (39) have
called "the trauma membrane." The Holocaust Memorial Yad
Vashem in Jerusalem and the Vietnam Memorial in Washington,
DC, serve as essential symbols for survivors to mourn the dead
and establish the historical and cultural meaning of the traumatic
events. Most of all, they serve to remind survivors of the ongoing
potential for communality and sharing. These observations also
apply to other survivor groups who have no memorial and no
common symbol around which they can gather to mourn and
express their shame about their own vulnerability.

Treatment Implications: Individual
Versus Group Psychotherapy

Most trauma victims benefit initially from individual therapy. It
allows disclosure of the trauma, the safe expression of related
feelings, and the reestablishment of a trusting relationship with
at least one other person. Patients can explore and validate perceptions and emotions and experience consistent and undivided
attention from one other individual. Provided that a degree of
safety can be established in the individual therapy relationship,
a trauma victim can begin dealing with both the sense of shame
and the vulnerability. Discussion of the traumatic events and
their impact on the patient's current life has an organizing effect,
allowing the patient to see value in the here and now. Horowitz
(40) pointed to the need to alternate between support and confrontation so that the patient can cover up traumatic material
when it threatens to become overwhelming and yet not wall off

the trauma during periods of constriction. Individual therapy allows for a detailed examination of a patient's mental processes and memories that cannot be replicated in a group therapy setting.

In individual therapy there is an inherent inequality: it is a relationship between a therapist, the "helper," who implicitly has answers and is not helpless, and the patient or client, who needs help and who may experience at least some passivity and possibly some sense of helplessness. This kind of relationship has both strengths and limitations. Initially it allows a sense of safety that encourages the fantasy of new strength: the relationship with the all-powerful therapist will allow the patient to regain a sense of control (41). However, this idealization tends to inhibit growth at later stages. A sense of personal usefulness is probably essential for a subjective feeling of control and meaning in one's life. The very nature of individual therapy precludes a sense of mutual support. Supportive individual therapy tends to reinforce dependency on the therapist and may decrease the subjective sense of mastery. Kobasa and Pucetti (42) found that executives who had suffered a myocardial infarction were most likely to make a good recovery if they had both a good social support network and an internal locus of control. Those with good social support but an external locus of control had the poorest prognoses of all groups studied. Because most trauma victims with PTSD have an external locus of control, supportive psychotherapy may not be helpful unless accompanied by other means of achieving mastery (see Chapter 10).

After infancy, support is usually earned by attention to the needs and desires of others. Individual psychotherapy does not require this, while group psychotherapy does and thus is less likely to foster dependence. It allows for more flexible roles, with mutual support and alternating positions of passivity and activity. In a group patients can start reexperiencing themselves as being useful to other people. Ventilation and sharing of feelings and experiences in groups of people who have gone through similar experiences promotes the experience of being both victim and helper. Even a trusting and secure relationship with a therapist who serves as a parental substitute does not necessarily enable the patient to assess his or her relationships with others accurately. In a group the therapist can facilitate reempowerment by encouraging mutual support and by exploring the patient's resistances to taking an active role.

Although no controlled studies exist, group therapy is widely regarded as a treatment of choice for many patients with PTSD, either as the sole form of therapy or as an adjunct to individual psychotherapy. It has been used for victims of incest (43), rape (44), spouse battering (45), and war trauma (46). Grinker and Spiegel (47) found that "the group more nearly approximates the state of the human being in a natural setting." When placed in a group of fellow sufferers, most war traumatized men were eventually able to express aggression, hate, love, and wishes without much guilt: "By working out his problems in a small group he should be able to face the larger group, i.e., his world, in an easier manner" (47).

People who come from abusive or neglectful homes are almost always hostile to, or suspicious of, authority figures; hence they are often difficult to engage in individual psychotherapy. This reluctance to depend on adults, coupled with the natural inclination toward peer group formation, is another reason why group psychotherapy is often the treatment of choice for individuals with a history of childhood or adolescent trauma (48). The temporary illusion of fusion in groups of individuals who share a common history of trauma and the relative anonymity of the group can afford temporary suspension of ambivalent and aggressive feelings, permitting spontaneous expression of emotions and memories that may be inhibited in individual therapy. Herman and Shatzow (43) stated that "in individual therapy it is difficult to come to a full resolution of the issues of secrecy, shame, and stigma." Short-term groups can be useful in decreasing anxiety and restoring hope, courage, and meaning in the life of the survivor. They may facilitate resolution of self-blame by allowing for external attribution. Parson (49) has explained the need for therapist activity such as modeling, assertiveness training, and reading assignments in such groups.

Groups of traumatized individuals are characterized by dependency rather than confrontation. Once group members overcome their initial distrust and shame, they rapidly establish a high degree of cohesion—a sense of us versus them (the dangerous world). Parson (49) stated that "only the group experience that is able to contain powerful projections, defensive splitting, and annihilation anxiety can reactivate the arrested development of these group members." He cautioned against the active exploration of aggression-dominated symptoms during the initial phases of group development.

Group members learn that they are similar in important ways and that they respond to one another as aspects of their own selves

(50). At first they use each other as mirrors to reflect traumatic memories and feelings, which allows a shared reliving of the trauma. Making the past public permits each patient to find personal meaning in the traumatic event (49).

Often groups of traumatized individuals initially resemble adolescent groups in many ways. They tend to be concerned with action rather than introspection. Group members are prone to use drugs to isolate affects generated by the group, and there is often intense splitting: leaders, organizations, or outside agencies are regarded as either all good or all bad. After a successful alliance has been formed with the group, individual differences and attachments slowly emerge, allowing members to break through their psychological numbing. Traumatized people must relearn the use of words to regain a sense of mastery over their emotions. Pines (51) states that "the process of communication is identical to the process of therapy. Patients learn to express themselves in language that has to be understood by their fellow members . . . gradually their problems become located in the group process and become recognizable by all the members of the group." By hearing others express their emotions verbally, and by learning how others manage to deal with the aftermath of trauma through reflection rather than action, many patients become capable of using similar maneuvers to deal with their own helplessness and pain.

The initial force binding the group together is the sharing of the trauma. The intense feelings generated by disclosure at first promote idealization of the leader, who is often credited with much greater power than the leader of other therapy groups. This idealization may seem gratifying for both therapist and members, but ultimately it operates as a resistance to overcoming the helplessness generated by the trauma because it keeps the locus of control outside the individual. Traumatized individuals sometimes elevate group leaders into cult heroes, perpetuating an illusion of the group's omnipotence through identification with a leader who is regarded without ambivalence. Idealization must be vigorously addressed and interpreted. Only after the group starts tackling the leader's real and imagined shortcomings can it really start to see itself as useful and powerful, and only then do group members regain a sense of individual effectiveness.

Traumatized persons need to abandon their identity of being a victim. This requires active reexposure and attention to other people's lives, interests, and difficulties. In the initial phases of homogeneous groups for trauma victims, group members tend to assume that they are all alike. Anyone who attempts to examine individual differences or who shows independence is likely to be met with hostility and invitations to leave. Engagement with others not similarly victimized is undermined. Parson (52) remarks that "since individuation is the goal of group treatment, persistent group we-ness is a resistance to growth and separateness."

It is crucial to avoid the formation of a group of victims united against a dangerous world, with an idealized leader who will protect the members against further harm. The pressure for sameness and fusion in groups of trauma victims led Parson (49) and Herman and Shatzow (43) to recommend time-limited homogeneous groups, followed by therapy in groups with mixed diagnoses. The time limit prevents regressive fusion but promotes rapid bonding and sharing of emotionally sensitive material.

The main task of the group is to explore its own interpersonal processes (50). Envy, competition, assertiveness, sharing, and intimacy are more readily evoked, discussed, and confronted in group therapy than in one-to-one therapy (53). In individual therapy, confrontation is easily seen as rejection rather than help; in a group, confrontation by one person can be balanced by the support and empathic identification of other group members. Many patients find it hard to disagree and express hateful or even just negative feelings in one-to-one relationships because they fear that the relationship will be jeopardized. In a group, the sharing of both confrontation and support often makes the examination of the negative transference vastly easier. Groups that focus on the relationships between the members allow new losses to be experienced as object losses with concomitant grief and sadness, rather than as narcissistic injuries with the accompanying feelings of helplessness, numbing, or vengeful rage.

The unique therapeutic virtue of the group is the opportunity it provides to experience, explore, and work through interpersonal relationships (51). The foundation for this is group cohesiveness, which, in turn, depends on how safe individual members feel with each other (48). The task of the group leader is primarily to be a facilitator of group cohesiveness, rather than a provider of psychotherapeutic attention to individuals. The leader must create an environment in which members can explore their relationships with each other and with the leader. Focus on extragroup issues usually promotes intellectualization and idealization, inhibits the sharing of affect, promotes regression, and leads to competition for the leader's attention (50). In contrast, a focus on intragroup issues usually promotes cohesiveness.

PTSD is not merely an unconscious intrapsychic libidinal conflict. Although the therapist is often drawn into serving the patients' dependent and narcissistic needs, posttraumatic symptoms themselves do not supply secondary gain. Anna Freud (53) emphasized that interpretation alone cannot undo the damage caused by traumatic experiences, even though it may clarify the past and help the patient to deal with the consequences of the trauma. Group psychotherapy reestablishes a peer group in which sharing and reliving of common experiences may facilitate entrance into a world of adult relationships where others can be regarded as both subjects and objects. By experiencing the effect of others on themselves and vice versa, patients can learn to modulate their responses to others according to today's requirements, rather than the demands of past trauma. This allows them to resume the process of growing to emotional maturity, which was arrested by the trauma.

References

1. Lindemann E: Symptomatology and management of acute grief. Am J Psychiatry 101:141–148, 1944

2. Krystal H: Massive Psychic Trauma. New York, International Universities Press, 1968

3. Krystal H: Trauma and Affects. Psychoanal Study Child 33:81–116, 1978

4. Erikson KT: Everything in Its Path: Destruction of Community in the Buffalo Creek Flood. New York, Simon and Schuster, 1976

5. Solomon SD: Mobilizing social support networks in times of disaster, in Trauma and Its Wake, Vol 2. Edited by Figley CR. New York, Brunner/Mazel, 1987

6. Baum A: Disruption during disaster. Working paper, National Institute of Mental Health Workshop on Mental Health Needs Assessment following Disaster. Bethesda, MD, National Institute of Mental Health, 1984

7. Lindy JD, Grace M: The recovery environment: continuing stressor versus a healing psychosocial space, in Disasters and Mental Health. Edited by Sowder BJ. Washington, DC, Center for Mental Health Studies of Emergencies (US Department of Health and Human Services Publication No 85-1421) 1985

8. Quarantelli EL: An assessment of conflicting views on mental health: the consequences of traumatic events, in Trauma and Its Wake, Vol I. Edited by Figley CR, New York, Brunner/Mazel, 1985

9. Davidson S: Human reciprocity among the Jewish prisoners of the Nazi concentration camps, in Proceedings of the Fourth Yad Vashem International Historical Conference. Jerusalem, Yad Vashem, 1984, pp 555–572

10. Becker E: the Denial of Death. New York, Free Press, 1973

11. Freud S: Group psychology and analysis of the ego (1921), in Complete Psychological Works. Standard Ed. Vol 18. Translated and edited by Strachey J. London, Hogarth Press, 1955

12. Eitinger L: Concentration Camp Survivors in Norway and Israel, Oslo, Universitetforlaget, 1964

13. Klein H: Delayed affects and aftereffects of severe traumatization. Israel Annals of Psychiatry 12:293–303, 1974

14. Des Pres T: The Survivor: An Anatomy of Life in the Death Camps, New York, Oxford University Press, 1976

15. Luchterhand EG: Sociological approaches to massive stress in natural and man-made disasters, in Psychic Traumatization. Edited by Krystal H, Niederland W. Boston, Little, Brown and Co, 1971, pp 29–54

16. Danielli Y: The treatment and prevention of long-term effects and intergenerational transmission of victimization: a lesson from Holocaust survivors and their children, in Trauma and Its Wake, Vol I. Edited by Figley CR. New York, Brunner/Mazel, 1985

17. Sullivan HS: Conceptions of Modern Psychiatry. New York, WW Norton & Co, 1940

18. Blos P: The Adolescent Passage. New York, International Universities Press, 1979

19. Offer D, Offer J: Three developmental routes through normal male adolescence, in Adolescent Psychiatry, Vol 4. Edited by Feinstein SC, Giovacchini PL. New York, Aronson, 1975

20. Erikson EH: The problem of ego identity. J Am Psychoanal Assoc 4:56–121, 1956

21. Kernberg O: The couch at sea: psychoanalytic studies of group and organizational leadership. Int J Group Psychother 34:5–23, 1984

22. Haley S: Some of my best friends are dead: the treatment of the PTSD patient and his family, in PTSD and the War Veteran Patient. Edited by Kelly J. New York, Basic Books, 1984

23. Sharp V: Adolescence, in Child Development in Normalcy and Psychopathology. Edited by Bemporad J. New York, Brunner/Mazel, 1980, pp 175–218

24. Aichorn A: Wayward Youth. New York, Viking Press, 1948

25. Elder GH: Military times and turning points in men's lives. Dev Psychol (in press)

26. Johnston J, Bachman J: Youth in Transition: Change and Stability in the Lives of Young Men. Vol 5: Young Men and the Military Service. Ann Arbor, Mich, Institute of Social Research, 1972

27. Elder GH: Historical change in life patterns and personality, in Life Span Development and Behavior. Edited by Bates PB, Brim OG. New York, Academic Press, 1979

28. Shatan CF: Bogus manhood, bogus honor: surrender and transfiguration in the US Marine Corps, in Psychoanalytic Perspectives on Aggression and Violence. Edited by Milman D, Goldman G. Springfield, Ill, Charles C Thomas, 1975

29. Lidz T: Nightmares and the combat neuroses. Psychiatry 9:37–49, 1946

30. Fairbairn WRD: The war neuroses: their nature and significance, in Psychoanalytic Studies of the Personality. London, Routledge & Kegan Paul, 1952

31. Moses R: Adult psychic trauma: the question of early predisposition and some detailed mechanisms. Int J Psychoanal 59:353–363, 1978

32. Fox RP: Narcissistic rage and the problem of combat aggression. Arch Gen Psychiatry 31:807–811, 1974

33. Kohut H: The Analysis of the Self. New York, International Universities Press, 1971

34. Modell A: Object Love and Reality. New York, International Universities Press, 1968

35. van der Kolk BA: Adolescent vulnerability to post traumatic stress disorder. Psychiatry 48:365–370, 1985

36. Laufer R, Brett E, Gallops MS: Post traumatic stress reconsidered: PTSD among Vietnam veterans, in Post Traumatic Stress Disorder: Psychological and Biological Sequelae. Edited by van der Kolk BA. Washington, DC, American Psychiatric Press, 1984

37. Bowlby J: Attachment and Loss. Vol II: Separation, Anxiety and Anger. New York, Basic Books, 1973

38. Lifton R: The Broken Connection. New York, Basic Books, 1983

39. Lindy JD, Titchener J: "Acts of God and man:" long term character change in survivors of disasters and the law. Behavioral Science and the Law 1:85–96, 1983

40. Horowitz MJ: Stress Response Syndromes, 2nd ed. New York, Aronson, 1985

41. Pines M: The frame of reference in group psychotherapy. Int J Group Psychother 31:275–285, 1981

42. Kobasa SC, Pucetti MC: Personality and social resources in stress resistance. J Pers Soc Psychol 42:168–177, 1982

43. Herman JL, Shatzow E: Time limited group psychotherapy for women with a history of incest. Int J Group Psychother 34:605–610, 1984

44. Yassen J, Glass L: Sexual assault survivor groups. Social Work 37:252–257, 1984

45. Rounsaville B, Lifton N, Bieber M: The natural history of a psychotherapy group for battered women. Psychiatry 42:63–78, 1979

46. Walker JI: Group psychotherapy with Vietnam veterans. Int J Group Psychother 31:379–389, 1981

47. Grinker R, Spiegel J: Men under Stress. New York, McGraw-Hill, 1945

48. Scheidlinger S: Focus on Group Psychotherapy. New York, International Universities Press, 1982

49. Parson ER: The role of psychodynamic group psychotherapy in the treatment of the combat veteran, in Psychotherapy of the Combat Veteran. Edited by Schzartz HJ. New York, Spectrum Publications, 1984, pp 153–220

50. Pines M: Psychoanalysis and group analysis. Int J Group Psychother 33:155–170, 1983

51. Pines M: Psychic development and the group analytic situation. Group 9:60–73, 1985

52. Parson ER: Posttraumatic accelerated cohesion: its recognition and management in group treatment of Vietnam veterans. Group (in press)

53. Freud A: A psychoanalytic view of developmental psychopathology. Journal of the Philadelphia Association of Psychoanalysis 1:7–17, 1974

CHAPTER 8

Amnesia, Dissociation, and the Return of the Repressed

Bessel A. van der Kolk, M.D.
William Kadish, M.D.

*The [traumatic] neuroses may proclaim too
loudly the effects of mortal changes, and may
be silent or only speak in muffled tones of the
effects of frustration in love.*

Freud et al. (1)

On Saturday, November 28, 1942, two days after Thanksgiving
and on the eve of the Boston College football classic, the Coconut
Grove nightclub, packed to capacity, went up in flames. It was
the worst fire disaster in Boston's history, killing 492 persons and
seriously injuring hundreds of others. Clinical observations about
the psychological sequelae of this fire gave rise to the classic papers by Lindemann (2) and by Adler (3). Lindemann defined trauma
as the sudden cessation of social interaction. In describing the
grief reactions of people who had lost loved ones in the fire, Lindemann did not study the reactions in the survivors of the traumatic impact of the fire itself. The fire remains part of the local
lore in Boston, and continues to be referred to from time to time
in the local press, usually in connection with subsequent disasters. We therefore were somewhat attuned to our patient Melody
D. when she started to make references to the fire in 1984, during
psychotic episodes for which she was hospitalized at the Massachusetts Mental Health Center. At that time the patient was a 55-

The case history in this chapter was written by Dr. Kadish, and the discussion
was written by Dr. van der Kolk.

173

year-old single woman who, as we will see, had no memory of having been in the fire herself, but whose dissociated reexperiences and reenactments of fire-related incidents had caused repeated psychiatric hospitalizations.

The Coconut Grove Fire

The fire broke out in the basement lounge, igniting certain decorating materials, which then released noxious gases. The combination of the rapidly spreading fire, the expanding volume of toxic gases, the overcrowded conditions, and the paucity of available exits contributed to the making of an unprecedented catastrophe. The main door to the nightclub malfunctioned on the night of the fire. It was a revolving door that got stuck as people tried to flee the building. Dozens of bodies piled up behind it and no one was able to leave that way. Another exit door was locked.

Ms. D. was then a 19-year-old single girl. The previous day she managed to get a job at the Coconut Grove and was thrilled to be there that Saturday night. It was exhilarating for her to be in the presence of the famous performers and glamorous guests, for she herself was a very attractive young lady and an aspiring dancer. As she recalled, at 10 p.m. she sat down in the main hall to see the band perform. Suddenly there was a commotion, and she looked up toward the ceiling.

> The wires—the fire was spreading in the wires. Then the whole room filled up with gases—choking gases. It looked as if the ceiling—the roof—were opening up—I saw people sitting there, not moving, with grotesque faces—and ash black, all black. I don't know how I got out.

It is not clear how Ms. D. escaped death. Perhaps she was helped out through the stage door. Perhaps she was one of several people who hid terrified in the kitchen freezer. She hesitatingly recalls feeling terribly cold, and remembers being in a crowded corridor in a hospital. Bodies were lying everywhere. But soon after she was released, she forgot about the event entirely.

After testifying at hearings in March 1943, she did not think about or explicitly recall the event for the next 38 years. When she did recall the tragedy, it was not in the form of a memory.

The Reenactment

In the summer of 1981, eight years after Ms. D. had returned to her hometown from an important sales position in New York City in order to help care for her ill father, she developed her first psychiatric symptoms. Over the years, her father had slowly deteriorated with at least one major depressive episode, which had required electroconvulsive therapy. He also suffered from a host of medical disorders. Ms. D. seemed to be unable to accept his deteriorating condition, and she insisted on his remaining independent by attempting to force him to return to work. He was intermittently incontinent, and he became increasingly unresponsive to her care. Rather than accepting the inevitable nursing home placement, she began to force-feed him. This caused him to become increasingly angry with her to the point that he told her that the worst day of his life was the day she was born. In her frustration and rage, she physically assaulted him on at least one occasion. The situation grew more desperate as the landlord took action to have them evicted from the building because the patient could no longer earn enough to pay the rent. When referring to this time, the patient said, "I tried to save my father from drowning, but he wouldn't let me."

On July 15, 1981, through other relatives' efforts, the father was taken to a local general hospital and the patient was brought to our mental health center on a civil commitment. She was calm and cooperative during the initial evaluation; her mental status was remarkable for its extreme guardedness and numerous delusions. She insisted that "gases are invading my body" and "electricity is spreading in my body" and that she was having other "crazy thoughts." During that admission Ms. D. received a diagnosis of atypical paranoid psychosis. However, a review of her behavior and speech during the 6 months of her hospitalization revealed a more intriguing syndrome. Although she did demonstrate loss of reality testing, delusional thoughts, and inappropriate behavior, there were periods of time, sometimes lasting days to weeks, when she would appear calm, behave normally, and engage in conversation in socially appropriate ways. At other times she would be seen talking to herself for hours. When asked what she was talking about, she once replied, "I lost five years somehow." Later, she gave further details. "I'm talking things over with myself. Which would be better—to continue this struggle to recall piece by piece the parts of my memory I have forgotten, or to live my life peacefully and let the pieces pop up? Each piece I remember just tells me how much I have forgotten." At yet another time, "I have to leave Melody behind, for a week I saw into who she was, and I was horrified."

In addition to this struggle over how to deal with lost memories, she also engaged in what, in retrospect, seem to be reenactments of the Coconut Grove fire. On one occasion the patient tried to gather everyone up to leave the hospital. "We're all moving out today," she ordered, "and I'm going to be the last one out, to make sure everyone gets out. All the doors are coming off today. No more doors!" On another occasion, she was observed singing patriotic songs very loudly. She explained, "There is a war out there. We won." She identified the enemies as the Nazis, thus confirming that the reference was indeed to World War II, which was taking place at the time of the fire. Another reference to the Grove event took place when the patient suddenly began questioning other patients. "How many women did you save from the fire? How many did you carry out?"

In February 1982, Ms. D's father died. She attended the funeral with her sister, and one week later she was discharged from the hospital. Her psychosis had "suddenly dissolved," although her doctor was not sure how or why. She continued to see her psychiatrist weekly for a year and returned to work. Then, in February of 1983, she was brought in by the police for disturbing the peace. Her behavior consisted of pulling fire alarms in numerous buildings and shouting at people to get out. (She later referred to this behavior as her acting like the town crier; she believed that her duty was to warn people of the impending danger). She was hospitalized but escaped days later. She changed her name and went to Florida, where she functioned for 2 months before returning to Boston and admitting herself voluntarily to another facility. There she was diagnosed as having bipolar illness and lithium was prescribed. She never took the medication, and again her behavior normalized and she was discharged. She had another episode requiring hospitalization in the summer of 1984, and she once again escaped.

Her last inpatient stay began in January 1985 when Dr. Kadish admitted her to the locked ward of our mental health center. The police brought her in from the supermarket, where she had been found yelling to all that "the gas from the ceiling will kill all the shoppers." When asked on admission what she had been doing, she stated, "I saved 1500 lives." For the next two months the patient remained grossly psychotic. She misidentified herself, had delusions of reference and of influence, consistently behaved as if the time were 1942, and eventually became extremely paranoid of staff, whom she thought were Nazis. Finally, after a prolonged medical guardianship procedure, she was started on antipsychotic medication. For 7 days there was no change. Then, on the eighth day, she spoke clearly to one of the attendants, and on the ninth introduced herself to her therapist by her proper name, apologized for her behavior, and inquired about the status of her apartment and her pet dog.

Early Experience

Before proceeding to an account of our remarkable therapeutic voyage, which continues to this day, one year later, it is important to elucidate some critical aspects of Ms. D.'s childhood, namely her relationship with her family and her physical illness. These two factors seem to play a prominent role in understanding the impact of the fire on her life. Ms. D. is the eldest of three daughters, born to a working class Jewish couple in Boston in the 1920s. It is quite likely that she was conceived before marriage and may have been responsible for the unhappy union of her parents. In any case, she recalls always being a hated child. "My mother never called me by my real name," she says (some nicknames she recalls are Blubber and Bim). She describes her father as a hard-working book dealer who was totally indifferent toward her. In his later years he clearly favored the patient's younger sister, despite the fact that it was the patient who sent him money and worked most actively in his behalf. The other sister was responsible, along with her sons, for taking all of the patient's possessions from her apartment when she came to Boston to help her father. In brief, the patient felt at best neglect and at worst betrayed and abused by every member of her immediate family. In the course of therapy she also reported episodes of actual physical abuse, consisting of her mother walking over her in high heels and engaging in hair pulling.

When the patient was 4½ years old, she developed a severe case of polio. What began as a sense of weakness and inability to walk progressed to total body paralysis requiring long-term hospital treatment. She was in a children's hospital for perhaps as long as a year, receiving for at least part of that time tube feedings and respiratory support. She remembers clearly only one incident from that time: being given a party by her relatives because she was able to wiggle a toe. For some time she was placed in a rehabilitation facility and vaguely remembers having to wear braces on her arms and legs. It was not until years later that she regained the full use of all her extremities and was able to return to regular school.

As a child Ms. D. really did "lose her body"; it was actually unmovable, unfeelable, and grossly distorted by tubes, braces, and probably an iron lung. She was faced with the prospect of death for a protracted period of time. One can speculate that the exaggerated isolation and physical immobility during these latency years significantly contributed to the patient's development of an extensive fantasy life and to the development of her capacity to dissociate. This actual experience of emotional isolation and threat of physical annihilation was compounded by the lack of reliable support from and synchrony with her family. She never developed a firm inner world in which she could experience herself as held and soothed. It is a cruel irony, but one paradigmatic of this case, that when the patient was finally well enough to return to school, her mother changed her name and insisted that she use this other name in school. Having at last recovered her body, she lost her name.

Therapy

Stage 1

The theme of the initial stage of Ms. D's therapy was loss. The patient stated clearly: "I haven't mourned my father's death." She spoke of what a great man he had been and how valiantly she tried to save him. She was never able to temper her idealization of her father or reflect well on her rage at him. Her body at times would shake with emotion as she recalled the affect-laden events related to her life with her father. She then moved from focusing on father-related losses to other profound losses. She touched on the loss of her material possessions, the loss of dignity involved in being a psychiatric patient, and living in a shelter for homeless women. In particular, she mourned the breakup with her boyfriend just before the time of the fire. It was a time of profound sadness; nurses' notes from the day treatment center report that the patient was "doing grief work" and that she was "appropriately depressed." Indeed, the patient herself, who after each of her prior psychotic episodes returned immediately to work, complained that she just didn't have the energy to pursue employment.

Stage 2

During the next three months the character of the therapy shifted to an almost total preoccupation with the traumatic event itself, the fire. She spoke about the Coconut Grove in every session; she brought in books about it; she went to the library to research the old newspaper articles. She often visited the site of the event (now a parking garage) and remarked that she felt very peaceful when she went there. She found this strange but clearly comforted herself by returning again and again to the site during these months. Initially she insisted she was at another club the night of the fire. As she related more and more details, her therapist began to wonder with her if perhaps she wasn't mistaken. Gradually, she became increasingly certain that she was there the night of the fire. This led to a highly productive phase of treatment, within which the patient was able to make cognitive connections between current symptoms and the traumatic experience. Together therapist and patient identified and made some sense out of the precipitants to her dissociative states, as well as to many of her lifelong idiosyncratic habits and ideas. For example, she was able to recall that one episode began when the radiator in her apartment was generating large quantities of steam, which she mistook for deadly gases. She also related her fear of wires to her belief about how the fire began, her fear of being in buildings with revolving doors to the tragedy of the revolving door at the Coconut Grove, and many other such examples. As she continued to make such connections, she reported frequently that she felt she was "becoming more of a person."

Stage 3

Despite the significant gains made in the therapy, Ms. D. remained convinced that the nature of her problem still wasn't really understood by the therapist. She repeatedly told her therapist in session after session, "Doctor, I lost my body. I've lost my physical identity." Initially the therapist thought that this, too, related to a near-death experience at the Coconut Grove. She was asked if she could recall any other time in her life, besides that, when she may have experienced similar sensations. It was at this point that she brought up her childhood illness and for the first time described the situation. (As best as could be determined, this subject had never been raised in any of her prior therapy.)

Unlike with the fire, her therapist had to take the lead in returning her attention to her childhood experience. She asked: "What does this have to do with it? Do you really think this is part of why I get sick?" She needed to be reassured that the therapist thought so, but that he could not be sure, and that he needed to know more about it. So she continued making cognitive connections between her psychiatric symptoms and her early experience. For example, when she was ill she developed a pyelonephritis, for which she was prescribed a very high fluid diet. She could now recall how bloated and edematous her body had been at the time and how her mother nicknamed her "Blubber." This recalled fact was related to her dissociated awareness of her body being "too big." A second example concerns the respiratory difficulties she experienced when ill. She is dimly aware of having tremendous trouble breathing and knew she was in the Children's Hospital for many months. These recollections led to her recognition that having a respiratory illness in adult life almost invariably led to some symptomatic episode. She told of an episode that occurred in New York during an otherwise good period of her life in which she experienced near total loss of strength and control of her limbs following a bad case of the flu. Also, she remembered that prior to her first hospitalization, she thought she had pneumonia and was put on erythromycin. As therapy progressed along these lines, Ms. D. and her therapist came to describe her illness as one of "horrible memories." This framework appealed to her, and it encouraged the production of further material. Each time she recalled something, an effort was made to relate the memory to other memories, and in particular to current symptoms. This strengthened her recognition of her symptoms as the undesirable emergence of horrible memories and increased her control over them.

At this writing, Ms. D. remains in therapy one hour per week. She takes no medication. She works full-time and has been promoted. She has resumed her friendships with her two closest girlfriends and frequents a local lounge where she enjoys a cocktail and conversations with men. Her goal is to develop a business of her own, or to once again become a manager of a shop as she had been before. Her attention to all aspects of her physical appearance is currently quite high, and in therapy this aspect of her identity is being explored. Whether this progessive improvement in her condition can be maintained is not a question that can be answered at this time. Perhaps, though, it can be said that the definition of her illness as primarily dissociative and post-traumatic, and the attendant treatment strategy of fostering gradual recollection of dissociated memories and their cognitive attachment to current symptoms provide this patient with the best possibility for long-term symptom control and adaptive function.

Discussion

The Discovery of the Relationship Between Amnesia, Dissociation, and Reenactment

In posttraumatic stress disorder the warding off of the return of unresolved psychological trauma becomes a central focus in people's lives. For over a hundred years psychiatrists have recognized the price that people pay for this walling off the memories of the trauma. Involvement with their surroundings becomes constricted, causing superficial or nonexistent love relationships. When the neat patterns of life are disrupted by loss of loved ones, physical illness, or other incapacities, the trauma often is relived in dissociated form, in nightmares, in overwhelming affect states, or in reenactments. Babinski (4), Janet (5), Breuer and Freud (6), and Freud (7) recognized that unresolved psychological trauma caused stress in later life to break through in the area of least resistance (4), and to be experienced as a recurrence of the original trauma. Janet (5) stated: "Stress is often experienced in later points in time much the same way as the actual earlier traumatic insult. The trauma remains isolated, more or less separated from all other ideas; it can envelop or suppress all else." The recognition of the danger of traumatic reexperiencing led Lindemann (2) to advocate acute crisis intervention to prevent a "walling off" of traumatic memories.

Freud's Early Work on Repression and Reliving

Dissociation of traumatic memories, alternating with uncontrollable actual or symbolic repetitions, are fundamental features of the trauma response (8). Since the time of Charcot, psychiatrists have noted the similarity between hysteria and the trauma response. In his early years, Freud ascribed a traumatic etiology to many psychiatric problems. Even after he abandoned the seduction theory of hysteria, around the turn of the century, he continued to be fascinated with the impact of overwhelming life events on the psyche. In 1920 (9), he declared that:

> The symptomatic picture presented by traumatic neurosis approaches that of hysteria . . . , but surpasses it as a rule in its

strongly marked signs of subjective ailment [in which it resembles hypochondria or melancholia] as well as the evidence it gives of a far more comprehensive general enfeeblement and disturbances of mental capacities.

Breuer and Freud (6) hypothesized that hysterical symptoms were caused by intense memories or ideas of events, which they termed psychic traumas. In 1893 they declared that "hysterics suffer mainly from reminiscences . . . the traumatic experience is constantly forcing itself upon the patient [and this] is proof of the strength of that experience: the patient is, as one might say, fixated on his trauma." They postulated that the memory of these traumas is unacceptable or frightening; hysterical patients use the defense mechanism of repression to remove the memory from consciousness. Breuer and Freud noted that the memories "originated during the prevalence of severely paralyzing affects, such as fright." Freud (7) stated that resulting psychic splitting is due to:

An incompatibility in their mental life—that is to say . . . the ego was faced with an experience, an idea, or a feeling which aroused such a distressing affect that the subject decided to forget about it, because he had no power to resolve the contradiction between the incompatible idea and his ego by means of thought activity.

Freud (10) quite categorically stated that:

The ultimate cause of hysteria is always the seduction of a child by an adult. The actual event always occurs before the age of puberty, though the outbreak of the neurosis occurs after puberty. The symptoms of hysteria can only be understood if they are traced back to experiences which have a traumatic effect.

Two years later Freud entirely abandoned the notion of a traumatic etiology of the neuroses. The determining factor in the genesis of hysteria was reframed as a fantasy elaboration of conflictual instinctual issues, rather than the repression of actual traumatic events. However, throughout Freud's life he remained preoccupied with the impact of actual trauma; the central theme of the last monograph published during his lifetime (11) was "the return of the repressed," the reenactment of unresolved childhood trauma in later life.

Freud's Later Contributions to the Understanding of the Trauma Response

Twenty years after abandoning the seduction theory, Freud (11) returned to the issue of psychological trauma. He noted the similarity between the fixation on the trauma seen in the war neuroses and in hysteria. Babinski (4) and Simmel and Ferenczi (quoted in 1) traced many of the motor symptoms of paralysis in the war neuroses to a fixation to the moment that the trauma occurred. Freud was struck by the fact that patients suffering from traumatic neuroses experienced a lack of conscious preoccupation with the memories of their accident. He postulated that "perhaps they are more concerned with NOT thinking of it." Freud (9) proposed that repression is the very cause of the fixation on the trauma and of the unconscious id's compulsion to repeat:

> We found that the perceptual content of the exciting experiences and the ideational content of pathogenic structures of thought were forgotten and debarred from being reproduced in memory, and we therefore concluded that the keeping away from consciousness was the main characteristic of hysterical repression.

Freud (12) further elaborated these themes, approximating the contemporary views on the central issues in the human trauma response: terror and helplessness. In raising the question: "When does separation from an object produce anxiety, when does it produce mourning and when does it produce . . . only pain," he touched on the multiplicity of expressions of the trauma response, including psychosomatic symptoms, much later further spelled out by Krystal (13) and others. Freud anticipated the biphasic response to trauma as formulated by Bowlby (14), Lindemann (2), and Horowitz (8).

Freud (12) described how posttraumatic anxiety (hyperarousal) becomes the source of the continuation of the emergency response. In anxiety-provoking situations, the patient expects renewed helplessness.

> The present situation reminds me of the traumatic experiences I have had before. Therefore I will anticipate the trauma and behave as if it had already come. Anxiety is therefore on the one hand an expectation of the trauma, and on the other a repetition of it in a mitigated form.

The Schreber Case

Freud did not have a chance to appreciate the full extent to which early experiences determine the form of later psychotic decompensation as well. His well-known discussion of Schreber's autobiography (15) formed the basis of an extensive description of the origins of paranoia. At age 51, the German judge Dr. Schreber developed delusions of having a mission to redeem the world and to restore it to its lost state of bliss. He thought he could fulfill this mission by being transformed from a man into a woman. Freud saw this emasculation fantasy as the earliest germ of the delusional system, which comprised a mixture of reverence and rebelliousness toward God. Schreber believed that God was the instigator of a plot against him; he was preoccupied with divine "miracles" which consisted of "being tied to the earth," being "tied to celestial bodies," or "fastened to rays." He also described a "chest compressing miracle," which he experienced as a horrifying assault on his body. Furthermore, Schreber accused his physician of attempting to murder him.

Freud explained Schreber's delusional system as an unacceptable passive homosexual longing for his doctor. Because this wish was unacceptable, Schreber defended against it by forming a paranoid delusion, with his wishful fantasy as the projected source of his persecution. Freud saw Schreber's preoccupation with the sun as a sublimated father symbol, and he postulated that Schreber's delusions had their origin in an unresolved childhood conflict between his ego and forbidden homosexual longings toward his father.

Thirty years after the publication of Freud's case discussion, Niederland (16–18) published a series of articles about Schreber's father, who had been a noted pediatrician in Germany in the middle of the last century. These accounts clearly revealed that young Schreber had been a victim of severe child abuse. The father had written a series of popular books about pedagogy that emphasized the need for proper posture and hygiene. His books were illustrated with a number of pictures depicting elaborate apparatus to which a child should be strapped to ensure proper posture and to prevent aberrant behaviors, such as masturbation. He advocated physical punishments for the slightest infringements on the rules and "at the earliest age . . . because the ignoble parts of a child's crude nature must be weakened by great strictness." He told his readers to get their children to volunteer for punishment to prevent "the possibility of spite and bitterness." Niederland (17) found that late in life, father Schreber had actually admitted that he drove some of his children into a state of complete submission and passive surrender. However, he had done this to develop a "better and healthier race of men." Niederland wrote: "the father, with no little apostolic grandeur, strives for the development of better health and hygiene in an earthbound way . . . the son, in his delusional elaboration of these concepts does so in an archaic, magical way." Clearly, the contents of the son's delusional system derive from an elaboration of early, futile attempts to gain his father's love and approval, and it incorporated the methods that disrupted the security of the attachment bond and the resulting pervasive sense of helplessness. Schreber's delusional system clearly illustrates both the continuation of his childhood terror into adulthood and the extent of his identification with the aggressor. A reinterpretation of the origins of the psychosis would speak much stronger for a desperate attempt on the part of a little boy to maintain attachment to an at once admired and terrifying father, than for a homosexual conflict. The son's obsession with the need to be turned into a woman can be readily understood in the light of the father's dread of infantile sexuality, expressed in words, and in his advocating strapping children to elaborate mechanical devices to prevent masturbation. Our knowledge of the effects of early disruptions of the attachment bond (see Chapters 2 and 4) make the issue of sexual conflicts here appear to be quite secondary. The psychosis was the reenactment of the infantile experience of terror.

Dissociation as a Response to Trauma

Dissociation as a response to trauma has been amply described in the literature (19–24). Except when related to brain injury, dissociation always seems to be a response to traumatic life events. Memories and feelings connected with the trauma are forgotten and return as intrusive recollections, feeling states (such as overwhelming anxiety and panic unwarranted by current experience), fugues, delusions, states of depersonalization, and finally in behavioral reenactments. Archibald and Tuddenham (25) found that reexperiencing of war trauma sometimes did not start until as long as 15 years afterward. In our patient, the time lapse was 39 years; she illustrates the timelessness and enduring power of unconscious mental life, in both its literal and its symbolic representations.

Dissociation is adaptive: it allows relatively normal functioning for the duration of the traumatic event and leaves a large part of the personality unaffected by the trauma. It is conceivable that amnestic dissociation for a traumatic experience remains adaptive throughout a person's lifetime without further psychopathological consequences. Freud was not optimistic about this possibility. His premise was that when a person represses important events "he is obliged to repeat the repressed material as a contemporary experience instead of . . . remembering it as something belonging to the past" (9). Freud (11) returned to this theme later:

> What children have experienced at the age of two and have not understood, need never be remembered by them, except in dreams. . . . But at some later time it will break into their life with obsessional impulses, it will govern their actions. . . . The precipitating cause, with its attendant perceptions and ideas, is forgotten. This, however, is not the end of the process: the instinct has either retained its forces, or collects them again, or it is reawakened by some new precipitating cause . . . at a weak spot . . . [it] comes to light as a symptom, without the acquiescence of the ego, but also without its understanding. All the phenomena of the formation of symptoms may be justly described as the "return of the repressed."

While Freud talked about instinctual drives, today many clinicians pay more attention to the formative experience of childhood attachments and the traumatic nature of separation and lack of validation in early life. In our patient, there was a serious, early disturbance in interpersonal relationships that almost certainly predisposed her to be vulnerable to subsequent trauma. It is as if the discrete external trauma, which threatened the existence of the body, resonated with the internalized traumatic interpersonal relationships, which threatened the existence of the self.

The case of our patient demonstrates the tremendous plasticity of dissociative phenomena. Her course included conversion reactions, fugue states, amnestic periods, derealization, depersonalization, reenactments, and psychosis. The variation in both type and severity of symptoms is impressive and illustrates the tremendous difficulty in reliably categorizing psychiatric illness over time. In addition, like most patients, her illness is a clinical kaleidoscope, with an etiology comprised of numerous pathogenic influences whose interconnections will probably never be entirely understood. In our patient's case there probably are important interconnections between traumatic events separated over time—

namely, family discord and possibly neglect, the polio, and the fire.

Our patient's story is a powerful example of the tendency to miss the diagnosis of severe dissociative illness and delayed post-traumatic stress syndrome. Despite the atypical features of her psychosis, the diagnoses throughout her first four years of treatment consistently included only bipolar illness, agitated depression with psychotic features, and schizophreniform psychosis. The defenses against the trauma, including dissociative phenomena, sensation seeking, emotional constriction, and drug and alcohol abuse cause great difficulty in recognizing the traumatic etiologies and reenactments in the symptomatology of many psychiatric patients (see Chapter 1). During periods of emotional constriction, when amnesia for the traumatic event, overinvolvement in work, and emotional distance may be the only symptoms, it is even more difficult to make the correct diagnosis. In Veterans Administration hospitals many war veterans with a history of severe trauma currently receive diagnoses of chronic schizophrenia or diagnoses denoting functional somatic complaints.

Treatment Implications

Traumatized patients are frequently very difficult to engage in psychotherapy. This probably is related both to a fear of attachment, which reawakens the fear of abandonment, and to the reluctance to remember the trauma itself. After intense efforts to ward off reliving the trauma, a therapist cannot expect that the resistances to remember will suddenly melt away under his or her empathic efforts. The history of the neglect of the trauma issue of psychiatry is probably as much related to the patients' efforts to forget as to the profession's reluctance to deal with the helplessness that accompanies the treatment of the sequelae of overwhelming life events. Many patients interrupt therapy and attempt not to have to deal with the issues related to the trauma. Our patient was no exception. It took her four psychiatric hospitalizations, and probably as many therapists, before she allowed the memories of the fire to be explored. Trust came slowly and probably was related to the therapist's empathy with her feelings that her father had been victimized by his family. They probably connected because of a shared cultural background and because loving feelings, probably dormant since the breakup just prior to the fire, were reawakened. Freud also was aware that loving feelings were essential for the task of therapy to be completed. This affection for the therapist was not acted out, as so often occurs in patients who have been traumatized within the context of the family. The therapist became a soothing object, whose words she learned to trust. This is reflected in her current use of the insights gained in her psychotherapy: through the words "It is only a memory," she is able to calm herself when aroused and reexperiencing trauma-related affects. Thus she is able to prevent full-blown dissociation. By using the therapist as a soothing object, the process is reversed and healing begins. A secure bond is established with another person; it is then taken in and utilized to hold the psyche together when the threat of physical disintegration is reexperienced. One can see how both the etiology as well as the cure of trauma-related psychological disturbance depends fundamentally on the state of the object relational world.

Once a patient can start remembering the trauma and is able to understand the connections between the events and subsequent emotional experiences, there is a gradual reduction in the intensity and frequency of the intrusive nightmares, reenactments, or anxiety and panic states. Interruptions of the treatment, often in the form of leaving therapy or escaping from the hospital (all illustrated by our patient), return the person to some form of denial and often prevent complete processing of the event. Failures to approach trauma-related material very gradually lead to excessive feelings of emotion, flooding, and retraumatization, usually accompanied by flashbacks or nightmares. The patient needs to be given control over the amount of information he or she is capable of divulging.

Our patient was able to regain her previous level of functioning, after approximately 40 years of relatively normal functioning and 5 of intermittent psychosis and dramatic deterioration. It is likely that, if she had not met a therapist who was able to understand the meaning of her symptoms and who wanted to know how she became who she was, she would have ended up another chronic patient, blended in with other chronic patients whose tales never got told.

References

1. Freud S, Ferenczi S, Abraham K: Psychoanalysis and the War Neuroses. New York, International Universities Press, 1921

2. Lindemann E: Symptomatology and management of acute grief. Am J Psychiatry 101:141–148, 1944

3. Adler A: Neuropsychiatric complications of Boston's Coconut Grove disaster. JAMA 123:1089–1101, 1943

4. Babinski J: Reformes, incapacites, gratifications dans les nevroses. Rev Neurol (Paris) 23:753–757, 1916

5. Janet P: L'automatisme Psychologique. Paris, Balliere, 1889

6. Breuer J, Freud S: Studies in hysteria (1895), in Complete Psychological Works. Standard Ed. Translated and edited by Strachey J. London, Hogarth Press, 1954

7. Freud S: Heredity and the etiology of the neuroses (1896), in Complete Psychological Works. Standard Ed. Translated and edited by Strachey J. London, Hogarth Press, 1954

8. Horowitz MJ: Stress Response Syndromes. New York, Aronson, 1976

9. Freud S: Beyond the pleasure principle (1920), in Complete Psychological Works. Standard Ed. Vol 18. Translated and edited by Strachey J. London, Hogarth Press, 1954

10. Freud S: The aetiology of hysteria (1896), in Complete Psychological Works. Standard Ed. Vol 3. Translated and edited by Strachey J. London, Hogarth Press, 1954

11. Freud S: Moses and monotheism (1939), in Complete Psychological Works. Standard Ed. Vol 18. Translated and edited by Strachey J. London, Hogarth Press, 1954

12. Freud S: Inhibitions, symptoms and anxiety (1926), in Complete Psychological Works. Standard Ed. Vol 20. Translated and edited by Strachey J. London, Hogarth Press, 1954

13. Krystal H: Trauma and affects. Psychoanal Study Child 33:81–116, 1978

14. Bowlby J: Separation, anxiety and anger. New York, Basic Books, 1973

15. Freud S: Psychoanalytic notes on a case of paranoia (dementia paranoides) (1911), in Complete Psychological Works. Standard Ed. Vol 12. Translated and edited by Strachey J. London, Hogarth Press, 1954

16. Niederland WG: Three notes on the Schreber case. Psychoanal Q 20:579–591, 1951

17. Niederland WG: Schreber, father and son. Psychoanal Q 28:151–169, 1959

18. Niederland WG: Schreber and Flechsig: a further contribution to the "kernel of truth in Schreber's delusional system." J Am Psychoanal Assoc 16:740–749, 1968

19. Hilgard ER: Divided consciousness: multiple controls of human thought and action. New York, John Wiley and Sons, 1977

20. Jaffe R: Dissociative phenomena in concentration camp inmates. Int J Psychoanal 49:310–312, 1968

21. Noyes R: Depersonalization in response to life threatening danger. Psychiatry 18:375–384, 1977

22. Fisher C: Amnestic states and the war neuroses: the psychogenesis of fugues. Psychoanal Q 14:437–468, 1945

23. Bliss EL: Multiple personalities: a report of 14 cases with implications for schizophrenia and hysteria. Arch Gen Psychiatry 37:1388–1397, 1980

24. Braun BG: Towards a theory of multiple personality and other dissociative phenomena. Psychiatr Clin North Am 7:171–193, 1984

25. Archibald H, Tuddenham R: Persistent stress reactions after combat. Arch Gen Psychiatry 12:475–481, 1965

CHAPTER 9

Retrieval and Integration of Traumatic Memories with the "Painting Cure"

Mark S. Greenberg, Ph.D.
Bessel A. van der Kolk, M.D.

Pathologies of memory are characteristic features of post-traumatic stress disorder (PTSD). These range from amnesia for part, or all, of the traumatic events to frank dissociation, in which large realms of experience or aspects of one's identity are disowned. Such failures of recall can paradoxically coexist with the opposite: intruding memories and unbidden repetitive images of the traumatic events. In the latter instances, the traumatized individual is compelled to recall the trauma involuntarily. After the acute stage of traumatic exposure, this is commonly manifested as a compulsive need to tell and retell the events that transpired. This tendency to reexperience, in either the verbal or visual realm, is generally understood as an attempt to come to terms with, or to integrate, the strong affects and somatic sensations invoked by the trauma into the fabric of one's life experience. This is often accompanied by a reaching out for interpersonal contact, an anchor that provides safety and stability. Alternatively, some trauma victims withdraw into a shell of self-imposed exile.

In chronic PTSD, episodic intrusive recollections can break through the amnestic barrier with life-like vividness in the form of nightmares and flashbacks (1, 2), accompanied by high levels

of subjective distress. As we have argued in Chapter 3, physiological arousal generally seems to precede such traumatic reliving
experiences. Further autonomic arousal, panic states, and dis-
orientation can then ensue. The state of sleep and the quality of
dream mentation facilitate the generation of eidetic images related
to the trauma (1). Perhaps the pictorial, emotional, and alogical
quality of dream mentation permit traumatic material to achieve
conscious representation in this altered state.

Infantile Amnesia

Schachtel (3) studied the phenomenon of infantile amnesia—the
universal inability to remember the first three years of life. He
argued that individuals could not recall their early childhood because the nature of the thought processes of the young child are
fundamentally different from those of adulthood. In his model,
the child develops thought structures, called schemata, which are
modified over time by maturation and life experience. These schemata serve as frames of interpretation that endow current experience with meaning. Furthermore, the process of remembering
consists of reconstructing past events using *presently* existing
schemata: "Memory as a function of the living personality can be
understood only as a capacity for the organization and reconstruction of past experiences and impressions in the service of
present needs, fears, and interests" (3). According to this model,
amnesia occurs when there is a mismatch between the cognitive
stage at the time that the event was experienced and encoded,
and the cognitive capacities at the time of recall.

   Schachtel stated that the acquisition of language is the crucial
factor in the construction of increasingly sophisticated schemata.
White and Pillemer (4) have claimed that memories do not appear
to be stored in narrative ("linguistic") form before the age of approximately 5 to 8. Other theorists, such as Bruner and Postman
(5) and Neisser (6) identified three distinct modes of thought:
enactive, iconic, and symbolic/linguistic. These three modes of
representation closely parallel Piaget's (7) notions of sensorimotor,
preoperational, and operational thinking. Over the course of development of the child, there is a shift from sensorimotor (action
codes), to perceptual (iconic) representations, to symbolic and
linguistic modes of organization of mental experience. Different
models posit differential availability of these three modes of representation in adulthood, but as a rule, symbolic/linguistic processing overshadows the sensorimotor and iconic. According to

Neisser (6) "childhood amnesia . . . is a necessary consequence of the discontinuities of mental functioning which accompany growth into adulthood . . . the cognitive accommodations which must accompany these transitions seem to make the past inaccessible."

Posttraumatic Amnesia

These cognitive developmental frameworks can be extended to account for posttraumatic amnesia throughout the life cycle. Amnesia can occur when traumatic experiences are encoded in sensorimotor or iconic form and therefore cannot be easily translated into the symbolic language necessary for linguistic retrieval. It is plausible that in situations of terror, the experience does not get processed in symbolic/linguistic forms, but tends to be organized on a sensorimotor or iconic level—as horrific images, visceral sensations, or fight/flight reactions. These then can be reactivated by affective, auditory (8), or visual (9) cues. This is analogous to the concept of state-dependent learning where information acquired in an aroused or intoxicated state is not available under normal conditions but returns when the altered state of consciousness is reintroduced (10).

Thus the degree of physiological disorganization, as well as the developmental stage during the traumatic experience, will affect the capacity for mental processing of overwhelming experience (11). The essence of the trauma experience is that it leaves people in a state of "unspeakable terror." The experience does not fit into existing conceptual schemata: it overwhelms. This precludes accommodation and assimilation of the experience. In contrast, the ability of emergency personnel to maintain composure and effective action in the face of catastrophic events is precisely because of overlearned coping responses that promote technical solutions. Of course, even among such well-trained people, some events may surpass their coping abilities (12).

Alexithymia, the incapacity to give symbolic/linguistic representations to internal affective states, may be a special case in point of "fixation" on the trauma. The cognitive style of "pensee operatoire" (13) relegates alexithymics to react to emotional stimulation with somatic sensations and motoric reactions. Krystal (14) postulated that alexithymia itself is a result of infantile catastrophic trauma that has rendered the individual fearful of affective states. This leads to a "dedifferentiation of affect," which is accompanied by a chronic blocking of subjective emotional experience and results in the indirect expression of affect through psychosomatic symptoms. Such individuals have a grossly impaired dream and fantasy life. Verbal psychotherapy is generally thought to be ineffective: they lack the language to communicate the internal milieu. Furthermore, one might speculate that the alexithymic cognitive style places a person at risk for PTSD because of impaired verbal capacities for coping with stress.

These various cognitive formulations provide a model for the pathologies of memory associated with psychological trauma without resorting to the psychoanalytic notions of motivated forgetting, censorship, and repression. Clinical experience shows that many traumatized people are aware of fragments of the traumatization but unable to recall specifics of the trauma, which often can be retrieved under hypnosis (15), during sodium amytal interviews (8), and after prolonged psychodynamic psychotherapy (16). Freud (17) was clearly correct in stating that when traumatic material gains partial representation, it is accompanied by anxiety, which can then trigger defensive maneuvers of suppression, avoidance, and flight. This anxiety can be viewed as a partial reliving of affective and somatosensory components of the traumatic memories, without the symbolic and linguistic representations necessary to place the trauma in its historical context.

In child psychiatry, the necessity for enhancing the child's underdeveloped verbal capacity has led to the widespread use of play therapy, which utilizes iconic representations and reenactments to access memories, needs, and wishes. Therapists of traumatized children have recognized this need by providing anatomically correct dolls to facilitate accounts of traumatic experiences. The projective hypothesis of psychological testing shares the same conceptual foundation: patients produce dynamically relevant material when they are asked to associate to ambiguous visual cues, such as Rorschach (9) and Thematic Apperception Test cards. This provides a channel through which to gain access to disturbing psychological material.

While the foregoing applies to normal individuals, there are important variations across individuals that require further consideration. The special developmental issues of blind, deaf, retarded, schizophrenic, and physically abused children are discussed in Chapter 4. On the other end of the spectrum, unusual cognitive gifts may also introduce variations; idiosyncratic cognitive schemata and modes of representations can influence the capacity to respond to overwhelming life experiences.

The present chapter will demonstrate how special cognitive resources outside the verbal realm can be reawakened and utilized, first to uncover and recall traumatic events, and then to transform the meaning of the trauma with resulting psychological growth. Images, scenes, bodily sensations, and emotions related to the trauma can be retrieved. This reversal of dissociation affords the patient an opportunity to recall significant autobiographical episodes and integrate the trauma into his or her personal history. In this process, the patient can transcend the trauma and cease the compulsion to repeat and reenact it.

A Case Example

Sharon L., a 30-year-old married woman, was referred for psychotherapy after she described crippling insecurities, compulsive behaviors, and unusual somatic symptoms to her endocrinologist.

On initial interview she was quite inhibited and self-deprecating. She maintained eye contact with difficulty and prefaced many of her statements with apologies for her inadequacy and for "boring" her therapist. She recited a litany of problems without pausing for reflection. During the next two sessions Sharon continued "pouring her heart out," but her extreme self-involvement and profound uncertainty made it difficult to engage her in a therapeutic interchange. Questions and requests for clarification brought a temporary halt to her monologue, and an apologetic "I don't know." At this early juncture, there was no indication that this patient would be able to tolerate and benefit from insight-oriented psychotherapy. She, herself, requested a behavioral approach to help her "calm down."

This assessment was altered when the patient came to her fourth session with the first three chapters of a highly imaginative and intricately developed novel spanning three generations of adventure in a preliterate Pacific Island tribe. She had established authenticity by painstakingly researching over 200 primary sources from the anthropological literature. She brought it in with the request that the therapist evaluate it and give feedback about whether it was "any good or not." While she readily acknowledged her authorship, and even expressed pride in her undertaking, her obvious achievement had made no impact on her self-image as an intellectually defective, "uncreative" individual. In contrast, she quickly overvalued her therapist in about every sphere of competence, and was unable to modulate her idealization, despite realistic occurrences that might have given other patients the opportunity for devaluation.

The patient positioned herself as a frightened girl with little expectation of approval from without. The traumatic origins of this stance did not become apparent until five sessions later when she reported the following dream:

> I am at a university museum. I work there. There is an exhibit of Hominid fossils and the curator says that he has a feeling some of them are missing. These bones are old and too valuable to remain hidden. I admit that I hid them, and I go with the curator to a secret closet, a low horizontal door with ornate carvings on it.

The patient's spontaneous interpretation of this dream is as follows: "I have 'skeletons' in this closet. Things about myself I want to forget and deny. Dr. G. is the curator."

While this dream (and others) obliquely alluded to a repressed trauma, the key to unlocking specific traumatic memories was unintentionally introduced when the patient casually mentioned that she enjoyed copying paintings and showed some examples of her work. When the therapist asked whether she could apply her obvious artistic gifts to generate a self-portrait, she was initially horrified and reluctant. However, several weeks later she spontaneously brought in a self-portrait and later that session said, "I think we need to talk about the seventh grade"—the year of her traumatization. Thus there was a large disparity between her rich creative capacity and exceptional talent of expression, witnessed first in a novel and subsequently in her paintings, and her constricted, inhibited, "uptight" self-presentation. This illustrates the principle that psychic trauma can selectively impair discrete modes of cognition, while other domains seemingly flourish (see Chapter 4).

The uniqueness of the present case lies in this patient's unusual pattern of cognitive strengths and weaknesses. Her superior ability to make private iconic images public in the form of illustrations and dream reports necessitated structuring psychotherapy as a "painting cure" rather than the traditional "talking cure." Samples of her illustrations are reproduced here as Figures 1–6 and will provide the structure for the unfolding of her case history. Matching the modes of therapy to the patient's cognitive abilities and limitations may be essential for trauma work.

Presenting Complaints

The patient's complaints and symptoms could be classified into four broad clusters: anxiety manifestations, somatic distress, severely compromised self-esteem, and complaints of cognitive and motor impairments.

Sharon was beset with phobic avoidance, obsessive preoccupations, and compulsive rituals. She avoided eating in public with familiar acquaintances and co-workers, although she could do so with aplomb in the company of total strangers or family members. She avoided driving, claiming she was unable to attend to the road and execute the motor aspects of driving simultaneously. She was anxiously preoccupied with her appearance, and this led to obsessive and ritualistic behavior such as frequent checking and rechecking her visage in mirrors and carrying extra sets of clothing and needles and thread in case she accidentally "tore" a piece of clothing. She avoided department stores because there were too many mirrors.

She noted a lifelong "math phobia." She had difficulty mastering the basic math concepts in public school and floundered in junior high school algebra and trigonometry. Her difficulty with numerical concepts and the anxiety generated by any work involving numbers caused considerable occupational limitations— she could not work *near* a cash register nor could she make change. The patient also exhibited prominent counterphobic tendencies. Although afraid of heights, she rock climbed with her husband. Although petrified of submerging her unprotected face in water, she frequently enjoyed recreational scuba diving.

Somatic symptoms included a panoply of autonomic manifestations: dizziness, tightness in the chest, palpitations, tachycardia, flushing, and uncontrollable sweating. Symptomatic episodes were not associated with panic attacks or fears of dying. She often awakened from sleep with extreme somatic discomfort. She had suffered from irregular menstrual periods throughout her life and complained of severe premenstrual symptoms including bloating, irritability, labile mood swings, and clumsiness. Most remarkably, having opted against parenthood, she underwent elective tubal ligation at age 21. Her endocrinologist had prescribed an estrogen–progesterone birth control pill with favorable response. Headaches were a frequent symptom, especially when she felt trapped in a situation that highlighted her insecurity. For example, while working as a substitute teacher for 15 weeks, she suffered daily, constant headaches.

An underlying lack of self-confidence pervaded her clinical picture. She was plagued with performance anxiety and chose to avoid situations implying evaluation, with resulting social and occupational constriction. For example, she hadn't shown her novel to anyone because she was afraid of the "verdict." She hadn't pursued formal art training because she was unsure of the extent of her talent. Her uncertainty was also revealed in her preoccupation with others' judgment. She continually sought feedback from the therapist. This ego-syntonic tendency to base her own self-esteem on an external criterion rendered her extremely vulnerable to devaluation. Over time it became apparent that this was not merely a defensive maneuver but rather was due to her *lack of capacity* for rendering and endorsing self-judgments. Her insecurities were born out of a lack of an internal scaling mechanism, combined with her readiness to seek out and internalize the judgment of a critical other.

Yet another cluster of symptoms involved a myriad of cognitive and motor complaints. Along with her previously noted difficulty with mathematics and calculations, she described several transient linguistic and speech errors including stuttering under stress, misuse of words, word-finding difficulties, and a tendency to generate spoonerisms.

In the motor realm she had difficulty executing complex gross motor activities. She remarked that she was always considered a poor athlete and learned to jump rope only with great difficulty. She claimed she could not dance. She noted that she had trouble dividing attention and carrying out tasks simultaneously. For example, when riding a bicycle, she had to stop in order to drink from the water bottle mounted on the frame. When walking up and down stairs, she felt she had to hold onto the handrail and look at her feet or else she was sure to lose her balance. These cognitive and motor lapses often occurred in the absence of social pressure and subjective anxiety.

In summary, the patient presented with multiple somatic, affective, behavioral, and cognitive complaints that fluctuated over time. These were not compatible with any one diagnosis. The diversity and variable character of PTSD manifestations has been emphasized throughout Chapters 1, 2, and 9.

Because of these prominent cognitive and motor complaints, and an academic history that raised the possibility of specific learning deficits, a neuropsychological analysis of her cognitive function was undertaken.

Results of the Neuropsychological Examination

Despite her marked performance anxiety, she was highly involved with the tasks and compliant with the demands of testing.

The results reported below are believed to be an accurate reflection of her mental status.

She used a deliberate and systematic scanning strategy on a Letter Cancellation Task, yet mild attentional lapses were noted—three target items in the left hemifield were omitted.

A survey of hand preference revealed mixed handedness. She wrote and painted with a sinestral orientation and threw a ball, hammered a nail, and cut with scissors with her right hand. The Finger Tapping Test, in which the patient is required to depress a telegraph key rapidly with each index finger, revealed mild to moderate slowing bilaterally, with clear superiority of the right hand. Stress gait demonstrated left-sided posturing. The Grooved Pegboard Test, in which the patient was instructed to place keyhole-shaped pegs into slots, confirmed a right-sided manual superiority. Thus the motor findings confirmed her self-report of subtle clumsiness, and provided strong evidence for anomalous dominance—the absence of the typical (dextral) cerebral organization.

Spontaneous speech was fluent, prosodic, and without obvious word-finding difficulty or paraphasic error. Repetition, visual confrontation naming, and word list generation were spared. A writing sample confirmed her left hand preference (with an inverted hand posture). There was no evidence of dysgraphia.

Her copy of the Rey-Osterreith complex figure, a complicated visual construction task, revealed carelessness and planning errors, mild distortion of outer proportions, and one frank error in copying an internal detail. These findings fall within the mild range.

Her immediate recall of the Rey diagram was strikingly empty, with a tendency toward reduplication. There was no significant change after a 20-minute delay. Immediate and delay recall of the simpler Wechsler figures were basically intact, suggesting that her visual memory deficits emerged when her capacity for absorbing visual information was exceeded.

Remote verbal memory was spared: she successfully retrieved 7 of 8 past presidents. However, on a 10-word 5-trial new verbal learning test, memory difficulties arose. She recalled 7 items on trial 1, then 7, 9, 10, and 8 across trials. This decrement in the learning curve seen on trial 5 was observed despite a highly systematic recall strategy. The patient noted, "My mind just went blank." There were no perseverative or intrusive errors. Delayed retrieval was basically intact, with the exception that the patient failed to retrieve the first word on the list. On a recognition task, she also failed to register that item as familiar. This is an example of an unusual failure of the primacy effect in memory.

Her abilities in the mathematical domain were assessed by the Arithmetic Subscale of the Wechsler Adult Intelligence Scale, in which the patient is required to solve one- and two-step problems without paper or pencil. She answered the easy items readily, indicating that she had acquired the basic math rules and operations. However, she gave up on two-stage problems involving percentages and fractions. When given a paper and pencil, she still had difficulty conceptualizing and setting up the problems for solution. When the steps of a particular problem were structured for her, she was able to perform the calculations readily. There was no spatial disorganization in her written numbers and columns.

In sum, cognitive testing revealed mild attentional, motor, and memory deficits and mild to moderately severe difficulties with mathematical concepts, in the setting of anomalous dominance. These findings were quite consistent with her academic history and strongly validated her complaints of difficulty performing everyday tasks that others found so effortless. These findings also place her long-standing self-deprecation and high anxiety levels in a somewhat new light. Lack of confidence in social and intellectual pursuits is quite common in adults who had focal learning difficulties as children. Furthermore, the presence of superior focal abilities—like being able to draw proficiently on an "Etch-a-Sketch" or draw one's dreams—can be seen as the flip side of the learning disability coin. It seems plausible that her focal cognitive weaknesses were compensated for by focal cognitive superiorities.

Over and beyond the chronic effect of discrete learning disabilities, it is likely that her high anxiety level sabotaged her cognition. Her retrieval failure on trial 5 of the Verbal Memory Task can be reasonably construed as being secondary to anxiety. Perhaps such transitory lapses of retrieval afford a brief glimpse into the mechanisms underlying dissociation and traumatic amnesia.

Historical Background

Sharon was of mixed Polish and French-Canadian extraction. Her mother, who died of metastatic breast cancer at the age of 58 in 1979, was the youngest of three girls and three boys. Four of her siblings suffered from tuberculosis and two succumbed at an early age. Sharon describes her mother as anxious, depressed, morbid, and "weird." Her mother was a virtual recluse during the last 15 years of her life. The patient took on the responsibility of nursing her mother as her health deteriorated, including bathing her and changing her ostomy bags. Sharon's father is the youngest surviving sibling in a family of eight. He quit high school to join the Navy and had a successful career as a salesman. He remarried five years after his wife's demise.

Sharon is the fourth of five children. She has three older brothers and one younger sister. Interestingly, her sister shares many of the same complaints and also experienced traumatization during early adolescence. One brother is described as "depressed and weird." Another is "shy, cynical, and can drink too much." A third brother has recently conquered alcohol addiction.

The patient describes her early childhood home life as hectic and unpredictable. The boys called the shots at home. They and their friends devised physical games in which the basic themes were domination, control, and power. They staged coed wrestling matches in the basement and tied up the girls on occasion. One variation in which the boys chased and captured the girls was known as "hunt the sister." The patient became quite adept at hiding and being "invisible"—under the covers, in closets, in the cellar, and in the garage. She was sometimes found hiding in these spots by a neighbor who was six years her senior and would then engage in children's sexual games.

Typically the patient would attempt to fend for herself, but was hopelessly outnumbered by the boys. Entreaties to her mother were met with incredulity and tacit if not explicit approval for the boys' "shenanagins." The patient remarked that "they could do no wrong in her eyes."

Sharon's earliest memories of her mother are those of being scrutinized and criticized on the basis of her physical appearance. Her mother would often compare her to famous actresses, feature by feature. There was constant advice and instructions on makeup, hair, and clothing. The mother imposed posture exercises in which the patient walked with books on top of her head. The patient's father balanced the mother's position by being supportive, but ultimately ineffective. He deferred to his wife on most matters of child-rearing policy. The patient currently exculpates him from any detrimental influence on her development. She tends to make excuses for him and expresses compassion for his marital plight. In situations of extreme threat, the father typically emerges to take effective action to protect his children. For example, it was he who confronted the school authorities after her attacks.

One conscious motive underlying her decision to undergo tubal ligation was to "prevent my mother's craziness from being handed down."

Sharon began "developing" in the latter part of the third grade. She felt "proud" like an "adult woman." She recalls her mother warning her at this time, "Don't let the boys touch you." In fourth grade she read "Sex and the Single Man" and was apprised of the mechanics of sexual reproduction by a relative of a friend. On the beach at age 10, her brothers and his cronies "admired and ridiculed" her in a bathing suit. At 11, she was molested in a funhouse by a group of boys. They "felt me up." She was paralyzed and afraid to yell. "Did I cause it?" she wondered. She still is curious about why she didn't react or resist. (Paralysis during the acute phase of stress may be a form of stress-induced tonic immobility mediated by the endogenous opioid system. Animals such as the oppossum are known for "feigning" death under predatory attack. Other species are capable of "animal cataplexy." A discussion of the opioid mechanisms in the physiological response to stress can be found in Chapter 2.)

In the sixth grade she got the reputation for being "easy," mostly because she looked the part—she wore miniskirts, fishnet nylons, and make-up to school. She developed a typical teenage crush on a male teacher. The other girls resented the attention she began receiving from the boys. At age 12 she began dating a high school student and they engaged in petting.

The psychosexual setting for the trauma to come was thus characterized by early sexual maturation, with high libido and much sexual curiosity and a dominant focus on her appearance and how others "saw her." There were strong, recurrent themes of exhibitionism and domination and humiliation.

The Trauma

Sharon began the eighth session reporting that she had awakened with crushing chest sensations. "I felt like I was being strangled." Suddenly, she recalled in graphic detail a traumatic incident from the seventh grade. After having been repressed for many years, the entire episode revealed itself in its entirety as she lay in bed. Sharon had been walking home from a friend's house in early October, one block from home, and was passing by a vacant lot. Two boys known to her for years yelled "slut" and "whore." She quickened her pace. They rushed her, threw her to the ground, jumped on top of her, and tried to strip off her clothes. "Their hands were all over me . . .

hitting me . . . trying to get at my zipper." She resisted as best she could. They threatened her, saying, "This isn't the end, slut. We are not through with you." She was shocked and amazed that these two boys she had known from the first grade had perpetrated this vicious assault. She felt guilty and "hurt, but *not* angry." She went home, changed her clothes, and told no one about the incident. Her contemporary obsession with changing clothes and with the idea that her clothes can be torn at any time (necessitating carrying needles and thread with her) can be seen as a partial reenactment of this traumatic episode.

Around this time she began being harassed by a tough girl in school, who threatened her with a knife on occasion and vowed to kill her. Because this girl was so physically large, she decided it was only fair to order a smaller substitute to fight Sharon. A fight was arranged following the Thanksgiving holiday. The patient was warned "if you don't fight, it will be worse for you." Sharon suffered in silence as the day approached, afraid to inflame the situation by going to the authorities or her parents. On the designated day she was grabbed at knife point after school and taken to a wooded area where about 100 people had gathered for the fight. The tough girl ordered one of her henchwomen to assault the patient. They kicked and punched and scratched and rolled on the ground to the delight of the assembled throng. The patient remembers scratching the other girl's face and drawing blood. All the while, the leader was exhorting "fight harder or else we will mess up your face so bad no one will ever look at you." Sharon remembers someone shouting something about her menstrual period, and surmises that they must have spotted blood on her undergarments. This compounded her sense of humiliation. During a lull in the action, a boy charged the two girls, threatening to "finish me off." The crowd cheered him, but the ringleader held him back. The patient then recalls the crowd disappearing. She was numbed and dazed, but relieved that she had survived. The leader then came up and said "what makes you think you can go?" She was then escorted to a nearby high school stadium, and one hour later was found walking outside of a friend's house stunned and disoriented. To this day, she has amnesia for the events that transpired during that 1-hour period.

When she stumbled into her house, her lips and nose bleeding and her blouse and stockings torn, her parents immediately panicked. "They couldn't deal with it." They called their daughter-in-law to help soothe the patient. Afterward the mother was not outraged and the patient could not understand why. The father went to school and confronted the authorities. There were no doctors or police involved. Paradoxically, the patient was greeted with respect and awe from her classmates when she returned to school about a week later. She was praised for taking part in an "historic fight."

But this was not the end of her victimization. Some months later she was attacked again by the same two boys who had thrown her to the ground in the vacant lot. This was by a mailbox only blocks away from her house. They had stalked her and watched her home and grabbed her at a time when she was alone. All she can recall is that she was knocked down. "I don't know if there was more to it." Again, she felt guilt and not anger following the assault.

She was haunted by the aftereffects of these incidents for the next 10 years. Her reputation as a "bad" girl was confirmed. The tough girls in school warned her that she was being monitored and would be punished for further indiscretions. One of her brothers "threatened to kill" her if he heard any more stories about her. She realized that the 16-year-old she had been dating was insincere when he dumped her and called her a "stupid 12-year-old slut." Soon after, she met her husband-to-be and began an exclusive relationship. He proposed to her shortly afterward at age 14. They have been together ever since.

Years later, just when she felt that things were settling down and the trauma was relegated to the past, her sister, who was then about 13 years old, was challenged to go into the boys' room at school on a dare. She did so, provoking a riot at the school. The sister was then labeled as "an easy tramp" and was subjected to the same types of humiliation, threats, and abuse over an extended period. The patient volunteered to protect the sister and escorted her to and from school, and interceded on her behalf with the school authorities. At one point she confronted the principal and demanded a transfer to a different school, which was subsequently granted. Sharon felt that she was somehow responsible for the abuse that her sister was experiencing.

During the two or three sessions in which the details of the trauma emerged, Sharon related the stories without affect. However, on the following session, she reported going home and crying all week long, having nightmares, and a marked enhancement of autonomic and somatic distress.

The Therapeutic Process

The key to accessing Sharon's artistic potential was revealed in the following transference dream, which was reported after cognitive testing had been performed and before the trauma had emerged:

> I am in a house. I can't decide what to do. I have a canvas set up in each room and an "Etch-a-Sketch" on every table. A man in his 30s is sitting on the brick steps below the side door. He is a professor. A group of my friends is standing with Dr. G. in the background. . . . I look out the kitchen window at the professor and I can see what he is writing. I begin to paint what he is writing about—the moon, sulfur fields, geysers, a volcano, and various mythic creatures from throughout the world. I can see a Neanderthal woman painting, writing on the cave wall or rock face.

One week later she again dreamed of the mythic scene described above. On awakening, she began to paint the scene on a canvas. She then brought a photograph of the canvas into her next session. It was a stark, serene, and timeless landscape rendered in searing colors. This was the very first time in her life that she had drawn something from within as opposed to drawing from a model. Her artistic talent was harnessed to what she *felt* and *imagined*, rather than what she saw. In doing so, her exhibitionistic tendencies were now utilized therapeutically in the service of the ego. Specifically, by first sharing her dreams verbally and then by explicitly drawing them and photographing her drawings and bringing the photos to therapy for analysis, she was reenacting her early predicament of being scrutinized by an external agent. Only this time, it was not her physical appearance that was subject to critique, it was her fantasy life and the deep structure of her personality. Moreover, after she quickly incorporated some basic principles of dream and symbol interpretation, she was able to reverse roles and become both the artist and the critic. In this manner, an observing ego gradually emerged. It was at this juncture that the specific traumatic memories (described in the previous section) were revealed following the introduction of her self-portrait into therapy. Figure 1 represents her self-portrait, after Norman Rockwell. She explained her nudity as an attempt to uncover hidden truths about herself. The obvious exhibitionistic quality of her self-portrait was *not* explored for fear of further inhibiting her nascent strivings for self-expression. A week later she presented Figure 2. This image is a poignant illustration of her sense of victimization and helplessness during and following her traumatic assaults. Her sense of paralysis and inability to resist is represented by the serpent which is lashing her to the tree. The ripped garments and dripping blood are undistorted

Figure 1

features of the attacks. Her sense of guilt for somehow provoking the incidents by her provocative dress can be inferred from the "crucifixation" theme.

The next stage of therapy was characterized by increasing self-awareness and tenacious self-exploration. She would bring in drawings and sketches and dreams along with detailed, type-written analyses of the symbols and the associations they evoked. Many of her associations were not to her autobiographical history, but were related to facts, words, and images she had learned while studying anthropology. At this stage, when the therapist would attempt to link a drawn symbol to other material she had pre-sented, she would often protest saying, "I didn't have that in mind when I drew it," or "That's *not* what I was thinking in the dream." Gradually she became more tolerant of the therapist's interpre-tative statements. She began breaking down names and dream words into complex verbal puns, which she would work and re-work. She produced such a volume of material at each session that the question of a hypomanic state was raised, and dismissed, when the patient denied other cardinal symptoms of mania. Sim-

Figure 2

ilarly, because of the tremendous outpouring of her writing and drawings, the diagnosis of temporal lobe epilepsy was briefly entertained and then rejected.

The patient continued to have good weeks and bad weeks. The latter were full of inhibitions, doubts, and feelings of victimization and helplessness. The former were suffused with a newfound sense of accomplishment and periods of freedom from crippling anxieties.

Less time was spent reviewing traumatic details and more time was spent on an analysis of her pretraumatic character, and early interactional patterns in the family that set the stage for her post-traumatic response. Instances of eccentric behavior and frank psychopathology were discovered in prior generations in both the paternal and maternal lineages.

In an attempt to render her self-deprecation more ego-dystonic, I suggested that she visualize her "bad me" and attempt to draw it. During the next session she produced "The Ogre"—a mutant half-woman half-bug being attacked by other insects (Figure 3). This image graphically depicts her sense of being exposed and vulnerable, as well as defective and unattractive. Having exorcised

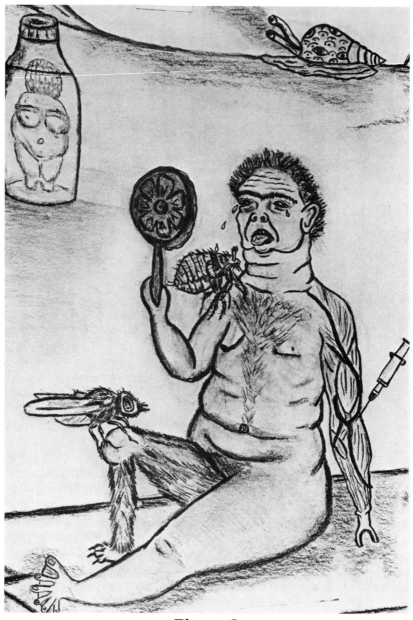

Figure 3

this demon, the patient was able to dissociate it from her sense of self, and it gradually became more ego-dystonic. When something new triggered her feelings of ineptitude or humiliation, she would say, "I felt like the Ogre again," whereas beforehand she would have said, "I am the Ogre."

As she began linking details of the recalled trauma with pretraumatic memories and familial and intrapsychic themes, she drew a chronology of her psychosexual development in a mural-like sketch (Figure 4). This scenic display of her past history ranges from her earliest recollections of being criticized by her mother (in the lower right) to her future fears of a childless and shattered marriage (upper right). The images are all linked by a tape measure, "because I'm always judging myself." The combination mannequin and eyeball represent the criticism and scrutiny she was subjected to by her mother. The bathtub scene represents early sexual stimulation from play with her brothers and their friends. The closet scene represents the episodes of fondling that took place with the older neighborhood boy. The year-long period after her "historic fight" in which she stayed home sick from school and hid in her bed daydreaming is portrayed by the bed scene, with the traffic light marking the corner of the street where the attack took place. The canine assault stands for the attack by her two former classmates in the vacant lot. The lovebird cage reflects her attachment and eventual marriage to her husband following the acute period of trauma. The piano, replete with neurons and a cup of coffee, symbolizes her therapist—a neuropsychologist. The tape measure ending in a question mark reveals her doubts whether therapy could liberate her from her disturbing past. Sharon describes the milk bottle as her "bottled-up creativity, and my biological desire for childbirth." The Ogre has cracked the bottle by throwing the mirror at it, as if to state that the patient's creativity and psychological development will be unlocked if and when she renounces her preoccupation with physical appearance. The cave painting portrays her wish to develop her intellectual gifts and further her creative pursuits. It is modeled on an ancient Incan fertility goddess, corresponding to the patient's strong maternal wishes, which began to become more manifest. The last series of images represents her fear that if she became less inhibited, her marriage might falter, causing her "heart to break" and a wedding band to fly off her hand. The moose on wheels represents her fear that her husband would abandon her and she would be left childless.

Having pictorially represented these various memories, intro-

Figure 4

jects, expectations, and conflicts, she was able to explore them articulately in the verbal mode. Thus again we see that conceptual/ verbal insight was made possible by the concrete visual representation of her internal milieu. The next month of therapy revolved around discussing and analyzing a half dozen additional sketches— all dealing with her conflicts surrounding life decisions (e.g., reversing her tubal ligation and raising children versus obtaining advanced schooling) and her libidinal development. This formerly shy and pathologically inhibited young woman began blossoming and acknowledging her own sexuality without guilt. Yet to the extent that eros was expressed, themes of thanatos were absent. This period was associated with increased intimacy with her husband, including a sharing of sexual fantasies and a newfound satisfaction with sexual intercourse. The patient reported that a long-standing aversion to semen also abated at this time.

Quite suddenly, without warning or explanation, the drawings ceased. Sharon began reporting having intense, vivid nightmares of victimization. It was as if her need to express herself visually found an outlet in nocturnal fantasy when the waking channel of illustration was shut down. At this time, on a hunch, the therapist began to actively solicit material with aggressive themes—material that was conspicuous for its absence up until now. The therapist challenged her to render her feelings of hurt, protest, and rage on paper. She remained inhibited and two months passed before she brought in her "anger image" (Figure 5).The image is a half young girl and half vicious baboon screaming in rage and tearing another baboon asunder. Only then was the patient able to verbalize her feelings of bitterness and anger over the assault she had experienced, and her frustration at being so vulnerable. She ventilated anger at the lack of protection she was afforded by others. These discussions led to a series of productive inquiries into eccentricities in the family that shaped her character.

The next several sessions involved the patient gradually "owning" her strong libidinous urges, which she slowly came to accept as part of her being. In this way, sexuality became divorced from sexual trauma. Furthermore, she was able to work through the guilt she had felt for "somehow" provoking her victimization. When she no longer blamed herself for inducing the assaults, she was more able to acknowledge her sexuality without feeling that she had "asked for it."

Figure 6 represents her most recent painting. It is a static representation of a dream she experienced. In the dream, she beckoned that the therapist follow her into a painting. They both dove

Figure 5

Figure 6

into this underwater canvas and explored the depths of the oceans, encountering various sea creatures—squids, sponges, and snails. They then surfaced on a sponge. The right of the figure depicts the therapist as disgusted by his encounter with the Ogre. The patient explained this as her fear that after revealing herself during the psychotherapeutic journey, the therapist would find her repulsive. Having expressed this fear in pictures, she was able to disown it verbally. This portrayal is a poignant example of the fear and anticipation of degradation that drives many traumatized patients from the therapeutic alliance. In the present case, the alliance was seemingly strong enough to withstand this irrational fear of abandonment.

At the present time, almost exactly 13 months after the initiation of therapy, the patient continues with weekly sessions and the alliance remains solid. She continues to draw and dream—expressing fantasies, recalling historical facts, and bringing unacknowledged aspects of the self to the surface. Amnesia still remains for portions of the traumatic incidents. The main shift in the therapeutic interchange has been a reduced emphasis on the trauma, and an increasing focus on the here and now as well as her future life plans. She is actively contemplating childbirth, and mulling over various career options. At this juncture, the patient has internalized and incorporated many therapeutic strategies and carries on self-analysis outside the therapeutic session. On the anniversary of the "historic fight," there was no new symptomatology, no regression, nor threats to the alliance. She represented her ability to internalize the therapeutic dialogue as well as her realistic appraisal of her therapist in a dream in which the therapist turned into a chimp who she carried about with her. Sharon explained, "I had overvalued you. You were superhuman. The chimp is subhuman. Now I think you are somewhere in the middle."

The patient has given her informed consent for this case study, and has actively collaborated in its preparation. This has been a positive experience for her.

Therapy continues with uncovering and exploration, with the ultimate goal of liberating her artistic gifts from their role as a conduit for emerging traumatic memories, and the expression of conflictual material. The Painting Cure is gradually effected as Sharon continues the transformation from patient to artist.

References

1. van der Kolk B, Blitz R, Burr W, et al: Nightmares and trauma: a comparison of nightmares after combat with lifelong nightmares in veterans. Am J Psychiatry 141:187–190, 1984

2. Brett EA, Ostroff R: Imagery and posttraumatic stress disorder: an overview. Am J Psychiatry 142:417–424, 1985

3. Schachtel E: On memory and childhood amnesia. Psychiatry 10:1–26, 1947

4. White SH, Pillemer DB: Childhood amnesia and the development of a socially accessible memory system, in Functional Disorders of Memory. Edited by Kihlstrom JF, Evans FJ. Hillsdale, NJ, 1979

5. Bruner JS, Postman L: Perception, cognition, and personality. J Personality 18:14–31, 1949

6. Neisser U: Cognitive Psychology. Englewood Cliffs, NJ, Prentice-Hall, 1967

7. Piaget J: Structuralism. New York, Basic Books, 1970

8. Kolb L: The posttraumatic stress disorders of combat: a

subgroup with a conditional emotional response. Milit Med 149:237–243, 1984

9. van der Kolk BA, Ducey C: Clinical implication of the Rorschach in Posttraumatic Stress Disorder, in Traumatic Stress Disorder: Psychological and Biological Sequelae. Edited by van der Kolk BA. Washington, DC, American Psychiatric Press, 1984

10. Eich JE: The cue dependent nature of state dependent retrieval. Memory and Cognition 8:157–168, 1980

11. Kihlstrom JF: Conscious, subconscious, unconscious: a cognitive perspective, in The Unconscious Reconsidered. Edited by Bowers KS, Meichenbaum D. New York, John Wiley and Sons, 1984

12. Wilkinson CB: Aftermath of disaster, collapse of Hyatt Regency Hotel Skywalks. Am J Psychiatry 140:1134–1139, 1983

13. Marty P, de M'Uzan M: La Pensee operatoire. Revue Français Psychoanal S27:1345–1356, 1963

14. Krystal H: Alexithymia and psychotherapy. Am J Psychother 33:17–31, 1979

15. Brown DP, Fromm E: Hypnotherapy and hypnoanalysis. Hillsdale, NJ, Lawrence Erlbaum Associates, 1986

16. Krystal H: Trauma and affects. Psychoanal Study Child 33:81–116, 1978

17. Freud S: Beyond the pleasure principle (1920), in Complete Psychological Works. Standard Ed. Vol 18. Translated and edited by Strachey J. London, Hogarth Press, 1959

From Victim to Survivor: A Stress Management Approach in the Treatment of Learned Helplessness

Raymond B. Flannery, Jr., Ph.D.

For clinicians actively treating the victims of psychological trauma, resolving the traumatizing event is at best difficult. We have noted repeatedly in this book the consistent biphasic protest/numbing response in humans to uncontrollable life events and that the more long standing the trauma, the more likely the victim will present with numbing: psychological constriction, depression, social isolation, anhedonia, and a sense of estrangement (see Chapters 1–3). Clinicians attempting to work directly on resolving the trauma itself will primarily encounter these signs of numbing in the victim. Frequently these patients will also use denial, intellectualization, and isolation as defenses, even when the therapist recognizes and probes the impact of the painful event. Some patients continue this avoidance as the treatment proceeds; many terminate as the effects related to the trauma are reexperienced in the treatment. As Lindemann (1) pointed out, patients frequently attempt to ward off the trauma, and thus set up the possibility of the trauma's being reexperienced as a dissociated event

---

The author wishes to acknowledge the intellectual rigor and assistance of Bessel A. van der Kolk, M.D. in the development of this chapter.

217

(see Chapter 9). Regardless of treatment approach, many clinicians experience intervening directly with the trauma as an event that often intensifies the patient's already compromised level of functioning.

As discussed in Chapter 1, many traumatized patients develop a psychological stance of "learned helplessness," a condition in which patients lose the capacity to appreciate the connection between their actions and their ability to influence the course of their lives. This perception of loss of control leads to a passive stance and either social withdrawal from, or clinging to, caregivers, family members, or mental health professionals.

Social support (2, 3) is often suggested as a buffer or modifier of these traumatic events. Yet social support alone may not always undo the passivity and may in fact aggravate it. Van der Kolk in Chapter 2 reviewed Bowlby's work on attachment and pointed out how attachment to parental figures who are themselves sources of external danger will lead to intensified imprinting with resultant increases in dependency and no lasting sense of mastery in their offspring. In examining the response of some executives to stress, Kobasa and Pucetti (4) found that men with good social support and an external locus of control (i.e., were more passive) coped less adaptively than those men with internal control (i.e., had a sense of mastery) and poor social support. Thus merely providing a supportive experience in the context of a feeling of helplessness may actually aggravate a patient's passive stance. Kobasa and Pucetti (4) found that men coped best with stress when they had both a sense of mastery (internal locus of control) *and* a good social support network.

While a high premorbid level of coping skills may mitigate feelings of helplessness, the essence of psychological trauma for all humans is being faced with uncontrollable overwhelming events where the person is helpless to affect the outcome of the event. Unresolved trauma causes this feeling of helplessness to become generalized; thus learned helplessness is often present in many patients with unresolved trauma (5).

In contrast, research on individuals who adapt successfully with life stress has shown that these stress-resistant persons have a strong sense of connection between their own actions, their feeling states, and their capacities to influence the course of their lives. These stress-resistant persons are characterized by having control and involvement in their lives, having a stabilized daily routine, and actively seeking out social support. While capable of negative affects when faced with adversity, a belief in their actions to resolve problems results in a general mood of well-being.

Teaching the stress management interventions of stress-resistant persons to those trauma victims with learned helplessness can increase active mastery of the environment and decrease avoidant behavior, social isolation, and depressive affect. Perceiving oneself in control of one's life and being actively involved with social support in daily life activities may then make the impact of the trauma less profound.

Learned Helplessness

Two models for understanding learned helplessness within the social learning paradigm have been formulated. Pavlov (quoted in 6) presented the first theoretical model. Speaking of the "defensive reaction" to denote the innate reflexive response to environmental threat, he hypothesized that, after exposure to repeated aversive stimuli, the cues associated with the trauma would themselves become capable of eliciting the defensive reaction in the organism by themselves. The findings generally support this theory and result in organisms that become passive (or helpless) in many situations because of the generalization gradient.

The second theoretical formulation is that of Seligman (7), which deals more specifically with the concept of learned helplessness. Between 1965 and 1969, Seligman and his colleagues trained 150 dogs to jump from one compartment in a shuttle avoidance box to an adjoining compartment to avoid receiving electric shock to their paws from the grid floor of this box. When the animals had successfully mastered this task, the researchers raised a barrier between the two compartments so that it was impossible for the animals to jump and avoid the shock. Their scientific goal was to create a situation analogous to human psychological trauma, a situation in which the organism was exposed to a painful stimulus from which there was no escape.

In two-thirds of the animals, Seligman (7) noticed performance decrements, increased passivity, disrupted normal canine routine, a loss of motivation, and the development of depression. He concluded that frequent experience with lack of contingency between response and outcome led the organism to assume it was helpless. This assumption then led to the organism's behavioral deficits and the appearance of a depressed state. He referred to this psychological state as "learned helplessness." To remedy this problem, his researchers turned off the current to the grid flooring and lowered the barrier between the two adjoining compartments with the expectation that the animals' natural curiosity would lead them to explore the cage over time and learn that it was now safe. When the animals were shocked, they lay passively in their cages, and defecated, urinated, whimpered, and showed signs of generalized distress. Yet now when relief could be obtained by merely moving to another part of the cage, these animals passively endured great suffering and demonstrated no curiosity in reexamining their cage environment. Seligman then began to drag the animals across the grid in an attempt to teach them that the cage was now a safe environment. While this second intervention was successful with some animals, other animals remained passive and withdrawn. These findings led him to reformulate his theory.

From 1975 to 1980, many investigators focused their attention of the meaning of the traumatic event to the organism. Garber and Seligman (8) provide an exhaustive review of this literature. From this extensive research on attribution theory, three factors that contributed to the perception of helplessness in traumatized organisms were identified. The first attribute concerned one's belief about one's control of the environment. Individuals who hold themselves personally responsible for a situation (even if no one could be reasonably expected to master it) were more likely to perceive themselves as helpless. While this is in contrast to the rape literature, which shows that women who blamed themselves (i.e., thought they could have controlled the outcome) had a much better prognosis (9), these results may be a function of measurement (see Chapter 9). The more common finding remains that persons holding themselves responsible are more likely to report feeling helpless. The second attribute related to the individual's perception of the length of the event. Situations perceived as long lived were more likely to induce helplessness than events perceived as short lived. The third attribute concerned the generalizability of one's capacity to function (stimulus generalization). While an individual might perceive him- or herself as unable to function in a specific situation, if the person then went on to assume that he or she could not function in a variety of highly similar situations, the probability of learned helplessness would increase. If a person is bitten by a dog and fears it, and then goes on to assume all dogs will bite, the feelings of helplessness become greater than if the person feared only the dog that had actually attacked.

Thus, in the revised theory, Garber and Seligman (8) hypothesized that individuals who lack contingency between response and outcome in painful situations from which there is no escape, who hold themselves personally responsible when in fact nothing can be done, who perceive the problem to be long lived, and who believe the inability to function will be widespread would be more likely to have performance decrements and depressed mood. Table 1 summarizes the characteristics of learned helplessness.

Van der Kolk and Greenberg (Chapter 3) argued about the possible neurological basis for these behavioral patterns of learned helplessness. They hypothesized that trauma victims with learned helplessness suffer from a vulnerability to experience subsequent arousal as a return of the trauma, and act with emergency responses appropriate to the original emergency. To avoid these emergency reactions, the victims shun involvement with people or events that expose them to the possibility of emotional arousal (7). While research is needed to evaluate this view more fully, it is a helpful beginning in understanding the possible physiological bases of psychological trauma.

In any case, since the passage of time and forced reexposure did not remedy learned helplessness (7), Garber and Seligman (8) then offered some additional theoretical suggestions for the treatment of this dilemma. One was to develop strategies to change the environment to increase positive outcomes. A second was to change the person's expectations of events from uncontrollable to controllable by training the person in appropriate responses. No specific interventions were presented at that time.

Finally, I believe that Seligman's (7) early research yielded a second and equally important finding that has received much less attention. Of the original 150 dogs, Seligman was unable to in-

Table 1. Components of Learned Helplessness and of Coping Strategies by Stress-Resistant Persons

Learned Helplessness	Stress-Resistant Persons
1. No perceived control	1. Personal control
2. Passivity: No task involvement	2. Task involvement
3. Disruption of basic life style	3. Adaptive lifestyle based on diet stimulant reduction/hard exercise/relaxation
4. Withdrawal from social support	4. Active seeking of social support
5. Mood: Depressed	5. Mood: Well-being

duce learned helplessness in one-third. In the presence of inescapable shock, these animals did not have the typical performance decrements and appearances of passivity found in many of the other animals. Attributing this resiliency to possible genetic or past learning experiences, his results documented that some organisms adapt successfully when confronted with the similar painful stimuli that render others helpless. This aspect of his work has not been systematically explored, yet there were some subjects that were not as vulnerable.

Stress-Resistant Persons

Beginning with the writings of Plato and Aristotle on the nature of the well-ordered soul, there has been a continuing interest in why certain persons cope successfully with the problems and sorrows of life, while others are overwhelmed and even crushed by these same events.

Certain aspects of this stress-illness relationship are becoming more clear. Illness onset does not appear to be a random event (9); stressful life events do seem to contribute to illness onset (10, 11), and there appear to be certain personality and coping strategies that result in successful adaptation and lessened probabilities of subsequent illness (12). Some of these factors are discussed in Chapters 1 and 2.

In an earlier paper, I have reviewed the stress-illness relationship as it is understood in the health psychology literature and have delineated the coping strategies most utilized by persons who successfully adapt to life stress (13). I refer to these individuals who utilize these strategies as stress-resistant persons. Even with methodological limitations (14–17) there is increasing empirical support to include four coping strategies as potentially adaptive in responding to adverse situations: 1) personal control, 2) task involvement, 3) certain healthful life-style choices, and 4) the utilization of social supports. These strategies are associated with lowered incidences of physical illness (13, 14), lowered amounts of anxiety and depression (18, 19), and increased longevity (20, 21). Since variables such as humor (22) and religious beliefs (23) are currently being assessed as potential moderator variables of life stress, these four strategies should not be thought of as exhaustive.

1. *Personal Control.* Personal control has at least two components (22): internal control and specific skills for specific situa-

tions. To have adequate mastery of one's life, one just needs to have an internal locus of control; that is, the perception that one is in control of one's environment and the rewards it offers. Individuals who primarily see themselves at the mercy of outside circumstances generally feel helpless and have less adaptive functioning. Secondly, individuals need specific skills to be effective in specific situations. The more specific experiences in coping with health, interpersonal, and financial problems, the better sense of mastery will the individual attain. Incorrect, unknown, or vague skills in solving problems increase stress and resultant passivity. Internal control and specific, effective skills in planful, organized self-directed activity have led in college students, working adults, and business executives to reduced anxiety and depression (11, 18, 24) and to develop a better sense of mastery (2, 24, 25).

2. *Task Involvement.* Reported by White (25) to be an important aspect of general competence, task involvement signifies becoming absorbed in the task and being guided by what the task demands. The task that is selected is personally meaningful and important to the individual, and frequently involves some sacrifice of short-term pleasures for long-range growth. Sometimes referred to as committed (11) or being industrious (26), these persons have a belief system that precludes passivity during times of adversity. Task involvement has led to improved health (26) with less anxiety and depression (10, 11) in college students and business persons.

3. *Lifestyle Choices.* Persons who adapt successfully engage in three behavioral patterns that appear to have demonstrated effectiveness in moderating the stress-illness relationship. First is the decreased use or general avoidance of the known dietary stimulants of refined white sugar, caffeine, and nicotine. The avoidance of these stimulants has resulted in less anxiety in working adults (27) and better health in a longitudinal study of Californians (20). Secondly, many stress-resistant persons engage in multiple periods of hard exercise each week, again a practice known to reduce stress in working adults (28) and athletically active adults (29). Finally, many stress-resistant individuals find time each day for a period of relaxation. While relaxation may include meditation, muscle relaxation, deep diaphragmatic breathing, imagery, or a hobby, relaxation itself results in decreased sensitivity to the stressors in an individual's psychological environment (30–32), a dampening of the organism's general level of arousal.

4. *Social Supports.* Stress-resistant persons utilize the social support of other people as a buffer in dealing with difficult situations (2–4). This social support may be obtained by being in a network of persons, such as a family unit, or by enlisting the help of specific others who may help in specific situations, such as a lawyer who would not be a family member (3). Personal relationships may provide companionship, empathic listening, information about resolutions, or instrumental help in solving problems (3). Singly or in combination, these aspects of personal relationships are frequently associated with reduced stress for working adults (2, 20) and executives and professionals (3, 4). However, these findings are not uniform, and social support appears to overlap at least with internal control (4) and early childhood attachment (see Chapter 2).

A summary of the adaptive coping strategies of these stress-resistant persons may be found in Table 1. The table shows that persons who adapt successfully are utilizing the very skills not employed by traumatized persons with learned helplessness. Stress-resistant persons exercise control over their lives, are task involved, follow a healthful life style, and initiate social support when dealing with life stress. These strategies result in less distress and a general sense of well-being.

These adaptive coping strategies are probably acquired in normal developmental stages in early life experiences with significant others with whom empathic understanding is possible, and where there is an interaction between one's actions and one's own life experiences. This allows for a sense of mastery over one's body (see Chapter 2), over one's cognition (see Chapter 4), and over one's fantasy life (see Chapter 6). As noted in Chapter 2, traumatized individuals frequently do not know their feelings, perceptions, and somatic sensations, and cope with their passivity through the use of chemicals.

What can be done to help those traumatized persons who do not have the fruitful, normal developmental sequencing? My hypothesis was that teaching the stress management strategies utilized by stress-resistant persons to traumatized victims with learned helplessness would improve the coping strategies of these persons such that they would have less hyperarousal and distress, and an increased sense of mastery and affiliation with others. It was a strategy to shift the psychology of learned helplessness to one of personal control by changing the environment to increase positive outcomes and to change the helpless person's expectation from uncontrollable to controllable by teaching specific skills, as Garber and Seligman (8) suggested.

The problem of helplessness in trauma victims first addresses the very essence of the trauma response: the loss of control over one's life. The resolution of the trauma itself may be less difficult to attain when the victims perceive themselves to be more in control of their lives and supported by a social network that renders them less vulnerable to life's adversities.

A Stress Management Approach in the Treatment of Learned Helplessness

Presented earlier in detail (13) and summarized here, the goals of this stress management approach are to develop adaptive coping strategies for common life stress events and to reduce somatic distress. The basic program incorporates four interventions:

1. The reduction of dietary stimulants (refined white sugar, caffeine, nicotine),
2. Hard aerobic exercise,
3. Relaxation exercises, and
4. A stress innoculation process (33) to master adaptive coping strategies.

This treatment approach is implemented in a group format. Groups of 8 to 10 persons meet for 8 sessions in this task-oriented program. Individual sessions are 1½ hours long, and all patients are initially screened for any medical problems that might present with symptoms similar to "anxiety" (e.g., hyperthyroid conditions) (34). Each patient is required to obtain a physical exam for medical clearance for the program's aerobic exercise component before the first group meeting. All groups are co-led.

During the first session, the patients are given a brief presentation of the physiology of stress and the characteristics of stress-resistant persons. The stress management interventions are outlined, and the session closes with each patient completing a series of basic self-assessment inventories including those for major life events (35) and daily hassles (36). Each patient receives a workbook that contains all the necessary information, self-report questionnaires, and forms required for the group's tasks.

Sessions 2 through 4 each focus on diet, hard exercise, and relaxation. Each session begins by initiating small changes over time in a patient's intake of dietary stimulants. Members are asked to decrease gradually their use of refined white sugar, caffeine, and nicotine in small incremental steps in each ensuing week. A gradual tapering process is encouraged to avoid withdrawal symptoms. Group time is next spent in the development of a hard (aerobic) exercise program tapered to individual need and interest, and consistent with any medical limitations. Members are taught warm-up/cool-down exercises; the importance of starting any exercise program gradually is stressed. All members commit themselves to three 20-minute exercise periods each week. The group itself goes for a brisk walk as a part of each meeting. Each session then concludes with relaxation exercises, as presented by Benson (30). Members sit comfortably in a quiet group room and breathe deeply and slowly. Members are free to add a pleasant image to the relaxed state if they wish. Members are encouraged to practice relaxation each day.

Sessions 5 through 8 continue the monitoring of dietary, hard exercise, and relaxation training compliance. Group time is set aside for brisk walks and a period of relaxation. As many group members have mastered the essentials of these tasks after four sessions, a stress innoculation procedure (33) is then added to each remaining session. The stress innoculation procedure seeks to train individuals in advance in basic coping strategies that are adaptive, and results in less stress. The procedure emphasizes direct behavioral action to reduce somatic distress (e.g., utilizing relaxation exercises before a stressful encounter) and the learning of specific skills to solve specific problems (e.g., asking the boss for a raise diplomatically). The procedure also delineates cognitive strategies to inhibit negative thinking, to keep the problem in proper perspective, and to provide self-praise for reasonable mastery. Common group stress innoculation tasks are chosen by the group and have included dealing with rush hour traffic, communicating with angry store clerks, and tactfully asserting one's self when an individual cuts into a line for tickets. It does *not* include the trauma situations themselves because this approach attempts to instill mastery in less aversive situations first.

Clinical Implementation

This chapter has focused on the signs of numbing that are seen in chronically traumatized individuals with learned helplessness. It has been postulated that the stress management interventions utilized by stress-resistant persons would increase personal control and a sense of mastery in trauma victims that would lead to less avoidant behavior, social isolation, and depressive affect. It was also noted that mastery of the environment with meaningful social supports might lessen the impact of the trauma for these victims.

While the first year of this program's development has focused on refining the treatment approach and in training staff, pilot study data are available on 68 patients in nine groups (6 of these patients withdrew). These groups were conducted in traditional outpatient clinic settings, a day treatment program for the chronically mentally ill, and the behavioral medicine program of the primary care unit in a general hospital. The psychological trauma suffered by these patients includes rape, incest, domestic violence, family alcoholism, and chronic mental illness.

Does this stress management intervention resolve the problem of learned helplessness in traumatized patients? Does it ameliorate the signs of numbing in the biphasic response to trauma? The patients reported less muscular tension and leg cramping, less sleep disturbance, less need of medicines for high blood pressure, less generalized anxiety, and less subjective distress. The patients became involved in tasks that demonstrated both mastery of the environment and improved social interpersonal links. They reported fewer family arguments, greater interpersonal cooperation in daily family chores, and being assertive in tactful ways with colleagues at work. One gave up smoking; one taught extended family members the relaxation exercises. The day treatment patients added decaffeinated beverages and fewer sugared snacks to their program. In the group meetings themselves, some patients paired off for the various between-session tasks; the group brisk walks became occasions for animated discussions among the members. These findings are consistent with previously cited research that these stress management techniques result in less hyperarousal and distress (20, 29–32), an increased sense of order and mastery (2, 4, 11, 18, 24–26), and improved social support (2–4, 20).

Does this new psychology of mastery with social support lessen the issues in resolving the trauma itself? This stress management is too new to permit an adequate answer to this question; however, one recent clinical example illustrates the direction in which we hope to proceed:

Patient is a 38-year-old married white female who came to outpatient clinic with chief complaints of agitated depression and feeling overwhelmed by her current life events. These included one teenage daughter being taken to court on a stubborn child petition, her husband's being confined to home with a chronic illness, severe financial problems, no help from her extended family, and the loss of her best friend through job relocation.

Patient vaguely reported early childhood. Both parents were alcoholic. There were many marital arguments, foster home placements, and general social confusion. Her mother refused to let her return home when she turned 18. Patient married an alcoholic, had one child, was verbally abused by him, and became divorced a few years later.

Patient's treatment plan included one-to-one psychodynamic therapy weekly and referral to a stress management group to help with her lack of mastery and her social isolation. She refused all medicines because of the chemical abuse in her family. The patient came to each treatment regularly. The psychodynamic therapy focused on her depression, and how to think through the issues with her daughter. In the stress management group, the patient demonstrated the initial steps in mastery and was a popular and accepted group member. After session 7 in the stress management program, she went to her individual therapist in tears and recounted a long history of sexual abuse by a family member.

While the more normal course of treatment is to spend an appreciable amount of time developing a therapeutic alliance with a trauma victim, this clinical example does appear to illustrate the usefulness of shifting the victim's psychology from one of learned helplessness to one of mastery.

How does this stress management approach resolve the problem of learned helplessness in trauma victims? This entire program proscribes passivity and rewards patients for taking control of their lives in small incremental steps. Group members comply with their own dietary contracts, engage in their own hard exercise programs, induce their own relaxation, and innoculate themselves to common stressful situations of their choice. In taking control of their lives in this planned orderly way, they are utilizing the adaptive coping skills of stress-resistant persons (2, 11, 18, 24, 25). These gains in personal control are enhanced by group cohesiveness (37) (see Chapter 7), which includes member acceptance, exchanges of information, and reinforcement for cooperation and successful outcome (37, 38). These interpersonal exchanges appear to be important components in developing social support. The patients report these groups as being fun, a setting where they can master something and do it at their own pace. The groups generally have high compliance with the various tasks, and this appears due in part to having fun with others. A group member makes a public commitment to the group to work toward mastery. This public commitment is the focus for gentle humorous chiding for nonattainment as well as social reward and genuine group excitement for mastery.

Basic clinical experimental research remains to be done to assess for whom this intervention is indicated and to determine which treatment components contribute to successful outcome. However, these early data do suggest that specific interaction with concrete outcomes and nonjudgmental feedback in a socially supportive group setting instills a sense of mastery that leads to the attenuation of learned helplessness.

References

1. Lindemann E: Symptomatology and management of acute grief. Am J Psychiatry 101:141–148, 1944

2. Antonovsky A: Health, Stress, and Coping. San Francisco, Jossey-Bass, 1979

3. Cohen S, Willis TA: Stress, social support, and the buffering hypothesis. Psychol Bull 98:310–357, 1985

4. Kobasa SC, Pucetti MC: Personality and social resources in stress resistance. J Pers Soc Psychol 47:839–850, 1983

5. van der Kolk BA, Blitz R, Burr W, et al: Nightmares and trauma. Am J Psychiatry 141:187–190, 1984

6. van der Kolk BA, Greenberg M, Boyd H, et al: Inescapable shock, neurotransmitters and addiction to trauma: towards a psychobiology of posttraumatic stress. Biol Psychiatry 20:314–322, 1985

7. Seligman MED: Helplessness: On Depression, Development and Death. San Francisco, Freeman, 1975

8. Garber J, Seligman MED (eds): Human Helplessness: Theory and Application. New York, Academic Press, 1980

9. Kirkpatrick DG, Veronen LJ, Best CL: Factors precipitating psychological distress among rape victims, in Trauma and Its Wake. Edited by Figley CC. New York, Brunner/Mazel, 1985, pp 113–142

10. Hinkle LE Jr, Wolfe HG: Ecological investigation of the rela-

tionship between illness, life experiences, and the social environment. Ann Intern Med 49:1373–1378, 1958

11. Flannery RB Jr: The work ethic as moderator variable of life stress: preliminary inquiry. Psychol Reports 55:361–362, 1984

12. Kobasa SC: Personality and resistance to illness. Am J Community Psychol 7:413–423, 1979

13. Flannery RB Jr: Towards stress-resistant persons: a stress management approach in the treatment of anxiety. American Journal of Preventive Medicine (in press)

14. Flannery RB Jr: Major life events and daily hassles in predicting health status: methodological inquiry. J Clin Psychol (in press)

15. Flannery RB Jr: Global versus restricted negative measure of life change events: methodological inquiry. J Clin Psychol 41:598–601, 1985

16. Dohrenwend BS, Dohrenwend BP: Stressful life events: their nature and effects. New York, John Wiley and Sons, 1974

17. Lazarus RS, Folkman S: Stress, appraisal, and coping. New York, Springer, 1984

18. Flannery RB Jr: Personal control as a moderator variable of life stress: preliminary inquiry. Psychol Reports 55:200–202, 1986

19. Johnson JE, Sarason IG: Life stress, depression, and anxiety: internal-external control as moderator variable. J Psychosom Res 22:205–208, 1978

20. Berkman LF, Syme LE: Social networks, lost resistance, and mortality: a nine year follow-up study of Almeda County residences. Am J Epidemiol 109:186–204, 1979

21. Enstrom JE, Pauling L: Mortality among health conscious elderly Californians. Proc Natl Acad Sci USA 79:6023–6027, 1982

22. Martin RA, Lefcourt HM: Sense of humor as moderator of the relationship between stressors and moods. J Pers Soc Psychol 45:1313–1324, 1983

23. Flannery RB Jr, Bowen MA: Religious values as a moderator

variable of life stress: preliminary inquiry. Journal of Pastoral Counseling 19:68–74, 1985

24. Bandura A: Self-efficacy: towards a unifying theory of behavioral change. Psychol Rev 84:191–215, 1977

25. White RW: Motivation reconsidered: the conceptualization of competence. Psychol Rev 66:297–333, 1959

26. Vaillant GF, Vaillant C: National history of male psychological health, X: work as a predictor of positive mental health. Am J Psychiatry 138:1433–1440, 1981

27. Farquahr JW: The American way of life need not be hazardous to your health. New York, WW Norton & Co, 1978

28. Kobasa SC, Maddi SR, Pucetti MC: Personality and exercises as buffers in the stress-illness relationship. J Behav Med 5:391–404, 1982

29. Sinyan D, Schwartz SG, Peronnet F, et al: Aerobic fitness level and reactivity to psychological stress: physiological, biochemical, and subjective measures. Psychosom Med 45:205–218, 1983

30. Benson H: The Relaxation Response. New York, William Morrow and Co, 1975

31. Boudrea L: Transcendental meditation and yoga as reciprocal inhibitors. J Behav Ther Exp Psychiatry 3:97–98, 1972

32. Wolpe JA: The Practice of Behavior Therapy. New York, Pergamon Press, 1971

33. Meichenbaum D: Cognitive Behavior Modification: An Integrative Approach. New York, Plenum Press, 1977

34. Anderson WB: Psychiatric emergencies, in MGH Textbook of Emergency Medicine. Edited by Wilkins EW, Denang JT, Moncoure AC. Baltimore, Williams & Wilkins Co, 1983, pp 402–418

35. Holmes TH, Rahe RH: The social readjustment rating scale. J Psychosom Med 22:205–208, 1978

36. Kanner AD, Coyne JC, Schaefer C, et al: Comparison of two

modes of stress management: daily hassles and uplifts versus major life events. J Behav Med 4:1–39, 1981

37. van der Kolk BA: Adolescent vulnerability to trauma. Psychiatry 20:365–370, 1985

38. Yalom I: The Theory and Practice of Group Psychotherapy. New York, Basic Books, 1970

Index